COOL MEN AND THE SECOND SEX

GENDER AND CULTURE

GENDER AND CULTURE

A SERIES OF COLUMBIA UNIVERSITY PRESS

EDITED BY CAROLYN G. HEILBRUN AND NANCY K. MILLER

Modern Feminisms: Political, Literary, Cultural
  Maggie Humm
Unbecoming Women: British Women Writers and the Novel of Development
  Susan Fraiman
The Apparitional Lesbian: Female Homosexuality and Modern Culture
  Terry Castle
George Sand and Idealism
  Naomi Schor
Becoming a Heroine: Reading About Women in Novels
  Rachel M. Brownstein
Nomadic Subjects: Embodiment and Sexual Difference in Contemporary Feminist Theory
  Rosi Braidotti
Engaging with Irigaray: Feminist Philosophy and Modern European Thought
  Edited by Carolyn Burke, Naomi Schor, and Margaret Whitford
Second Skins: The Body Narratives of Transsexuality
  Jay Prosser
A Certain Age: Reflecting on Menopause
  Edited by Joanna Goldsworthy
Mothers in Law: Feminist Theory and the Legal Regulation of Motherhood
  Edited by Martha Albertson Fineman and Isabelle Karpin
Critical Condition: Feminism at the Turn of the Century
  Susan Gubar
Feminist Consequences: Theory for the New Century
  Edited by Elisabeth Bronfen and Misha Kavka
Simone de Beauvoir, Philosophy, and Feminism
  Nancy Bauer
Pursuing Privacy in Cold War America
  Deborah Nelson
But Enough About Me: Why We Read Other People's Lives
  Nancy K. Miller
Palatable Poison: Critical Perspectives on The Well of Loneliness
  Edited by Laura Doan and Jay Prosser

GENDER AND CULTURE READERS

Modern Feminisms: Political, Literary, Cultural
  Edited by Maggie Humm
Feminism and Sexuality: A Reader
  Edited by Stevi Jackson and Sue Scott
Writing on the Body: Female Embodiment and Feminist Theory
  Edited by Katie Conboy, Nadia Medina, and Sarah Stanbury

SUSAN FRAIMAN

COOL MEN AND

THE **SECOND SEX**

COLUMBIA UNIVERSITY PRESS / NEW YORK

COLUMBIA UNIVERSITY PRESS

Publishers Since 1893

New York   Chichester, West Sussex

Copyright © 2003 Columbia University Press

All rights reserved

Library of Congress Cataloging-in-Publication Data

Fraiman, Susan.

    Cool men and the second sex / Susan Fraiman.

      p.   cm. — (Gender and culture)

    Includes bibliographical references and index.

    ISBN 0–231–12962–9 (cloth) — ISBN 0–231–12963–7 (paper)

     1. Men—Identity. 2. Men—Attitudes. 3. Gender identity. 4. Masculinity.

I. Title. II. Series.

HQ1090 .F73 2003

305.31—dc21   2002041257

Columbia University Press books are printed on permanent and
durable acid-free paper.

Printed in the United States of America

Designed by Lisa Hamm

c 10 9 8 7 6 5 4 3 2 1

p 10 9 8 7 6 5 4 3 2 1

FOR CORY

CONTENTS

PREFACE: THE UNCOOL MOTHER

Pose of supreme indifference, eyes hidden behind shades, habits of transgression, irreverence as a worldview—the allure of coolness is something we know about from high school and think about through a store of images supplied by books, music, television, and movies. My project here is not to pin down the meaning of coolness, much less trace its cultural origins or various manifestations. Rather, setting a particular notion of coolness beside the dilemmas of gender gives me a way of talking about a troubling phenomenon: the fact that, more than thirty years after the dawn of the second-wave women's movement, after decades of intensive feminist scholarship in almost every field, after the promotion of at least some feminist scholars to positions of eminence, after the emergence of a body of feminist film theory now central to film studies, and after the infiltration of most aspects of movie production by women—after all this, there is not only a predictable and well-documented right/center backlash against feminism but also, incredibly, a lingering, systematic masculinism among some of the best-known, left-leaning, evidently "cool" cultural workers, many of whom explicitly ally themselves with women's concerns.

This book examines a number of filmmakers and scholars—Quentin Tarantino, Spike Lee, Brian De Palma, Edward Said, Andrew Ross, Henry Louis Gates Jr., Eve Sedgwick (and a cluster of other queer theorists)—famous in recent decades for breaking the rules and disrespecting the status quo. Setting trends in cinema; challenging received views of race, class, nation, and sexuality; radically transforming traditional scholarship—these figures are "cool" by virtue of their celebrity and widespread influence, and because their names have been synonymous with bracing, left intellectual work or brazen innovations in popular culture. They are also, I am arguing, cool in their style of "maleness." For while my final chapter on queer theory includes other female scholars in addition to Sedgwick (Judith Butler and Judith Halberstam), these women resemble the men who precede them in affirming a kind of dissident, hip masculinity, which typically phrases itself over against a more conventional "feminine." I am talking, then, about "cool male" ways of speaking that often but not always—and certainly not by any anatomical necessity—occur in writings by biological men.

My thinking about coolness takes note of Peter Stearns's view of American cool as a middle-class ethic of emotional restraint that began to predominate in the 1920s (*American Cool*, 1994). I am likewise grateful to Richard Majors and Janet Billson, who discuss coolness as a strategy deployed by African American men (*Cool Pose*, 1991).[1] For me, however, coolness is primarily a mode of masculinity that crosses racial lines, though of course it is contingent on many factors, including race. I use "coolness" to describe a "male" individualism whose model is the teen rebel, defined above all by his strenuous alienation from the maternal. Coolness as I see it is epitomized by the modern adolescent boy in his anxious, self-conscious, and theatricalized will to separate from the mother. And it goes without saying that within this paradigm the place occupied by the mother is by definition uncool. So I agree with Stearns that twentieth-century American cool is characterized by wariness of strong emotion in general and maternal fervor in particular—a drawing back from the intensity of mother love so sanctified by the Victorians. In our less feeling era, we are all in some sense overweaned, leather-wearing toughs. Antimaternal coolness is nevertheless most strongly evident and virulent in the formative stages of conventional maleness. The cool subject identifies with an emergent, precarious masculinity produced in large part by youthful rule breaking. Within this structure of feeling, the feminine is maternalized and hopelessly linked to stasis, tedium, constraint, even domination. Typed as "mothers," women become inextricable from a rigid domesticity that bad boys are pledged to resist and overcome. A defining quality of coolness, then, is that a posture of flamboyant unconventionality coexists with highly conventional views of gender—is, indeed, articulated through them. The project of my book is to make the logic of coolness visible as a political contradiction in the work of various influential contemporary artists and intellectuals more widely known for their bold opposition to aesthetic and ideological norms.

The tension between radical class views or defiant antiracism or artistic/cultural innovation on the one hand and commitment to women's liberation on the other has a long and complicated history in the United States. Even when there has been an express desire on the part of "cool men" to include women and to question male domination, in practice a traditional division of labor, a double standard of sexuality, and analyses assuming a male perspective have tended to prevail. Not that women haven't participated in and been inspired by left politics or bohemian circles and succeeded in voicing feminist concerns within these contexts. As we know, first- and second-wave feminists came of age in the abolitionist and New Left movements, respectively, and were able to garner some support from men as well as women belonging to these movements—certainly more than could be had from mainstream or conservative institutions. And Christine Stansell has recently argued that bohemian New York from 1890 to 1920 was a mecca not only of many modern arts but also of genuinely modern notions about male and female roles (*American Moderns* 225–72). Nevertheless, the overriding ethos of progressive movements and bohemian milieux in this country has often been largely and sometimes fundamentally at odds with gender revolution—thus the pattern of eventual secession from groups centered on issues of race and/or class in order to focus on women.[2] The examples offered by this book, especially those involving cutting-edge academic discourses, suggest that such an ethos continues at times to underpin (and undercut) left thinking today.

To mention just a few of the precedents for my current cool men and their apprehensions about women, the feminine, and feminism: what Heidi Hartmann has famously called the "unhappy marriage of Marxism and feminism" was apparent as early as the 1860s on the occasion of the First International. There the Americans split internally over "the woman question," and Marx himself recommended expelling those who, following Victoria C. Woodhull and others, tied the emancipation of women to that of workers and dared give precedence to the former (Buhle xiv). By the time of the Second International in 1907, August Bebel had elaborated the socialist analysis of women's oppression outlined by Engels's *The Origins of the Family,* and the Communist Party officially urged support for women's suffrage. Yet Bebel's analysis served primarily to assimilate women to male-centered economic paradigms, without accounting for the specificity of women's work (unpaid domestic labor topping off a day of low-wage labor), much less the subordination of all women within the spheres of reproduction and sexuality (Buhle 180–84).[3] And even support for the vote was warily framed to distinguish the socialist position from that of middle-class suffragists shunned, like feminists generally, as merely reformist (Buhle 218–22). Sixty years later, what Robin Morgan termed the "ejaculatory politics" of the New Left did little to improve on the masculine legacy of the old. A particularly vicious example of Left hostility to feminist agendas occurred at the 1969 Counter-Inaugural Demonstration in Washington, D.C., where speeches by Marilyn Webb and Shulamith Firestone were met by male comrades chanting, "Take her off the stage and fuck her!" In response, Firestone along with Ellen Willis promptly founded the Redstockings, one of the first radical feminist groups in the United States. Their reasoning was carefully elaborated by a letter Firestone composed for *The Guardian*: "Fuck off, left. You can examine your navel by yourself from now on. We're starting our own movement" (Echols, *Daring*, 114–20).[4]

Elizabeth Cady Stanton and Lucretia Mott said essentially the same thing to male abolitionists back in 1840, when they and other American women delegates attended but were barred from participating in the World Anti-Slavery Convention in London. Infuriated by their second-class status within the abolitionist movement, Stanton and Mott went on to organize the first conference on women's rights, held in Seneca Falls, New York in 1848. We should certainly acknowledge not only the staunch support for women's rights of such key antislavery men as Frederick Douglass but also the racism of much white feminism in the contentious period following the Civil War. Nevertheless, it is equally true that the years preceding the passage of the Fifteenth Amendment saw men with cool racial views (including Douglass) willing to postpone working for the interests of black as well as white women while seeking to enfranchise and otherwise empower black men.[5] The privileging of black masculinity would continue to characterize antiracist efforts of the twentieth century, beginning with the casual sexism of the civil rights movement, quite in keeping with 1950s norms, and taking on more earnest masculinist overtones with the Black Power movement's emergence in the 1960s. A case in point was Casey Hayden's and Mary King's anonymous 1964 critique of sexism within SNCC (Student Nonviolent Coordinating

Committee), to which Stokely Carmichael infamously replied that "the only position for women in SNCC is prone" (Rosen 882–83).[6] As we will see in my sections on Spike Lee and Henry Louis Gates Jr., Black Nationalism's identification of racial and political authenticity with *virility* is residual within antiracist discourses of the 1990s, even those whose explicit theoretical frameworks might seem to argue otherwise.

As for the cultural avant-garde, the bohemians most responsible for putting "cool" on the map were, of course, the Beats. The masculinity they patented in the 1950s drew both on the stylized nonchalance of black male jazz musicians (Miles Davis's *Birth of the Cool* came out in 1949) and on the macho surliness of white working-class men. Exemplifying Norman Mailer's "White Negro" (1959), they revered jazz genius Charlie Parker, and like the rest of their generation had a weakness for the kind of underclass or outcast characters popularized by Marlon Brando and James Dean. Anticipating the figures featured in *Cool Men*, the example of the Beats suggests once again that revolt against white, bourgeois values may coexist easily with traditional, subordinating views of women. The Beats were, indeed, rather notorious in this regard; Kerouac was a deadbeat dad, Burroughs a uxoricide, and the project of their circle was to glamorize a nomadic male camaraderie in principled flight from women and their supposed conventionality. As Barbara Ehrenreich describes the Beat sensibility, "Women and their demands for responsibility were, at worst, irritating and more often just uninteresting compared to the ecstatic possibilities of male adventure" (54).[7] Coolness in the pages to come has all of these various connotations: a self-conscious and in many ways productive nonconformity; an appeal to African American and working-class men as embodiments of an authentic, renegade masculinity; an air of cool-tempered autonomy; an investment in male homosociality; and a careless if not hostile attitude toward women and their demands. The idea of being cool is seductive, and few of us, male or female, are not a little susceptible to the fear of being uncool. At the same time, thanks to several generations of feminist scholarship, we on the left are now well positioned to recognize both the gender exclusivity and the ideological incoherence of coolness as a mode of rebellion. I hope the following chapters will succeed in fostering such a recognition.

IN TERMS OF MY OVERALL ARGUMENT, coolness is neither causal nor more than loosely descriptive. It works well to account for the moral schema I find in Andrew Ross, which celebrates rowdy male youth, from rappers to hackers to soccer fans, while neglecting girls and often implicitly demonizing women. Whether in his first, signature work of cultural studies, *No Respect: Intellectuals and Popular Culture* (1989); in short pieces written for *Art Forum*; or in later books on environmental discourse, sons for Ross are positively aligned with the hip, popular, and transgressive, while the feminine and feminist are not only maternalized but gentrified so that, as for the Beats, women become enforcers of bourgeois regimes. Ross's intellectual trajectory—from his training in feminist film theory at the University of Kent to his realignment with British cultural studies at Illinois State— might also be read as a swerve away from the mother of contemporary film criticism (Laura Mulvey) into a tradition originating with the study of Rude Boys and Teddy Boys, among other boy subcultures.

This career pattern is even more pronounced in Henry Louis Gates Jr., who appears in his work as the most strongly mother-identified of all my subjects. For Gates too eventually makes the shift from claiming women's writing to profiling men and prioritizing the "crisis of the black male." Never such an unrepentant bad boy as Ross, Gates has developed as a public figure in a way that (echoing the trajectory of personal development narrated by *Colored People*, 1994) has gradually increased his distance from the maternal. Moreover, if his flight from the feminine is full-blown by the 1990s, it is incipient even in his earlier work, where Gates arguably aspires to master as much as to honor the black mother's voice. My discussion of Gates elaborates this claim by focusing on his first two, groundbreaking works of scholarship, *Figures in Black* (1987) and *The Signifying Monkey* (1988). I would also note that for Gates the stakes of coolness are raised by constructions of African American masculinity that, while mythologizing black mothers, dismiss the mama's boy and authenticate the muthafucka.

Likewise for Spike Lee, racial agendas produced by and feeding back into ideas of black masculinity ultimately trump the desire, expressed in his early movies, to advocate for black women and sympathize with feminism. My reading places his film *School Daze* (1988) alongside two contemporaneous white texts—the 1989 Central Park jogger case and Brian De Palma's movie of the same year, *Casualties of War*. All three map race and gender by means of a narrative about rape; juxtaposed thus, white and African American male texts appear to have racially specific but nonetheless interdependent ways of deploying the rape tale. Lee's story of life at an all-black college, which culminates in racial protest along nationalist lines, does so in part by reiterating the trope of the violable female body. His insurgent racial politics coexist uneasily in this movie, as in *Do the Right Thing* (1989) and *Jungle Fever* (1991), with a gender schema that, ostensibly feminist, nevertheless reduces women to either trophy or injury in a race war between men. More generally, this second chapter underlines a presupposition of *Cool Men* overall: the belief that masculinities are necessarily inflected by race—by notions, for example, about whiteness as well as blackness, by the tensions that affiliate as well as alienate white and black males.

This brings us to Edward Said, whose magisterial *Culture and Imperialism* (1993) reveals, like the work of Spike Lee, a contradiction between fresh racial paradigms and rotten gender ones. While very much in agreement with this book as a whole, I am disconcerted by the primacy given to Jane Austen, which serves to give a domestic and feminine cast to the whole of nineteenth-century imperialist culture. Women like Austen should, of course, be implicated along with men for creating English-centered textualizations of "home," but Said goes beyond this to discredit European culture by implicitly gendering it as female. Nonwestern resistance cultures, by contrast, are strongly marked as male, thereby restoring masculinity to those subordinated by Orientalist paradigms. Reversing the gender assignments of colonizer and colonized, Said resembles Ross in offering a left critique that lines up opposition with the "masculine," domination with the "feminine." We might also liken Said as an Orientalized male to Gates as a black male closely identified both with his mama and with the Caucasian cultural elite. For these two men, masculinism may be in part a panicked response to being racialized as inadequately male.

Of all my texts, Quentin Tarantino's *Pulp Fiction* (1994) illustrates the structure of cool feeling in the most bared and primal terms. Indeed, in Tarantino the flight from mother love and intimacy generally is unmitigated by even pro forma appeals to feminism. Rebellion and innovation are, in his case, formal and aesthetic rather than ideological; as a result, he doesn't exemplify what is often cool's political incoherence but instead dramatizes quite starkly the male developmental logic underlying the cool persona. In the opening chapter on *Pulp Fiction*, I invoke Freud's analysis of the child's game of Fort!/Da! to help describe and derive the sexual politics not only of Tarantino's famously cool characters but also of a narrative style determined to keep us all cool. The violent alternation in *Pulp Fiction* between scenes of relationship and scenes of relationship shattered suggests to me the reeling in–and–throwing out dynamic linked by Freud to a child's effort to master separation from "his" mother. I am interested, then, in thinking about violence in Tarantino's most popular film as a matter less of theme than of narrative rhythm. Borrowing an image from the movie, I propose the *adrenaline shot* to describe a narrative structured by body-jolting shifts in tone and genre. The aim is to protect a kind of cool masculinity endangered by too much intimacy or domesticity. The effect is a hierarchy in which rupture and departure take precedence over daily routines aspiring to closeness and continuity, and as with Said, the repudiated, domestic register is coded female. I begin with Tarantino, then, because he offers such a vivid anatomy of "cool" as male rebellion against an "everyday" seated in relationships and implicated in an original dependency.

Perhaps it will strike some as counterproductive and unseemly to mount a series of critiques not only of charismatic filmmakers but also of some of the most brilliant and progressive intellectuals working in the United States today. For this reason, I want to stress how deeply indebted and strongly allied I am to all of the scholarship I discuss. It is precisely because these works have contributed so significantly to left thinking about race, popular culture, colonialism, and heteronormativity, and because they often align themselves with feminism, that I hold them accountable for any and all traces of misogyny. Intensely aware of the merits of my texts, I have tried at every turn to make my comments—though frequently negative, and stemming from a clear and passionate position on my part—both nuanced and fair in their judgments. I offer these thoughts, then, in the spirit of left self-criticism, especially in the final queer theory chapter, where I take up a formation in many ways continuous—chronologically, intellectually, and ideologically—with my own training in and loyalty to second-wave feminist theory. Indeed, without collapsing the two, I would say that queer theory now occupies the place feminist theory did in the early 1980s, so that its paradigm shift is also in some sense a generational development, and this book is finally, as it concludes, a meditation on gender studies in its own right as well as an estimation of its influence (or lack thereof) on other fields.

What I perceive in the newest wave of thinking about gender and sexuality is a tendency to recenter men, male desire, and masculinity. As I am not the first to note, in addition to making the risks and pleasures of male homoeroticism central, many of the most influential theories of queerness appear to mark their most vaunted values (mobility, transgressive sexuality) as male, and those most degraded (stasis, normative sexuality) as female. In this 1990s discourse, the young, hard, female-to-male transsexual is heroic, while the sagging, female-identified lesbian feminist is made to appear an unhip holdover from the 1970s. Posed against a "maternal" frequently conflated with the "biological," queer theory in the cases I cite recalls the repudiation within cultural studies of "mothers" by rebellious "sons." I close this chapter and the book as whole with a reading of Leslie Feinberg's novel *Stone Butch Blues* (1993). While Judith Halberstam has recently discussed the novel's transgendered protagonist as a case of "female masculinity," my analysis shifts the emphasis to bring out what I call, instead, Jess's "butch maternity." By mixing up the category of cool "butchness" with a positive sense of "maternity," I offer this final section as an alternative to the logic of coolness, which prefers to keep these strictly segregated.

ONCE, AFTER A TALK I gave on Andrew Ross and his writing on soccer, the audience began heatedly debating the pros and cons of soccer players and soccer fans. Because I criticize this soccer-positive piece, I was seen as disliking the game itself. But this, I feel, is to mistake the object of my critique. What concerns me in *Cool Men* is often not the explicit topic being handled but rather the way, in handling it, certain quite subtle gender codes are called into play. Here, for example, Ross defends soccer as a manly sport against what is implicitly described as its feminization by U.S. corporate sponsors. In some cases (Henry Louis Gates and Judith Butler come to mind), I take up texts that are sincerely bent on transforming gender categories but turn out, upon closer reading, to rely nonetheless on disparaging views of the "feminine." So my problem in the Ross chapter is not with soccer but with the way Ross discusses it. And I would add (staying with Ross as an example of my procedure throughout), nor is my problem with Ross himself so much as his rhetorical strategies. Needless to say, I have no animus against my figures as people. What I mean to protest are cumulative textual effects, unexamined and incongruous patterns of sexism just beneath the surface of works purporting to be oppositional (and sometimes feminist).

There is another reason I do not see this book as being about actual people in a personal sense. As I say, I am interested in cultural artifacts, and even the biographical or autobiographical materials I occasionally use exist at some remove from their subjects. Further, virtually all of my figures have the kind of celebrity or iconic status that causes their names to resonate be-yond their bodies and even beyond the bodies of their work. Said, Ross, Gates, and Butler, in particular, are that new breed of celebrity dubbed by Jeffrey Williams "academostars," whose glamorous visibility evokes the world of film but takes a form finally particular to the campus and confer-ence circuit (191). The much-discussed phenomenon of academic celebrity in the United States is relevant to this project in several ways. First, while I resist those moments in David Shumway's "The Star System in Literary Studies" that resonate with conservative attacks on contemporary theory, I agree with him that "too often these days, the name of a star is enough to guarantee our assent to all manner of highly questionable assertions" ("Re-visited" 176). Not that stars are more likely than others to make dubious claims, but star assertions may be less open to questioning, especially when no longer put forth as arguments but invoked as theoretical shorthand or embedded as casual assumptions within other people's work.

I would say this is particularly true when the star being cited, the scholar who is citing, and the reader of both are all genuinely committed to the po-litical and intellectual projects of antiracism, antinormativity, antiessential-ism, etc. In such cases, to disagree is to risk appearing to disavow these op-positional projects, thus positioning oneself as decidedly "uncool." The other, more dire risk is that of adding fuel to the fire of right-wing cultural warriors, for whom the stars mentioned above are symbolic markers on the political landscape, no less than for us on the left. For this reason, before a conservative or even mainstream audience, I myself would readily defer the goal of left self-criticism and rush to defend each and every one of the aca-demic figures mentioned in these pages. The fact that my subjects articulate important progressive agendas with all the heightened authority of "stars" has therefore worked to curtail criticism from feminists who understandably appreciate the personal and political advantages of a left united front. In this sense, the celebrity of my cool scholars makes the interventions that follow both more difficult and more urgent.

Another point I would make about the star system in academia concerns its gender politics, and here I disagree with Bruce Robbins in "Celeb-Reliance," who represents this system in opposition to the patrilineal old-boy network. Once again I would echo Shumway in remarking that greater mobility for nonwhite and/or female scholars coexists with but is unlikely to have been *caused* by the cult of celebrity ("Revisited" 178). Indeed, it seems obvious that, within the star system, faculty continue to be hierarchized by gender as well as race—whether in the disparity stressed by Sharon O'Dair ("Academostars Are the Symptom; What's the Disease?") between those in the teaching trenches and those with more research opportunities or, at the top of the heap, between what Tim Spurgin (in "The *Times Magazine* and Academic Megastars") calls lower-level "stars" and the handful of "megastars" who make the *Times*. As Spurgin notes, seven of the eight megastar theorists profiled in the Sunday *Times Magazine* between 1990 and 1994 were men, and the detailing of Gates's Mercedes and Stanley Fish's Jaguar merely furthered the impression of megastardom as "a boy's club" (230). Since 1995 only two more such profiles have appeared. Both featured women (Martha Nussbaum and Elaine Scarry), and both, in a departure from earlier profiles, represented their subjects less as intellectual powerhouses than "curiosities, eccentrics, and weirdos" (Spurgin 234). More recent profiles of Eve Sedgwick and Marjorie Garber were not only shorter and less prominent (buried in the Saturday "Arts and Ideas" section) but also more gossipy. Explaining this decline of the genre and this diminished view of the star, Spurgin asserts that "gender would seem to be a factor" (234–35). The upshot, for our purposes, is that academic stardom, at least at its very highest level, appears to be gendered male. The megacelebrity of my subjects is thus an important component of their "cool masculinity," and their "cool masculinity" is, in turn, conducive to their favorable depiction as academic celebrities, especially in prestigious publications such as the *New York Times Magazine*.[8]

Celebrity is, finally, a category in terms of which the distance between Hollywood and the Ivy League is loosely bridged, my filmmakers and professors brought into some kind of contiguity. Lee and Tarantino act in their own movies; Said is a talking head on the evening news; Gates narrates a documentary on Africa for PBS; and sooner or later they all get interviewed by Charlie Rose. Tarantino works hard to be lowbrow, Said cannot help being highbrow, but in the popular imagination they float together in the ether of the small or silver screen. Common celebrity ground notwithstanding, I would like to note that my first two chapters on movies proceed rather differently from the next four sections on academic discourses. Whereas chapters 1 and 2 describe ways that female characters are deployed within cinematic texts (as figures connoting a dangerous intimacy, between men as objects of rape, etc.), the remaining chapters look less at images of women than at metaphors of gender organizing scholarly texts on imperialism, pop culture, black literature, and sexuality. These metaphors, I argue, work against the grain of texts professing feminism. In the film chapters, by contrast, I read with rather than against the grain of movies whose sexual politics are more obviously ambiguous. They nevertheless prepare for the rest not only by thematizing coolness and white masculinity but also by hinting at the gender figurations to come: the coding of racial authenticity as male, claustrophobic domesticity as female; the association of masculinity with rebel sons, femininity with retro moms; above all, the casting of cool men as protagonists, women as the second sex.

Readers will notice that my closing chapter, "Queer Theory and the Second Sex," ranges over several theorists and so breaks with the pattern of focusing on a primary figure. Yet all of my chapters are about discursive formations, represented by but hardly confined to a single individual, and in this sense chapter 6 is less anomalous than it may initially appear. Chapters 1 through 5 do indeed center on specific men, but they are men chosen because of their emblematic relation to a larger field—because they have played such shaping and highly visible roles that they are easily taken, by their colleagues, audiences, and the popular media, to stand for major artistic or scholarly movements. Tarantino, for example—dismantling plot, splicing genres, and recycling cultural trash in a much-imitated manner—supplies a shorthand for Hollywood postmodernism, while the name "Spike Lee" references the renaissance in black film kicked off by his 1987 work, *She's Gotta Have It.* This is even more true of the scholars, among whom Said is founding father and *éminence grise* of postcolonial studies, Ross the poster boy (and whipping boy) for cultural studies, and Gates the mogul of multiculturalism. Each tells us something about the formation he represents, without by any means exhausting or being coextensive with it.

For there are, of course, numerous feminists doing work in all of these fields, and it would not do to discount them. Broadly speaking, I situate myself within both queer theory and cultural studies, and my postscript pays homage to some particularly notable scholars producing feminist knowledge within these and other left paradigms, without whom my own work would neither exist nor mean. The larger-than-life celebrity figures criticized here nevertheless cast extremely long shadows; thus chapter 6 considers the Judith Butler *effect*, an influence that exceeds and may even distort what Butler has written but nevertheless hangs on her name and on common understandings of her work. In short, while strongly affirming the overall goals and methods of these various theoretical discourses, I use my iconic figures to represent significant tendencies within them—strains of thought that, by subordinating the "feminine," work against their otherwise revisionary projects. And in every chapter I ask: Why, across so many hip academic fields and cultural forms emergent in the wake of the women's movement, does gender remain a sticking point, a site of strangely anachronistic views?

I WOULD LIKE TO THANK the University of Virginia for three Summer Research Fellowships and two Sesquicentennial Fellowships. I am also grateful to the Society for the Study of Narrative Literature, whose annual conference was the occasion for trying out much of this work. In addition, I am deeply indebted to those who generously read and commented on all or part of this book at various stages: Eileen Boris, Jennifer Crewe, Rita Felski, Jonathan Flatley, Judith Kegan Gardiner, Carolyn Heilbrun, Heather Love, Deborah McDowell, Nancy Miller, Tania Modleski, and Jeffrey Williams. Columbia University Press has been fearless in its enthusiasm for what others regarded as a disconcerting project, and I appreciate their confidence. The kindness and wisdom of Chris Reppucci and Steve Greenstein have been beyond measure. Eric Lott has been a shrewd interlocutor, partner in political crankiness, and encouraging friend throughout. I am eternally grateful to my parents for their ongoing support. This book is lovingly dedicated to my son, Cory, who at ten years old is already adept at ironizing his coolness.

Several parts of this book have been previously published. Chapter 2 appeared as "Geometries of Race and Gender: Eve Sedgwick, Spike Lee, Charlayne Hunter-Gault" in *Feminist Studies* 20.1 (spring 1994): 67–84. Chapter 3 appeared as "Jane Austen and Edward Said: Gender, Culture, and Imperialism," *Critical Inquiry* 21.4 (summer 1995): 805–21. A portion of chapter 4 appeared as "Andrew Ross, Cultural Studies, and Feminism," *the minnesota review* 52–54 (2001): 239–47. I am grateful for permission to reprint them here.

COOL MEN AND THE SECOND SEX

1

QUENTIN TARANTINO: ANATOMY OF COOL

Jules (to Pumpkin): "Tell that bitch to be cool!
Say, bitch be cool! Say, bitch be cool!"
—Quentin Tarantino, *Pulp Fiction* (1994)

When I began to write about Quentin Tarantino, I was right away confronted by coolness. With his white-Negro persona; his appeal to insiders through arcane allusions (if not plagiarisms); his stylish, matter-of-fact handling of appalling violence; and his youthful cult following, Tarantino, especially the Tarantino of *Pulp Fiction* (1994), has an undeniable aura of cool. A self-advertised bad boy, Tarantino gets off on aggressively flouting formal and thematic conventions. What happens if we push out the borders of a gangster film to include some slowed-down chitchat lifted from a situation comedy? What happens if we borrow a low-brow story and deconstruct its linear plot beyond all recognition? What happens if we show a woman being stabbed in the chest and make it funny as well as therapeutic? (OK, so the weapon is a hypodermic needle.) Puckishly raising such questions, Tarantino aligns himself with a risky, defiant expressivity, making his critics appear timid and prudish by comparison. The age and gender dynamics of Tarantino's reception as "cool" was brought home to me by a University of Virginia panel on *Pulp Fiction* that, tellingly, attracted a larger audience and many more undergraduates than most such scholarly events. During the discussion period, someone referred, with eye-rolling impatience, to "our mothers," and the phrase quickly became audience shorthand, passed along from one young fan to another, for those outside the movie's magic circle—those probably too uptight to see it in the first place, and too unhip to "get it" if they did. To dissent from Tarantino's project was apparently to be discredited, in a very specific way, as *maternal,* and realizing this, I began, in the antinomy of cool men and mothers, to find the topic of this book.

COOL MEN, ORDINARY WOMEN

More than just an aspect of Tarantino's directorial mystique, within the world of his films coolness is a state either lived or coveted by virtually all his male characters; it is also, I will be arguing, a state whose masculine rhyme and reason is dramatized by the plot of *Pulp Fiction.* For Tarantino's heisters and mobsters, the hallmark of coolness is steely self-control, its pay-off control over others. "I need you cool. Are you cool?" says Mr. White (Harvey Keitel) to a ranting Mr. Pink (Steve Buscemi) in *Reservoir Dogs* (1992). And though Mr. Pink responds, "I'm cool," his skeptical partner suggests he splash water on his face. "Take a breather," Mr. White advises him evenly (20). Likewise, in the tense finale of *Pulp Fiction,* Jules (Samuel Jackson) instructs "Pumpkin" (Tim Roth) to calm the hysterical Yolanda (Amanda Plummer): "Tell that bitch to be cool! Say, bitch be cool! Say, bitch be cool!" (181). "We're gonna be like three Fonzies," Jules continues. "And what's Fonzie like?" "He's cool?" poor Yolanda guesses through her tears. "Correct-amundo," Jules replies. "And that's what we're gonna be, we're gonna be cool" (182).[1] In his streetwise black masculinity, Jules is head teacher in the school of cool, and the pale, volatile Yolanda is at the bottom of the class. Offering her the example of Fonzie, good-hearted, white ethnic greaser of *Happy Days,* he dumbs down coolness to a level she can grasp. For if Jules is the real thing, then between him and the white woman on the spectrum of cool characters lies the white man, in particular the white hipster emergent in the 1950s whose putative coolness derives from an impersonation of blackness.[2]

But black and white are not the only terms underwriting the cool/uncool binary in Tarantino. As the lines above demonstrate, a failed relation to coolness is further signaled by "pink" and by "bitch," confirming what we have already seen to be the specifically masculine character of Tarantino's ideal. The race and gender politics of white male coolness prove, indeed, to be closely intertwined. Take the previous example of Mr. White. Insofar as cool hinges on assumptions about race that are never explicit in *Reservoir*

Dogs but strongly implied by the men's code names (various colors), Mr. White's pallor marks him as uncool and thus, by analogy, as "feminine." In a male homosocial subculture parsed by race, Mr. White would seem to be as lowly and vulnerable as the incarcerated Mr. Blonde, pictured by Nice Guy Eddie with "black semen . . . shootin' up his butt" (51). All this changes, however, in the pseudo-hetero context created by his admonitory relation to Mr. Pink, which conveniently enables Mr. White to regain his maleness and his coolness, even to acquire a degree of "blackness." We might, in short, imagine Mr. White leaving behind a racial schema in which he is uncool; entering a gender schema in which, compared to "pink," he crosses over into the cool; and finally reentering the racial schema as, if not black, then considerably blackened and passably cool. Coolness for Tarantino, and those enraptured with him, thus involves a distinctly masculine desire for mastery, in which domination of the feminine is tied up with white male anxiety about, among other things, black masculinity. One of my primary goals in what follows is to localize Tarantino's allure by exposing its inextricability from white male need. *Pulp Fiction*'s violence, I will argue, is driven by an interest in exploring male vulnerability, along with an only partly self-conscious compulsion to restore men to a state of cool imperviousness.

Unlike in movies by Brian De Palma or David Lynch and Hollywood fare generally, the object of violence in *Pulp Fiction* and *Reservoir Dogs* is rarely the body of a woman within the diegesis. Female bodies are, in any case, few and far between in the first two movies directed as well as written by Tarantino.[3] Instead, as the moniker "Mr. Pink" suggests, he is more preoccupied by the aspect of manhood repudiated as "feminine," and this, not women per se, is what he courts and what he tortures. But the scarcity of female characters in *Pulp Fiction* does not mean that women are entirely absent or spared. For my purposes, the precise quality and function of their presence is figured by a moment in the motel room of Butch and Fabienne (Bruce Willis and Maria de Medeiros) when the camera closes in on a TV screen bursting with bombs (104–6). As in most of Tarantino's films, the landscape on the tube is a war zone and ostensibly all male. In the foreground, however, shimmers Fabienne's reflection as she stands there brushing her teeth, half attentive to the killing fields. This coupling of the daily and banal with the horrendous occurs often in Tarantino, who typically rhymes "burger" with "murder" to produce both comic and sinister effects.

Perhaps less intentional, however, is the way he relegates women, and Fabienne in particular, to an "ordinary" that for him is essentially unnarratable. The story of men mutilating each other disturbs Tarantino, but it alone has the power to make his camera whir and his film reel turn. Unlike the harmless things women do—standing, brushing, watching—male violence counts as "action," and, as I elaborate below, it is what counts in movies like *Pulp Fiction* and *Reservoir Dogs* as the "real." Tarantino's women, by contrast, may serve as origin and destination of plot for an action figure like Butch, but (as in western narrative generally) they themselves are largely outside of plot. At best, they are like Mia (Uma Thurman), whose role in *Pulp Fiction* is as short-lived as her role in the doomed television pilot; Tarantino too gives her a single joke before she is dropped (17–18, 57). More frequently they are Fabiennes, devoted to small gestures made within small spaces, spectral presences hovering just offscreen.

My project in this chapter is to claim Fabienne as not only a spectral but also a spectatorial presence. By insisting on a female subject position outside Tarantino's frame, by legitimating, as it were, the scorned perspective of "our mothers," I hope, first, to explicate violence in *Pulp Fiction* as part of a logic constitutive of "cool" white masculinity; and second, to observe that a "realism" based on this logic serves to discount other possible realisms. Tarantino, I will argue, invokes a narrative idiom appreciative of the ordinary and intimate, only to nullify this along with the women who represent it.

THE ADRENALINE SHOT

One means of getting at *Pulp Fiction*'s violence might be to count its bodies and inventory its weapons. Following Butch, who goes through a hammer, bat, and chainsaw before choosing a samurai sword to unzip Zed (128), we could enumerate ways of getting whacked in Tarantino. I want, instead, to offer a trope that makes violence a matter of form as well as theme. As a figure for the syntax of violence in this movie, I propose the adrenaline shot. Literally, this is the shot that Vincent Vega (John Travolta) stabs into Mia Wallace's heart, jolting her out of her overdose (78–81). The overdose occurs at the climax of a long sequence involving Vincent and Mia that promises, in countless ways, to end in sex (48–69). The nervous jealous-husband jokes, Mia's coked-up pouts, and Vincent's narcotized sermons to himself all point in one direction. At Jackrabbit Slim's, his body defamiliarized by heroin, Vincent samples Mia's five-dollar shake and does the twist in his stocking feet with a kind of slow-motion, sensual amazement. No less than Vincent, we are astonished to find ourselves on a dance floor at all in a movie such as this, and the resulting pleasure of this musical interlude has lowered our guard by the time we get back to Mia's.[4]

But then, suddenly, instead of sex we get death, or something very close to it. One minute Mia is sultry with anticipation, the next she's a bloody mess, sexy as an emergency room. The effect on the audience is jarring, to say the least. Has the foreplay quickened our pulses? Have our hearts opened in expectation of intimacy? Tarantino throws the switch and gives us a face turned inside out. All narratives rely to some degree on suspense and on surprise. Most place obstacles between lovers. But this body-jolting extremity of disappointment, this violent injection of antithesis, is what I call narrative as adrenaline shot. Violence in *Pulp Fiction* is thus not only a signature motif but also a narrative rhythm or mode, and the adrenaline shot is not only the jab Vincent gives Mia but also the director's cinematic method, a way of organizing visual materials.[5]

Porn films splice together a series of mininarratives, each one building to a climax known in the industry as the "money shot." Tarantino, I am suggesting, replaces this with a series building again and again to the adrenaline shot. It is not always, as with Mia and Vincent, a case of *coitus interruptus*; elsewhere we get simply *coitus superfluous*. For example, in the motel sequence featuring Butch and Fabienne, the two make love, but instead of peaking here the narrative climaxes with the eruption of Butch's violence over his father's gold watch. In one frame his childlike lover is completing her toilette and planning her breakfast; in the next she is cowering in the corner while Butch destroys the furniture (108–13). The whole idea of this scene is to smash its domesticity with the spree of murder, torture, and rape that immediately follows.

Before the credits even roll, Tarantino gives us a proleptic instance of this pattern (7–13). A young man and woman (Roth and Plummer) who call each other "Pumpkin" and "Honey Bunny" are seated in a diner. He speaks energetically while she humors him, and the mood is comfortably conjugal. The woman smiles a lot in a lazy, purring, postcoital kind of way and at one point puts her head down on the table. They are talking about robbery, but the scene is more about being a couple, waking up side by side, drinking coffee, making plans. Then Tarantino sets up his adrenaline shot. The man and woman lean across the table and kiss; next they murmur endearments; and finally, in a flash, they leap to their feet with guns drawn and faces contorted: "Any of you fuckin' pricks move and I'll execute every motherfuckin' last one of you!" (13) The camera freezes on the woman yelling this—an image of murderous rage—before cutting to the credit sequence.

Tarantino shows us the diner couple agreeing to rob the restaurant, preferably without bloodshed, so their explosion into threats shocks us less than Fabienne's ruined morning, pains us less than Mia's near death and horrifying revival. Still, the essential logic of this opening episode may be seen to anticipate the other two insofar as all involve a burst of violence that works to disperse heterosexual closeness and ironize the little things that lovers do and say.[6] Pumpkin and Honey Bunny's pet names for each other, Butch and Fabienne's baby talk, Vincent and Mia's awkward flirtation all seem lightweight, if not absurd, faced off with death, as if the stuff of Harlequins were put in the ring with Homer. Intimacy apparently puts coolness at risk, and the director responds with a paradigm swerve designed to break up and disparage it. One effect of the adrenaline shot is thus to establish a hierarchy valuing disruption over connection, unexpected crisis over daily ritual—a hierarchy in which, as it were, a heroic mode displaces and subordinates a domestic one. Needless to say, these modes are gendered.

As for the gay male desire that is everywhere in Tarantino, this desire generally represents not only another stay against heterosex but also, in turn, a threat to the heroic mode. Here too the adrenaline shot intervenes to dispel the dangers of intimacy. Take the early scene, for example, in which Vincent and Jules stroll down a dark hall together, their large bodies overlapping in the narrow space. Their talk drifts from fondling the boss's wife to foot massages between men, until they find themselves in front of a closed door (19–21). Here everything stops for a beat. Then the gangsters resume walking, the conversation rewinds to adultery, and when Vincent and Jules return to the door a moment later, they come not to pleasure but to shatter the bodies of four men.[7] In this foot massage–turned–massacre, the adrenalizing jolt comes when a dialogue full of wit, affection, and fine discriminations about the everyday pulls up short, and we find ourselves in a room certain that only death will get us out of it. Inside the death chamber, moreover, the pairing of these extremes is parodically replayed, the endearing details of daily life forced into company with high-tech weaponry. But while before we were asked to enjoy the way different cultures package their beef patties, perceiv-

John Travolta and Samuel Jackson keeping cool in Tarantino's *Pulp Fiction* (1994).

ing at the same time that we are all God's children in consumption, now discussing the relative merits of Big Kahuna Burger becomes a way of taunting
men about to die. In this new situation, the reassuring normalcy of days
hung on cholesterol and corporate logos, which Tarantino often appears to
value, is made suddenly irrelevant and even despicable. My point, once
again, is that his lurch from the daily to the deadly, from closeness to separation, works finally to trivialize the former. Everything becomes banal in
contrast to the high meaningfulness of butchery, and this banality is implicitly labeled "feminine" or, in this case, "effeminate."

The precedence of a murderous "male" economy over a "female" one of
desire and domesticity is comically inverted by the section called "The

Bonnie Situation" (135–70). Here Vincent and Jules, who must be the first gangsters in history to clean up after themselves, pull off the road and attack their bloody car with all manner of household cleaners. "Get the Windex, do a good job," Harvey Keitel as "The Wolf" admonishes them (155). In this suburban topography of garages and gourmet coffee, bedroom sets and linen closets, hit men worry about bloodstains on a white towel and shrink in fear from the nozzle of a garden hose. Deadliness is next to cleanliness on Bonnie's turf, and the worst fate imaginable is divorce. For a moment, intimacy threatens to outrank mastery, and for once a woman coming home is more eventful than a man going off to war. Finally this section is funny, however, precisely because it so ludicrously upsets the norm. Like people pulling carts in which animals ride, men scrubbing frantically before the wife gets off work belong to a topsy-turvy world that, by definition, cannot be sustained; indeed, dependent for its humor on continual reference to the conventional order, in the end it may simply reinforce this. Predictably, neither Bonnie nor her story actually materializes, and our heroes, freshened up and victorious in the fight against dirt, soon reclaim the road.[8]

GONE/THERE

It is true, I acknowledge, that Vincent and Jules leave Bonnie's house deprived of the black suits Tarantino likens to "suits of armor."[9] It is also the case that this section sets up the movie's epilogue, which returns to the diner of the opening scene and proceeds to illustrate Jules's conversion to nonviolence. We might be tempted, therefore, to think that Tarantino's crooked tale goes straight after all—his bad dudes trading in their armor for sandals, guns for diplomacy, coolness for gentle dorkiness—and more than one critic has asserted as much. Charles Deemer, for example, hails *Pulp Fiction* as a subtle departure from Tarantino's earlier screenplays, because for the first time "redemption is possible" (82). Cynthia Baughman and Richard Moran likewise argue for an accent on redemption not only in Jules's choice of charity over tyranny but also in directorial manipulations of time that, on a formal if not moral level, interrupt a robbery and (by concluding with events before his death) bring Vincent back to life. Yet the irony of Baughman and Moran's elegant reading is that it actually devotes far more space to figures like Butch and Vincent, who are not redeemed, than it does to

Jules, who ostensibly is. These critics also admit that the character who engages us most is probably not the reconstructed Jules but rather his doomed friend, Vincent (109)—in part because Jules reforms himself right out of a role in those middle sections (2 and 3) presumed to occur after he exits the criminal life (110). Much as *Pulp Fiction* would imagine an alternative to violence, its narrative idiom is such that it cannot pursue the story of a character like Jules once he lays down his gun.[10] This idiom, organized by what I have called the adrenaline shot, is motivated not by the possibility of redemption but by the inevitable repetition of violence.

Tarantino does, with some regularity, resurrect characters and actors from movie to movie, so that Vic Vega (alias Mr. Blonde) dies in *Reservoir Dogs* but comes back as Vincent Vega in *Pulp Fiction*. Harvey Keitel, who plays Mr. White in the first film, is also reanimated in the second as Winston Wolf. And Tim Roth, dying throughout *Dogs* as Mr. Orange, is similarly returned to the fray as *Pulp Fiction*'s Pumpkin. Yet these examples serve only to support my claim that rebirth in Tarantino may be less about salvation than compulsion. Like Zed's sadistic sidekick, Maynard, who sprays his victims awake in order to torture them some more (123), all Tarantino really does is put people back in the ring for another round of abuse.

The adrenaline shot is characterized, in short, by two things: a lurch from feminizing intimacy to heroic alienation; and repetition. The reasons and pleasures behind it are illuminated, I suggest, by Freud's famous remarks concerning a child's game of Fort!/Da! (8–11). As Freud understands it, this game originates in painful separation from the mother, which the repetition of "Fort!"/"Da!" (gone/there) manages in several ways. First, it symbolically casts the mother out in order to stage her joyful return. Freud noted, however, that the game's return phase (Da!) was usually omitted, leading him to stress a second motive: that of reimagining an event in which the child is uncomfortably *passive* as one in which he is, far more pleasurably, *active*. Finally, there may be a punitive aspect to the child's repeated gesture, insofar as it preemptively and vindictively expels the abandoning mother.

Though all children presumably share anxiety about abandonment and need to achieve a degree of separateness, Nancy Chodorow's work in object relations suggests that modern western masculinity is shaped by an especially urgent mandate to depart and distinguish itself from a primary female figure (104–8). Boys may therefore have a heightened investment in the task of separation. For this reason, I have followed Freud's use of "he" in narrating the Fort!/Da! dynamic, taking the maleness of his particular protagonist to symbolize a wider social pattern.[11] My point about *Pulp Fiction* is that Tarantino's adrenaline shot would seem to derive from similar, markedly "male" fears and to involve a similar assembly of strategic responses. Like the anxious toddler, Tarantino mimes again and again the violent loss of close relation, and the effect of his playful simulation—at least for those in tune with his story—is the transmutation of passive into active, vulnerability into mastery, pain into pleasure. As he preemptively disrupts one intimacy after another (between Pumpkin and Honey Bunny, Jules and Vincent, Vincent and Mia, Butch and Fabienne), the original desire for connection is virtually written over by a desire for separation, which accedes in its own right to the status of the pleasurable.

Tarantino summarizes the emotional achievement of the Fort!/Da! game in another way as well, as if he can't get enough of the alchemy producing masculine power out of impotence. One of his favorite moves is to take a man from tyrant to tyrannized and back again, sometimes in the course of the story but often in a matter of seconds. Butch, for example, kills another boxer and seems to have outfoxed the mob boss, Marsellus (Ving Rhames); but then, crossing an open lot to get his watch, he appears defenseless as an overbold child; moments later, he kills Vincent with the mobster's own weapon.[12] The subsequent dungeon scene begins with Butch on top of Marsellus; next shows him bound and gagged by the pawnshop sadist, Maynard; and concludes shortly thereafter when Butch cuts Maynard dead. Marsellus, for his part, begins as the mystified, omnipotent Godfather; goes on to suffer a rape imagined by this film as the ultimate male humiliation; and finally not only masters Zed but also, thanks to Tarantino's scrambled chronology, is next shown poolside, restored to all his pre-rape splendor. Old Testament avenger Jules, too, survives a round of bullets and proceeds to overpower Pumpkin, the armed robber who, in turn, is suddenly unmanned by a gun to the head. Lastly, there is Vincent, shot while shitting, only to be revived by a flashback that has him exiting the can and pointing a weapon at Honey Bunny.

In every case but Pumpkin's, these oscillations between male abjection and omnipotence resolve in favor of the latter. When completed in a hectic split second, they resemble adrenaline shots in their shock value, though here the director merely repositions his characters while remaining within a single modality. But whatever their time frame, in swinging from infantile helplessness to homicidal fury, converting some characters into agents while displacing the fate of passivity onto others, these sudden reversals distill the adrenaline shot's underlying psychodrama. That psychodrama, I have argued, issues from a sense of male vulnerability in relationship, and its outcome, over and over, is a strong dose of remedial violence.[13]

SOFT MEN, PULP FICTION

As we have seen, the vulnerability that *Pulp Fiction* finds so fearfully "uncool" is gendered female and must be forcefully repudiated by its male characters. In addition to the boy child's trouble with relation/separation outlined above, as well as the white man's humiliation by his myth of black masculinity, there are several other aspects of Tarantino's work that raise the specter of feminization and so require the masculinizing intervention of violence. First, perhaps because Tarantino was trained as an actor, his work is notably self-conscious about actors and acting: *Reservoir Dogs* has a long flashback of the undercover cop learning his lines (70–73); *Pulp Fiction* shows Jules and Vincent "getting into character" before their hit (22); and in all his screenplays, Tarantino's habit of alluding to other films calls attention to the craft involved in his own. Stressing the movieness of his movies, Tarantino accentuates Hollywood's mode of framing the bodies of actors "to be looked at," displaying men as well as women in ways that cultural codes of spectatorship consider "feminine."[14] Moreover, the spectacle of the male body, present but repressed in most films by an aggressively heterosexual focus on female bodies, is unusually difficult to overlook in Tarantino's typically male worlds. Calling attention to men as objects of the gaze, Tarantino not only puts them where classic cinema and social norms say women should be but also, dangerously, makes possible their contemplation by other men.

Pulp Fiction, though it pays glancing attention to Uma Thurman's curves, is especially smitten with the hard, boxer's body of Bruce Willis playing Butch. After his big fight, for example, we see Butch jump half naked into a cab, strip off his gloves, and breathlessly towel off his streaming, well-muscled chest. Looking through the windshield and past a darkly glamorous cab driver (Angela Jones), the camera does not gaze *at* her so much as identify *with* her, so that we focus together, as if in the rearview mirror, on the hunk changing clothes in the back seat. The classic male gaze is likewise disoriented in the subsequent motel scene, which has Fabienne fully dressed during sex while Butch is conspicuously shirtless. Tarantino follows this with a view of Fabienne described in the screenplay as "swallowed up" by a terrycloth robe. Behind her, meanwhile, "Butch is inside the shower washing up. We see the outline of his naked body through the smoky glass of the shower door" (101). Here in the shower, earlier in the cab, and also in the slow dolly around and around the boxer in a phone booth (95), Willis's eroticized body is pinned behind a pane of glass that tropes nothing so much as a camera lens. Seducing us with the sight of this character, Tarantino underlines both the cinematic cliché (a woman silhouetted in the shower) and his own innovative re-gendering of it.

To my way of seeing, John Travolta as Vincent is also especially arresting. There is something about his lazy-eyed fleshiness in this film that pleases me, notably in the section called "Vincent Vega and Marsellus Wallace's Wife." We are, in any case, explicitly urged to take him as a visual object by the scene in which Vincent picks Mia up at her house. The original screenplay begins with voyeuristic shots of Mia dressing and only afterward has her filming Vincent with a camcorder (43–48). The completed film revises this sequence, however, making Mia a largely disembodied voice and panoptical gaze (48–51). Up until the last moment, we see only her lip-sticked lips speaking into an intercom, her back as she sits in front of multiple video screens, and her hand manipulating the camera controls to track Vincent's movements. Our view of him (in color and on his level) is inter-cut with hers (in black and white from above): together we watch him navigate his stoned and self-conscious way around the plush, white living room. Finally, to drive the point home, Tarantino shows the gangster examining a portrait of Mia but shoots it from the portrait's point of view, looking down on Vincent earnestly impersonating a man who knows a little something about art.

So even when positioned as spectator, Vincent is denied visual authority. And his role in this section as object rather than subject of the look is reinforced by the subsequent dance scene, which deliberately recalls not only *Grease* but also the spectacle of Travolta gyrating his way to stardom in *Saturday Night Fever.*[15] As I have suggested, the framing of Willis and Travolta for display and the relative absence of women thus framed goes against the grain of sexual as well as gender norms. Add to this the paucity of women available to mediate male relations, and you get in *Pulp Fiction* a homosocial world in which gay desire is always on the verge of coming out. Unfortunately, for this basically conventional director, such brinksmanship only heightens the level of violence required to deny the triple threat of male objectification, female desire, and love between men—all the more reason, then, for the gory end to Mia's story.

Pulp Fiction troubles conventional masculinity in still one more way. Its self-congratulatory recycling of pop cultural materials insists on the movie's own status as popular entertainment. Ostensibly shunning the art house crowd, it chooses to identify instead with the lowbrow sensibilities of greasy food, politically incorrect cartoons, and crime fiction. Likewise, Tarantino's most important models span a range of popular movie genres: 1930s gangster films, 1940s noirs, 1960s spaghetti Westerns, 1970s blaxploitation and Bruce Lee movies. Slashers are another formative influence: *Psycho* (1960), *The Texas Chainsaw Massacre* (1974), and on down to the seventh circle of mutilation-and-dismemberment flicks. What all of these genres share is an aspiration to sweaty palms and raised pulse; all are thrillers in the sense of attacking the very nervous systems of their viewers, and their investment in bodily response connects them to two other denigrated types: pornography and the weepie. Aiming to move audiences in quite literal, corporeal ways, *Pulp Fiction* not only represents onscreen but also imagines its viewers as opened, effluent, palpitating bodies. On the one hand Tarantino revels in the messy, gutsy immediacy of a film tradition descended from the Victorian "sensation" novel; on the other hand, however, he seems uneasily to recognize these genres—which "pulp" not only their characters but also their most hardened spectators—as feminizing.[16]

I have argued that Tarantino's method of administering repeated adrenaline shots may, like the Fort!/Da! game, address certain male needs. Yet the rush of feeling the shots produce also goes against the grain of manliness; culturally speaking, jolted nerves, along with penetrable cavities and dripping orifices, belong to women. And although (or because) this film primarily addresses sensation-seeking men, it pays homage to the cultural norm through the scene that inspired my trope, in which the body jump-started by adrenaline is not actually male but female. Meanwhile, the masculine counterpart to this oozing, punctured feminine is represented by the much-discussed briefcase that Jules and Vincent kill for. My own answer to the cult question, "What's inside the briefcase?" is interiority—that is, defended, mystified, male interiority. Much valued, much vaunted, and never finally shown, this radiant, indefinable softness is locked within a hard, exterior shell. Even Jules, who wants to lose the baggage of a barricaded self, walks out of the movie clutching it still (187). It is into this world of female bodies so soft they dissolve and male bodies so hard they feel and reveal nothing that *Pulp Fiction* tentatively admits the ambiguous "Gimp": a figure for the unmanly man who willingly, wordlessly submits to every sensation the movie cares to inflict (125–28).[17] The Gimp embodies the first, vulnerable moment of what I have called the adrenaline shot and the sex/gender confusion of the captive male viewer overwhelmed by feeling. At the same time, The Gimp's beating by Butch and death by hanging suggest once more Tarantino's ongoing need to master this vulnerability and murder this ambiguity.

There is, finally, another breach of gender laws raised by Tarantino's putative embrace of the popular.[18] For as Andreas Huyssen, among others, has argued, mass culture and its fans have long been sneeringly described as "female." In this sense, *Pulp Fiction*'s publicity shot of Uma Thurman, lolling in bed with a bad novel, does more than use cleavage to sell tickets; it also recognizes that women stretching back to Emma Bovary have been seen and derided as the archetypal consumers of pulp (Huyssen 188–90). In the actual story, however, it is not Thurman's character but Travolta's who goes to the bathroom at two key moments with a copy of the pulpy *Modesty Blaise* (117, 176). Note too that while a little research proves the author of this text to be a man (Peter O'Donnell), its very visible cover, like the Thurman poster, features a woman's face. Locating popular fiction in the bathroom, Tarantino reinforces its association with shit, already suggested by the dictionary meanings of "pulp" that preface the movie: moist, shapeless matter; also, lurid stories on cheap paper.[19] What we have, then, is a series of damaging associations—pulp, women, shit—that taint not only male producers of mass-market fiction but also male consumers. Perched on the toilet with his book (176), Vincent is feminized by sitting instead of standing as well as by his trashy tastes; preoccupied by the anal, he is implicitly infantilized and homosexualized; and the seemingly inevitable result is being pulverized by Butch with a Czech M61 submachine gun (117–18). That this fate has to do with Vincent's reading habits is strongly suggested by a slow tilt from the book on the floor directly up to the corpse spilled into the tub.

Huyssen concludes optimistically that postmodernism has all but collapsed the gendered hierarchy between art and schlock so typical of modernism (201–6). *Pulp Fiction* demonstrates, however, that even an open pulpophile like Tarantino may continue to feel anxious and emasculated by his preferences.[20] His response is to savage the body unmanned by fiction like his, so that Travolta's flaccidity is superseded by Willis's hardness. The movie's concluding flashback to the diner offers still another antidote. In this version, Vincent gets to emerge from the men's room *sans* book, gun drawn and ready for action. Rewriting the "earlier" assassination scene, Tarantino now asserts not only Vincent's vitality but also his virility, spelled out in particular contrast to Honey Bunny— the "bitch" who proves no-tably "uncool" under fire. "I gotta go pee! I want to go home," she whimpers, aiming unsteadily back at Vincent (185). As it turns out, would-be shepherd Jules spares her life and Pumpkin's, but not before the bathroom, the leaky body, and the pulpy read have all been realigned with the biolog-ically female.

VIOLENCE AS THE REAL

Whiteness, closeness to women, closeness to men, bodily display, bodily sensation, the cheap thrills of mass culture—*Pulp Fiction* shows men made as vulnerable as "women" by all of these and then disowns any hint of cross-gendering by killing the character in question, arming him, or otherwise in-troducing the *deus ex machina* of sudden violence. Tarantino's signature move, I have argued, is to shatter again and again the intimacies of break-fast, bedroom, or banter with a hammer blow of death, and the result is a narrative jagged as broken glass. It is not simply that Tarantino creates gangsters or cowboys or warriors of some sort within an adventure story type that any three-year-old could recognize as "male." The logic of the adrenaline shot dictates, rather, oscillation between a "male" economy of emergency and a "female" one of the humble everyday. What distinguishes Tarantino is the adjacency in his films of epic levels of violence with what he himself describes as the little facts of "real life." He explains in an inter-view, for example, that Mr. Orange of *Reservoir Dogs* bleeds to death with excruciating slowness because "that's the reality. If someone is shot in the stomach, that's how they die" (Dargis 19). Similarly, one of his fantasies is to take *The Guns of Navarone*, keep "the thrills and the spills," but add char-acters who "would be human beings, with a heartbeat, who would talk about things other than just blowing up the cannons" (Dargis 16). For Tarantino, in short, "real-life" touches authenticate death while making bad dudes more plausible as such. Consequently, though of course his violence is not real, one might fairly say that it aspires to a kind of realism. And if quotidian details make violence more believable, Tarantino's corollary is that violence makes for a truer everyday. Defending his use of violence in neonaturalist terms, he reasons, "Violence is part of this world and I am drawn to the outrageousness of real-life violence." Take the example of a man in a restaurant picking up a fork and stabbing his wife in the face. "That's really crazy and comic-bookish," he comments, "but it also happens" (Fuller xiv–xv).

My concern with this epistemology, as I've already suggested, is the way it naturalizes and prioritizes violence as "the real." My problem with Tarantino isn't that he actually kills people or encourages his viewers to do so, but that his brand of realism sees a fork in the face as the ultimate sign of "reality." In Tarantinoland, romance isn't true unless there's killing involved, and vanilla sex belongs to the fantasy world of Jackrabbit Slim's. Men I've talked to generally get into the notion that Tarantino mixes up dinner and murder with an even hand. But I don't agree that Mia's face after overdosing—smeared with what looks like cum—is about some mystical contiguity of sex and death, yoking the occasional with the ultimate. To me, as I've said, it looks like death *instead* of sex, just as every adrenaline shot mentioned above makes violence the main event and all else mere prelude and pretense. The privileging of violence as the real stuff of stories is particularly clear in the Butch section ("The Gold Watch"), from which I take my closing example. When the boxer finally returns to Fabienne, he comes from having butchered three men and fled from sadists; she, meanwhile, ate buttermilk pancakes (they didn't have blueberry) and can't begin to fathom his ordeal (132–35). That the movie shows us his story and not hers is both cause and effect of its conviction that Fabienne's little appetites and fears are off the metaphysical map and wholly implausible as plot. Tarantino, once again, does more than give us violence. He gives it to us over against a realism of pancakes and incomprehension of violence epitomized by Fabienne and explicitly denigrated by *Pulp Fiction* as sentimental, genteel, small-minded, and naive. To this I would reply, standing up for depictions of lives ranging narrowly between good sex and a pay cut, that sometimes a fork is only a fork.

2

SPIKE LEE AND BRIAN DE PALMA: SCENARIOS OF RACE AND RAPE

Ever since Eve Sedgwick's *Between Men: English Literature and Male Homosocial Desire* (1985), the erotic triangle in which two men bond over the body of a woman has proved more compelling for literary and cultural critics, and certainly more demonstrable, than that mysteriously attractive triangle near Bermuda. In Victorian novels and postmodern movies, the Sedgwickian triangle—the woman between men—seems to meet us at every turn. Surely this is one reason the more exclusive male homosociality of *Pulp Fiction* and *Reservoir Dogs* strikes us as so raw and bold; though we have seen that Tarantino dares not follow through on his theme of ties between men, we should also give him credit for being less tempted than most to triangulate and dress these up as heterosexual rivalries. Turning away now from such Tarantinoisms as Mr. White cradling (before killing) the bleeding Mr. Orange, this chapter takes as its starting point what is more often, in our culture, the strategic mediation of such relationships by a third, female party. Proceeding through a series of three-sided scenarios drawn from American culture at the onset of the 1990s, I develop Sedgwick's typology so as to schematize relations not only of gender and sexuality but also of race.

We have already seen, in our reading of *Pulp Fiction*, the extent to which white men gain access to "coolness" through the assumption of a phantasmatic black masculinity. In his public persona, the characters he plays, and the characters he conjures, Tarantino stages quite frankly his identification with the hip vernacular of African American males. This chapter, by contrast, explores the attempt by white men not to embrace or embody black men but rather to master them. It considers cultural narratives driven not by cross-racial identification so much as by white male domination and black male protest. What both chapters share is the sense that masculinities are significantly shaped by racial impersonations and antagonisms.

SEDGWICK'S WORK DRAWS, of course, on Lévi-Strauss's famous reasoning about exogamous marriage: that male-headed groups exchange women in order to bind themselves to each other in relationships of reciprocity and kinship. Like money or words, brides are circulated for the purpose of organizing and extending masculine society. The result is what Gayle Rubin has called the "traffic in women," in which men are designated as givers, women as gifts. "It is the partners, not the presents," Rubin notes, "upon whom reciprocal exchange confers its quasi-mystical power of social linkage" (174). Luce Irigaray, in "Commodities Among Themselves," has also commented on the implications of this traffic for the commodity: "Woman exists only as an occasion for mediation, transaction, transition, transference, between man and his fellow man" (193). Although Rubin points out that gift exchange may involve male rivalries and disputes as well as diplomacy, the emphasis of all the analyses above is on the role women play in fostering positive conjunctions between men—in bringing them together as affines, political allies, economic partners, and, in Sedgwick's formulation, cohorts of a "potentially erotic" kind. This formulation suggests, briefly, that in a modern patriarchy such as ours—based on male ties but at the same time violently homophobic—men will be required to route their intimacy through women. Elaborating on René Girard's study of erotic triangles in European fiction, Sedgwick's important argument only makes explicit the assumption, intimated by precursor accounts, that what women mediate is basically men's *desire* for each other.

Sedgwick is particularly concerned to take up this triangular paradigm "not as an ahistorical, Platonic form, a deadly symmetry from which the historical accidents of gender, language, class, and power detract, but as a sensitive register precisely for delineating relationships of power and meaning" (27). As evidence of the way racial ideologies, for example, can shape and splinter sexual meanings, she observes that *Gone With the Wind* (book and film) automatically construes the vaguest black male–white female encounters as "rape," while refusing to perceive white-on-white sexual assault as anything but "blissful marriage" (9–10). And in numerous brilliant readings Sedgwick goes on to show how literary representations of male homosocial desire are variously inflected by shifting, historically specific constructions of class, male homosexuality, gender, and English imperialism. Yet in spite of this self-conscious and elucidating attention to the way erotic triangles get tossed on historical seas, there is a sense in which their significance for Sedgwick remains the same: they are always essentially about the forbidden love of men for men. What I wish to do in this chapter is to insist on some of the other meanings that may inform this configuration, meanings that in Sedgwick are perhaps too readily subsumed by the trope of attraction between men. I will also, in my conclusion, urge our renewed attention to the women who are both pivotal and incidental to this paradigm. Anticipating my concerns in chapter 6 (which returns to Sedgwick and her predominance in the field of queer theory), I finally shift away from a between-men model that, as Sedgwick herself readily admits, has little to say about female subjectivities.

Let me begin by repeating that men's ties to each other are frequently characterized not simply by uneasy desire but also by political domination on one side and resistance to that domination on the other—that race and racism, for example, cross and complicate relations between men so that the erotic, while undoubtedly present, may no longer be the predominant affect or agenda.[1] Sedgwick does not leave conflict out of these relations, but in her account hostility and violence are essentially the signs of a highly charged but unrecognized intimacy. Thus "the magnetism between the rivals in *Our Mutual Friend,* although intense, has to be inferred from the very violence of their hating intercourse" (181). In a homophobic society, the Freudian logic by which same-sex "rivalry" and "love" are complementary, even equivalent, intensities (and the privileged subtext is sexual) can clarify a good deal. I do not deny that domination and desire are sometimes inseparable bedfellows. Yet it seems important to explore the way women also mediate rivalries between men that cannot be wholly assimilated to "love." In the American imagination today, women are often at the nexus of male struggles that, however eroticized, are more fully explained in terms of attempts both to enforce and to oppose white supremacy.

My first four scenarios represent a set of interlocking variations on this theme. Each is centered on a woman's rape and emblematic, I think, of a story we tell ourselves about race relations in this culture. I have tried to render them with some degree of subtlety and specificity, even while abstracting their triangular logics of race/gender so as to offer them as general types. In these abstracted terms, they delineate the following geometries. One, white men dominating men of color through a narrative involving a white woman's rape. Two, the same racial domination only this time involving a woman of color. Scenarios 3 and 4, shifting from a white male to black male subject position, are ostensibly parallel to the first two. In 3, African American men resist the oppression of white men through a narrative involving the rape of a black woman. And in 4, resistance to racial domination turns on the rape of a white woman. These latter African American examples are both drawn from early movies by Spike Lee, in which the staging of racial strife and the call for racial justice are paramount. Yet as with Edward Said, Andrew Ross, and Henry Louis Gates Jr., as well as queer theorists Lee Edelman and Judith Halberstam, Lee's hip racial politics ultimately depend, I will argue, on the continued marginalization of women and the feminine. For instance, in ways that will be echoed by subsequent chapters, his movie *School Daze* (1988) associates racial coolness and authenticity with masculinity, while projecting racial conservatism and betrayal onto the female body. And of course all four scenarios I discuss not only relegate women to merely intermediary roles but also work to define them, above all, as objects of male sexual violence. This chapter closes with a fifth scenario challenging the tendency to narrate race through heterosexual rape. My conclusion offers an alternative model of international and domestic race relations represented, for a change, through women whose interlocutors are other women.

SCENARIO 1: THE CENTRAL PARK JOGGER

I would start by returning, in effect, to Sedgwick's image of Scarlett O'Hara and the specter of the black rapist. "The Central Park jogger" was the name given by the press to a woman raped, beaten, and left for dead in Central Park on April 19, 1989. The woman was young, white, and an investment banker at Salomon Brothers; those arrested and ultimately convicted for the crime were young, black or Hispanic, and working class. My concern here is not with the actual assault, whose brutality is obvious and whose historical details remain, in any case, elusive.[2] I am interested, rather, in the way this event was narrated by the white, male-dominated media, the ideologies that were filtered through it, and the allegorical meanings accruing to it over time. Lingering in the news for the next eighteen months (three of the defendants went on trial in the summer of 1990, two in the fall of 1990), the jogger became, among other things, a locus of white panic about crime in New York City. The woman's job, her use of leisure hours for aerobic exercise, and especially her young, blond femaleness combined to render her a symbol of privileged intactness suddenly violated. Beyond their horror at this particular rape, the class of New Yorkers accustomed to moving through the city sealed off from violence by whiteness and wealth were enraged by what they read as a general attack on their entitlement to be invulnerable.

The racism underlying their rage was barely disguised by the pseudo-sociological media inquiry into an alarming phenomenon known as "wilding." From what I can remember and imagine, the term originated something like this: a reporter from a white newspaper drove up to East 110th Street and quickly assembled around him a group of neighborhood kids eager to comment on the recent crime. One of them made what may in fact have been a reference to a popular song of the time, Tone Loc's "Wild Thing." The newsman misheard and gravely reported that for young black and Hispanic youths to go on a group spree of premeditated rape and maybe murder was a well-known practice referred to in street argot as "wilding." The effect of this widely publicized construct was implicitly to pathologize black culture, to justify any irregularity in the obtaining of videotaped confessions from four of the accused, and to rationalize further Bernard Goetz-style preemptive strikes against groups of nonwhite male teens who ride the subways or use the parks.[3]

This logic—in which the myth of the black rapist stalking white womanhood becomes a blanket excuse for the execution of black men by white men—has, of course, a long and ugly history. The journalist Ida B. Wells exposed and condemned its racism in a series of pamphlets published between 1892 and 1900, a period during which the rate of lynchings had reached more than a hundred per year. Only about one third of these involved accusations of rape or attempted rape, but all were at some irrational level justified to whites by the imagined black threat to "their" women. The case of Emmett Till, a fourteen-year-old boy murdered in 1955 for whistling at a white woman, is only the most notorious example of subsequent lynchings thematized along these lines. And the pattern prevails, as is now common knowledge, not only in the backwoods of the unreconstructed South but also in the contemporary criminal justice system, which continues to punish black-on-white rape more harshly than any other type.[4] So I take the Central Park jogger case to stand for one paradigm of American racism, available during slavery but crystallized in the period following Reconstruction and still influential today, in which white men's control of black men is mediated by the always-about-to-be-violated bodies of white women.

In this scenario, racism primarily (though not only) on the part of men and directed primarily at men operates alongside sexism in three respects. First, it makes white women coextensive with their sexuality, which is, moreover, taken to be tremblingly passive, never active and initiating. It assumes that no white woman would ever choose a black (or any) lover, and it estimates women's value in terms of their newness or usedness as sexual goods, making rape less the violation of a female body than a trespass on male property. Above all, it perceives white women as frail, vulnerable, and wholly dependent for protection on chivalric white males.[5] Second, by fixing on the specter of the black stranger-rapist, it obscures what is actually the far more habitual crime of white-on-white acquaintance rape. As antirape activists continually stress, the great majority of rapes are committed by men known to their victims and belonging to the same racial and class group (Estrich 11–12). And finally, by fetishizing the white woman as the quintessential victim of rape, it ignores the rape of black women altogether, by white and black men both. As the black community was quick to point out, the most salient fact about the story of the Central Park jogger is that it became a story at all, when daily violence against black women goes virtually unreported.[6] Angela Davis suggests further that, since "the mythical rapist implies the mythical whore," the jogger scenario may even encourage the rape of black women, insofar as it supports the convenient view of black people as naturally lascivious (191).

Before moving on to my next scenario, I would like to point out that a similar logic—what we might call the white chivalric fallacy—is frequently at work in imperialist American wars waged against a racial Other. Here too, white women back home may be taken to represent decency and security, made to symbolize the intact national body, which must be shielded from penetration by dark, alien forces. Outright aggression is once more framed as "protection," the bombardment by white men of an enemy imagined as nonwhite and male once again justified in the name of white women. Yet these women are, for the most part, not participants so much as symbolic currency in the exchange of firepower between men. Indeed, as Virginia Woolf argued in *Three Guineas* and more recent polls have seemed to confirm, women (like other disenfranchised groups) are apt to feel they have little to gain and much to lose from bids for national supremacy. The 1991 war in the Persian Gulf, to take an example concurrent with my texts, invoked the white chivalric fallacy on several mutually reinforcing levels. Certainly it generated televised images of a feminized home front—small midwestern towns waving with yellow ribbons and corn-fed women trying to keep back the tears. Saddam Hussein was perfect as the swarthy psychopath, and to Americans raised on generic images of Arabs as terrorists, it hardly mattered in emotional terms what particular country he was from or that other Arab states were on our side.[7] Yet the difficulty in this case of making even Hussein's melodramatized villainy extend to our own backyards also required a clever recasting of the scene. As Susan Jeffords argued at the time (following linguist George Lakoff), the helpless victim of this "rescue scenario" was less our own virgin land than Kuwait, an American satellite whose much-reiterated "rape" by Iraq cried out for our intervention. Jeffords derived this model not from that of lynching for rape but from an even older national story conjoining race and gender: the captivity narrative, popular in the late seventeenth and early eighteenth centuries, in which a Puritan woman must be rescued from her savage Indian captors by the heroic Puritan man ("Protection Racket" 10).

There was one more, less obvious variation on the logic of chivalry produced by this episode of aggression in the Gulf. Appropriating "feminism" for jingoism, U.S. news reports cast at least some Islamic women in the role of wannabe westerners. Subjected by Islamic men to a bizarre sexual confinement, such women cried out for salvation by a kinder and gentler American sexual politics. Underneath the chador, these stories implied, is an American soul struggling to free itself from the barbaric Arab male. This version of the rescue scenario with western "feminism" in the white chivalric role, while arguably enabled by an Orientalist strain of feminism (as well as Middle Eastern gender practices), was basically an opportunistic act of impersonation by the mainstream media, serving at once to rationalize our military invasion and to project home-team sexist guilt onto faraway lands.[8]

SCENARIO 2: CASUALTIES OF WAR

I refer here to Brian De Palma's 1989 Vietnam movie (screenplay by David Rabe). Like the press coverage of the rape in Central Park, *Casualties of War* narrates a real atrocity, first reported in 1969 by Daniel Lang: the kidnapping, gang rape, and murder of the South Vietnamese woman Phan Thi

Mao by four American soldiers, which took place in 1966.[9] Once again, however, I am less interested in the facts of the incident than in the way they have been mythologized by the dominant culture. In De Palma's myth, the story begins with the betrayal of Americans by innocent-seeming South Vietnamese villagers who turn out to be murderous Viet Cong. As a result of a surprise ambush, the squad's fearless and beloved black sergeant, Brown (Erik King), is shot down just weeks before his tour is over. Brown's mutilated body, anguished face, and pathetic bravado all serve to focus, for us and for his buddies, an image of the slant-eyed enemy as the incarnation of deceit and depravity. According to De Palma, the Viet Cong's malignant and triumphant maleness is further indicated by their monopolizing of the Vietnamese whores on a night when the grieving Americans are desperate to get laid. The vicious attack on the woman here called Oahn (Thuy Thu Le) follows soon thereafter.

In this scenario, then, the body of the Asian female, site of the Viet Cong's imagined mastery, is quite naturally transformed into the site of the Americans' "revenge." As in the lynching model above, white men's assault on darker men is staged not as aggression but as reasonable defense or retaliation, and once again this racial domination is achieved by means of the rapeable female body. That rape is a weapon of war is hardly news. As Susan Brownmiller recounts in *Against Our Will,* rape has been the victor's prerogative since *The Iliad* and has long been tolerated if not encouraged in spite of official prohibitions (31–113). I take *Casualties of War,* therefore, to figure a racialized version of a military truism: that rape is an effective means of waging war and one of its oldest rewards. To summarize and schematize my argument so far, both triangulated scenarios 1 and 2 uphold white privilege and pivot on the objectified figure of a woman. From a white male perspective, in the jogger scenario this woman is white, she is "ours," and "we" are protecting her from "them." This is what I have called the chivalric fallacy. In the De Palma scenario she is "yellow" (or some other deviation from "white"), she is a condensation of our racial hatred, and we are raping her. This story type is structured by what I call rape as a weapon of war.

The violence against women in the latter case is obvious, but *Casualties of War* adds an interesting twist to the role played by the victimized character Oahn. For De Palma's film dramatizes not only rationalized American violence against an Asian woman who stands for the Asian enemy (rationalized insofar as the rapists themselves are seen as "casualties" of war's moral chaos) but also American guilt about this violence. Perhaps De Palma—having butchered so many women of (techni)color in his earlier films—is working out some personal guilt as well. In any case, the protagonist of *Casualties* is a fifth soldier, Private First Class Eriksson, played by Michael J. Fox, who witnesses the rapes and murder but refuses to participate in them. In fact, he befriends Oahn, tries to help her escape, and eventually succeeds in having her four assailants court-martialed. The result is that male America gets to see itself as the winsome hero of *Family Ties*, while Oahn, in addition to being physically abused, is deprived even of the right to struggle and speak on her own behalf. De Palma portrays her as nothing but helpless terror— she's like a wounded child or animal—incapable of outrage and reliant on Eriksson even to prompt her escape. In a particularly implausible scene she clings to him, refusing to flee unless he goes with her. Later, as she lies broken in a gully, he braves a hostile military hierarchy in order to win her justice. For this gallantry the Asian woman (refigured as an Asian American student in the movie's frame) absolves America of guilt and reassures Eriksson that the "bad dream" of our violence against Vietnam is "over now." Any anger the Oahn figure might have toward Americans in uniform is obscenely written over as gratitude. De Palma's feat is to enable this woman's brutalized and silenced body to mediate both American men's savagery toward the Vietnamese and their fantasy of being forgiven for it.

The incident on which *Casualties* is based occurred in 1966: between the assassination of Malcolm X in '65 and that of Martin Luther King in '68, between the Watts riots of '65 and the Detroit riots of '67, at a time when violent protests against racism exploded in more than a hundred urban neighborhoods. Scenes of Vietnamese huts and American inner cities aflame blur together in our national memory. More to the point, when *Casualties* was released in the summer of 1989, New York City was still at racial odds over the April jogger incident, and white fears ran high that the opening of Spike Lee's *Do the Right Thing*—in which a black man is strangled by police and white property is set afire—would make the summer very hot indeed. Given that the United States was and continues to be embattled over issues of race, and given the disproportionately large numbers of African Americans who saw combat in Vietnam, it seems inevitable that representations of Vietnam and wasted "gooks" would also bring up America's peculiar history of subordinating blacks. I want to suggest that the oppression of African Americans, white investment in and guilt about this, is introduced as still another subtext of *Casualties of War*, by means of numerous implicit equations between the victimized Asian woman and the victimized black man.[10]

First and most obviously, Brown (his very name a crude marker for "coloredness") meets a gory fate that is an ante-type for the Vietnamese woman's; in the slasher-film idiom De Palma speaks so fluently, their murders are part of a single series. So while De Palma invents Brown and his death largely as a rationale for the later rape and murder, the relation between them is one not only of cause and effect but also of structural equivalence. The deaths of Brown and Oahn mark the two points of greatest visual and emotional stress in the film, pairing these two figures as the most overt "casualties" of the war. Second, as frame opens onto inner story, the Asian American woman who prompts Eriksson's flashback gives way, in his mind, to shadowy figures patrolling a jungle; the first one to emerge into view is a black commander we later meet as Lieutenant Reilly (Ving Rhames), and he speaks the movie's first words. Reilly's association with the woman is subtly reinforced by the fact that they both (and no one else in the movie) wear glasses. The effect of this conjunction is to hint that, at some deeper level, Eriksson's and De Palma's guilt-ridden dream is not about the Asian woman or Vietnam at all, but about the black man and race relations between men in the United States.

In his only extended scene, Reilly responds to Eriksson's report of the Oahn atrocity with a seemingly irrelevant story of his own about racism back home. Denied a bed in a white hospital, Reilly's wife delivered his son on the reception room floor. Reilly's righteous anger only got him locked up in the white man's jail, an experience that eventually taught him that "what happened is the way things are." "So why try to buck the system?" he concludes, finally addressing Eriksson's complaint by advising him to just "forget about it." What interests me here is that Reilly's story actually, at this point, displaces Eriksson's about Oahn. For De Palma chooses not to dramatize Eriksson's report to Reilly, implying instead that it has already occurred when the film cuts to Reilly's office. This scene opens with, and indeed consists of nothing but, Reilly's narrative. Consequently the crime *reported on screen* is not, in fact, the crime against Oahn but the crime against black Americans, represented by the black husband and father. Stressing Reilly's impotence and resignation before racial injustice, the movie once again stages the guiltiness of white masculinity only to reassert its superiority. It is in pointed contrast to both Reilly and Oahn that De

Palma's Eriksson courageously pursues his court-martial, showing that he, if not they, has the balls to "buck the system." Thus the white hero simultaneously redeems himself as a champion of the oppressed and reoppresses them by proving that he alone can speak on their behalf.

As for the relationship between the Asian female and African American male narratives, this returns us to my larger point, for in a sense the entire story of Oahn's violated body operates as a cover for the antecedent story of white men's guilty but relentless domination of their black brothers. The feminized Vietnam material mediates, as it were, an underlying drama of racial conflict between American males. Susan Jeffords stresses the appearance of cross-class and interracial fraternity as a key component of Vietnam narratives, heterogeneous men allying to exclude the feminine (*Remasculinization* 54–86). Yet I am arguing that one subtext of *Casualties* is the absence of interracial fraternity: a struggle to preserve racial hierarchies among men that does not exclude so much as rely upon the feminine as a switching point.

SCENARIO 3: *DO THE RIGHT THING*

We move at this point to black male subjectivity. Spike Lee's 1989 film, *Do the Right Thing*, is in many ways a compelling meditation on the complexities of racism—its smartest move being, in my opinion, the director's controversial refusal either to condone or absolutely to rule out the use of violence in fighting the powers that be. Yet *Do the Right Thing* nevertheless shares with many other antiracist representations the assumption that racism, as well as the struggle against it, is something that happens exclusively between men.[11] There are no white women in this movie; the mother of Sal's sons is curiously absent from the Italian family romance and its racist ways. And the women who are present generally function as a kind of Greek chorus to the main action, chiding men to be responsible and keening in the aftermath of destruction men have wrought. The opening shots of Rosie Perez, in which she wears boxing gloves and does a pugilistic dance to Public Enemy's "Fight the Power," seem all the more merely decorative given the fact that, in the ensuing drama, women never even enter the ring of racial combat. The relegation of women to the political sidelines is explicit in Lee's previous movie, *School Daze*, where the battle over divestment at Mission College is waged between two male students—a black nationalist (Dap) and a fraternity president (Julian)—while their female counterparts claw each other over men and hair.[12] In *Do the Right Thing*, Mookie (Spike Lee) is a delivery man for Sal (Danny Aiello), Italian owner of a pizza joint in the mostly black neighborhood of Bedford-Stuyvesant. Sal likes Mookie's sister, Jade (Spike Lee's real sister, Joie Lee), and in the resulting dynamic the female character serves chiefly to bring out underlying racial tensions in Mookie's relations with his boss. The contradiction of Lee's film is therefore that it launches a radical attack on the racism enforced by our first two scenarios while also apparently reproducing their location of the female between antagonistic males.

The film illustrates, we might say, another manifestation of the chivalric fallacy in which this time *black* men rally to protect "our" women from "them." Thus we get Mookie's annoying paternalism toward Jade, when he warns her to stay away from Sal because all Sal wants is sex. Although Jade protests, Mookie's view is glossed and legitimated by the graffiti visible on the wall behind them, which reads TAWANA TOLD THE TRUTH. Of course, in one important sense Lee is right. Tawana Brawley—the black teenager who in 1987 accused several white men of raping and defacing her and whose story was later discredited—did tell the truth; for if the facts of her particular case have been hard to ascertain, we can nevertheless say with certainty that Tawana's story accurately represents the sordid and elided history of white men's sanctioned rape of black women. To insist on this truth is clearly a necessary counter to the use of rape as a weapon in the war against black people. At the same time, however, another effect of this formulation—by Mookie/Lee or by Alton Maddox, Vernon Mason, and Al Sharpton (who represented Brawley)—is to raise the violated black female body as a kind of flag in the black man's fight against racism. What seems like a campaign on the black woman's behalf may assign her once again to silence and passivity, to a symbolically mediating and spoken-for position that works against her in several ways.[13] First, it imagines her (not unlike the Southern belle) as the helpless victim of male aggression, without desires and defiances of her own. Second, even as it articulates her racist and sexist abuse by white men, it obscures the extent to which black men abuse her as well. We can see this, I think, in the Tawana Brawley case, in which the black male version of her narrative automatically discounted the theory that Tawana told her story in the first place because she was late coming home and wanted to avoid being beaten by her black stepfather.

Spike Lee cautions Joie Lee. Graffiti in the backgrount reads, "Tawana told the truth." From Lee's *Do the Right Thing* (1989).

SCENARIO 4: *SCHOOL DAZE*

If the chivalric fallacy of scenario 1 is echoed by the paternalistic defense of Tawana Brawley or Jade, so the use of rape as a weapon of war in scenario 2 is echoed by Lee's 1988 film about black college life, *School Daze*. In an interview with Henry Louis Gates Jr., Lee argued that to represent homophobia and sexism onscreen is not necessarily to endorse them, and may actually be, as Gates proposed, "an effective way of critiquing them" (182–83). I think that *School Daze* does attempt to critique the traffic in black women among black college men, summed up by the fraternity pledges with their chant of "pass the pussy." This argument culminates with Dap (Larry Fishburne), the movie's moral authority, condemning his cousin Half-Pint (Spike Lee) for accepting Jane (Tisha Campbell) as a sexual gift from Julian (Giancarlo Esposito)—for proving himself to his fraternity brothers by what amounts to a rape. More than this, I find *School Daze* quite knowing, in the Sedgwickian sense, about the way this kind of traffic articulates brotherly love. There is, for example, a humorous moment on the darkened dance floor of the "Da Butt" beach party when two men trade partners and, in the process, "mistakenly" embrace each other.

Yet if *School Daze* seems aware that black women may, to their disadvantage, mediate black men's homosocial desires, it has far less critical distance on the strategic function of Jane's rape in the movie's war against racial injustice. Lee makes this scene painful to watch and certainly seems to lament Jane's violation. At the same time, however, *School Daze* associates the light-skinned sorority queen with white domination and corrupt racial politics to an extent that virtually requires her punishment and exile. Whereas campus activist Dap Dunlap epitomizes racial integrity—"No white blood in me," he jokes in mock-African tones, "my stock one hundred percent pure"— Jane and her similarly complected clique are taken to embody not centuries of forced miscegenation but simply a blamable wannabeism. And though Dap's friends tease him about his inflexible Africanism, the movie's call to "Wake Up" seems finally to validate notions of racial purity as well as pride. For what *School Daze* urges blacks to wake up *from* is a messy history of complacency before and complicity with ruling-class whites, which is almost entirely projected onto women whose complexions are lighter and whose hair is straighter. The effect is a gendering of politics and a moralizing of gender that we will see again and again throughout this book. Like Said's anticolonialism, Ross's hedonist populism, Gates's deconstructive vernacular, and the perverse resistance of queer theorists like Edelman, black nationalism in this film—what is understood to be genuinely radical and ideologically *cool*—is strongly coded as masculine, in large part through its distance from a particular female embodiment represented as *uncool*.

This helps to explain why the depiction of Jane's extreme humiliation seems ultimately more punitive than sympathetic, and why (unlike her male counterpart, Julian) she is not included in, much less redeemed by, the film's final vision of a campuswide awakening to black solidarity. While this last, heavily stylized scene of perfect African American community is bathed in the light of dawn, *School Daze* (like Julian) leaves Jane crumpled and alone in a dark room. To rape and reject the light-skinned woman is, the film implies, to strike a blow for racial freedom. Such logic is, I think, related if not equivalent to that of the young Eldridge Cleaver, for whom the white woman stands between black men and their white masters as a kind of fatal attraction, making her rape "an insurrectionary act" (22).[14] As in *Casualties of War*, this emotional reasoning once again makes the torn body of the "otherized" female a trophy, signifying victory over the enemy male.

In sum, scenarios 3 and 4 represent black men resisting white male domination by invoking the vulnerability of black women or the violability of white/light women taken to stand for white privilege. Even such powerfully antiracist polemics as Spike Lee's appear in this sense to rely on the same configuring of gender as scenarios 1 and 2, the same relegation of objectified black and white women to the no-man's land between men. In ideological terms they are riven by internal contradictions—oppositional in regard to race, conventional in regard to gender—making them continuous as well as discontinuous with the white male texts considered above. For the black chivalric fallacy would seem to map neatly onto the white version, as the use of rape as a weapon of war appears common to black and white men alike. Nevertheless, the structural similarities I have outlined do not mean that black sexism can simply be conflated with white sexism. What I would emphasize, rather, is not the similarity so much as the *interdependence* of white and black constructions of masculinity: if white rapists logically produce black chivalry, so white chivalry virtually invites a retaliatory use of rape as a weapon of racial self-defense. What appears at first glance to be a simple symmetry, parallel sexisms, is arguably a case of cause and effect, in which the racial agendas of white masculinity generate a mirroring black inverse. The relation of these white male to black male texts is not, in truth, symmetrical so much as chiasmic—and the cross between them is burning.

SCENARIO 5: CHARLAYNE HUNTER-GAULT

Throughout the 1980s and well into the 1990s, Charlayne Hunter-Gault of PBS's *MacNeil/Lehrer Newshour* made a nightly, national appearance as a woman between men. Until MacNeil retired in 1995, Hunter-Gault added what felt like texture to the flatness of Robin MacNeil and Jim Lehrer; they anchored the show, and she seemed, somehow, to anchor them. From July

1990 through May 1991, as war raged in the Persian Gulf, Hunter-Gault was in the middle of another pairing as well—as were we all: squeezed into the tight spot between George Bush Sr. and Saddam Hussein.[15] Yet wartime has proved, especially in the twentieth century, to be a time of increased opportunities for women, the positionings of male and female more unstable than ever. I close this chapter by turning to a series of televised interviews from this period of military conflict, occurring not long after the news reports and movies discussed above. Conducted by Hunter-Gault with three women in the American air force—Susan Brown, Theresa Collier, and Prayon Meade—they will serve, I hope, as a figure for geometries of race and gender beyond those examined thus far.[16]

The Hunter-Gault of those months, particularly in the unsure weeks before war actually broke out, before the total accession of aggressive virility, was on the move in the Middle East. I recall shots of her striding through a sandy landscape, seemingly at home amid professionals preparing for battle. Instead of still and studio-bound, her hair and casual clothing are in motion around her. Interviewing her subjects at a base in Dehran, Saudi Arabia, Hunter-Gault looks comfortable in pants, a sweater over her shoulders and sunglasses on her head. The servicewomen are wearing fatigues and combat boots, sitting or leaning on a military vehicle, with planes visible and audible in the background. Two of the women are white, two are black. From the pale, red-headed Susan to the blond Prayon, honey-colored Charlayne, and dark-skinned Theresa, they suggest a veritable rainbow coalition of womanhood.

What strikes me, of course, is that here are women in the news, on the screen, not between men but between other women. It feels unfamiliar, this conversation about war in which all of the voices are female. The usual furrow-browed face of PBS is nowhere to be seen. Inviting them to share their feelings about the uncertainties, stresses, and costs of violent conflict, Hunter-Gault is more group facilitator than grim war correspondent. "How about you, Prayon, what about that boy child of yours?" she asks (16 Jan. 1991). "You don't like war," she offers in response to Theresa's apprehensions (11 Feb. 1991). Calling them by their first names, Hunter-Gault develops with the women an apparently common language about children left behind, uncooperative husbands, dislike of violence, and the ambition to be fighter pilots. Even on the eve of the war, when male soldiers interviewed were hunkered down, intoning military mantras about "doing a job," all the women speak openly about how scared they are. One of my favorite moments—because it occurs, poignantly, at the end of this interview with combat looming, and because it's so much in the idiom of "just us girls"— is when Prayon signs off with, "When we get back to the States, we'll do lunch" (16 Jan. 1991).

The final interview takes place on American soil, and at its conclusion the four women do, in fact, head off to share a meal. Yet we should have no illusion that what happens when women of diverse colors get together is simply "lunch," much less uncomplicated sisterhood. They come together here as participants in an international, racialized struggle, and their very black and white Americanness cannot but refer (as in *Casualties of War*) to ongoing racial struggles at home. It is evident, for example, from Hunter-Gault's question about women in Saudi society that Arab women are wholly and mysteriously Other to the Americans (2 Oct. 1991). "I haven't seen one," Prayon says. "I don't know any," Theresa agrees. Lacking any direct information, the servicewomen waver between glad-to-be-me-isms and a curious envy of the unencountered female. "I heard they have it real good over here, real good," Theresa comments. This is followed by an eager chorus: they have maids (Prayon); they have chauffeurs (Theresa); their husbands buy them expensive jewelry (Prayon); they're put on a pedestal (Theresa). Only Susan interjects, "They can't go to the gym." As earlier tones of superiority ("Over here, you're like, you don't see how a society has done it for so long") give way at this point to desire and resentment, the bewildering racial/cultural differences between American and Arab women seem suddenly to be rearticulated in terms of more familiar domestic differences of class and race. It is as if all the privileges associated with ruling-class white femininity in the States are projected wholesale onto the blankness of the Arab female, who is therefore looked up to wistfully even as she is scorned. A similar class/race rift between women is also invoked by the reference to "maids," who are not themselves regarded as Saudi women, but only as part of the luxury surrounding those women whose femininity is recognized as such.[17]

Subtle divisions emerge, moreover, among the interviewees themselves. I notice, in particular, a tension between Prayon and Theresa over their relationship to the United States, beginning with the second interview (16 Jan. 1991). As our planes prepare to bomb Baghdad, Prayon asserts that the United States is going to "kick butt," because "we've got an advantage like you would not believe." Prayon says she believes this "personally," and also "being American." Theresa responds with considerable irony: "Yeah, being

American, apple pie, you know. I'm just as patriotic as the next person, but you know . . . ," and she goes on to express doubts and fears about the war's outcome. A month into the war, Theresa is again more willing than her compatriot to be critical of the United States. She disagrees with Prayon's feeling that the conflict is "one man [Saddam Hussein] messing up the lives of millions." "I feel he's wrong," Theresa explains, "but it takes two to tango, you know" (11 Feb. 1991). And finally, in the postwar interview back home, at least one basis for Theresa's more examined and ambivalent citizenship becomes explicit. It is Theresa speaking:

> The first image that I saw after leaving Saudi Arabia was the police beating the hell out of Rodney King in L.A. and that really pissed me off. Excuse my French, but I couldn't believe it. I'm like, here I am, spent eight months over here to protect "my country" but yet people are getting beat, you know, people are getting beat for no apparent reason at home. (15 May 1991)

Without ever mentioning race, Theresa makes clear that she identifies less with those Americans kicking butt in Baghdad than with those getting beat in L.A., and she tells us she plans to leave the military. "I've gone to work for my country," she says. "Now let me stay home and work for my people." The gap opened up here between "my country" and "my people" is evidently not present for Prayon, whose first thought on her return is "What a great country!" It is also worth noting Theresa's casual reversal here of the sexual politics we saw in Spike Lee; now the violated body symbolizing racial injustice is male, and Theresa responds by going to work as a political subject, preparing to fight the power in her own person.

If Susan seems somewhat left out of all this, her relative obscurity in these interviews figures for me another line of fracture among women. As the only "single" woman, she is excluded from the extensive discussions of marriage and motherhood. She is eloquent, however, on why men resist the idea of women as fighter pilots:

> I think a lot of men out here still think they need to protect us, protect their mother or girlfriend or a woman. That feeling is still very much alive and that's going to take a long time to get rid of, but the women are ready. We're ready. (11 Feb. 1991)

Given this clarity on the chivalric fallacy, no wonder, as we saw earlier, Susan seems to be on a different planet in the exchange cited above about pampered Saudi wives. I choose to take Susan's investment, rather, in going "to the gym" as a sign of something else—of living and working (out) the female body against the grain of compulsory heterosexuality. In terms of sexuality, then, as well as race and class, it should be clear that domination in America, and opposition to it, is not a matter between men only, however much our most widely circulated cultural myths imagine it as such.

I began by asking how sustained attention to the American racial imaginary might reinflect Sedgwick's powerful model. I hope my typology of scenarios evoking race and rape has shown that the traffic in women may involve male status as well as eros. But my goal in describing dominant gender mythologies, black as well as white, is not only to demystify them but also, finally, to contest their use of women primarily to mediate transactions brokered by males. As I elaborate further in chapter 6, I mean finally to urge gender and sexuality studies away from the alluring Sedgwickian triangle and back to women—to slighted representations of our bodies and ourselves, the geometries of our relations, however problematized and embattled "we" may be. By making women figure, I would like this last scenario to symbolize women's particular complicity with racism and other exploitations, to gesture toward the specificity of female domination and defiance, and to suggest the elements of power and desire that characterize women's uneasy and undying ties to each other.

3

EDWARD SAID: GENDER, CULTURE, AND IMPERIALISM

SEE JANE SIT

What is it about Jane Austen that makes headlines? *Mansfield Park* (1815) takes up relatively little space in the vastness of Edward Said's *Culture and Imperialism* (1993), yet one reviewer after another has seized on Austen's novel as emblematic of the cultural tradition Said shows to be inextricable from European colonialism.[1] Topping Michael Gorra's full-page review in the *New York Times Book Review*, for example, is the eye-catching question, "Who Paid the Bills at Mansfield Park?" Gorra goes on to highlight the discussion of Austen as "one of the best chapters" in Said's book (11). Irving Howe, in the pages of *Dissent*, though denying the relevance of colonial Australia to *Great Expectations*, lingers approvingly over Said's suggestion that slavery in Antigua is the dark underbelly of *Mansfield Park* (558). Likewise John Leonard, reviewing *Culture and Imperialism* for *The Nation*, begins his analysis of Said's sequel to *Orientalism* with a striking image of Austen: "See Jane sit, in the poise and order of *Mansfield Park*, not much bothering her pretty head about the fact that this harmonious 'social space,' Sir Thomas Bertram's country estate, is sustained by slave labor on his sugar plantations in Antigua" (383). His next paragraph renders Said on Albert Camus in similar terms, as a character in his own imperialist primer ("Watch Al run away"), but by then the device has lost its sting. And while reviewers friendly to Said repeatedly cite Austen as definitive proof of his claims, hostile reviewers invoke her with even greater vehemence as the figure most implausibly tied by Said to imperialist wrongdoings.[2]

If, as Leonard implies by omission, Jane Austen is not only "pretty" but "little," why the apparently big role in Said's exposé of the canon's partnership with imperialism? For one thing, as W. J. T. Mitchell notes in his piece for the *London Review of Books*, Said himself places Austen first in his lineup of cultural suspects (11). He does this, I think, partly for chronological reasons, arguing that not only the venturesome *Robinson Crusoe* (1719) but also the stay-at-home novels beginning with Austen prepared the way for Kipling's and Conrad's more overt colonial thematics later in the nineteenth century (*CI* 75). But Mitchell suggests another explanation for the foregrounding of Austen that Gorra, Howe, and Leonard un-selfconsciously reproduce: "The choice of *Mansfield Park* (and of Jane Austen) as Said's opening literary example is a way of forcing this issue [of the novel's complicity with colonialism] into the open" (11). For it is, as Mitchell observes, because of the tacit sense precisely of Austen's "littleness," the genteel narrowness of her concerns, that word of her hand in the plundering of Antigua gets our attention. A similar logic is at work in Eve Sedgwick's notorious linking of "Jane Austen and the Masturbating Girl" (1991). Juxtaposing *Sense and Sensibility*'s screening of sex with nineteenth-century anti-onanist writings, Sedgwick herself, no less than the journalists who wagged their heads, plays upon the oxymoronic scandal of such a pairing. In spite of much revisionary work on this author, the yoking of gentle Jane to sex, subversion, or slavery still has the power to shock, registering thus the persistence of Austen's reputation for piety as well as the ongoing violence of debate between proponents of various new Austens and defenders of the old. One context for these remarks about Austen's place in Edward Said's influential book is my own investment in the woman writer that feminist critics have variously and laboriously wrested from the fray—a contradictory figure neither pretty nor little, with widely engaged interests and independent views, more self-conscious and profane than the flatly conservative figure of *Culture and Imperialism*. Another context, of course, is my sense that Said's use of Austen as an emblem of imperial views participates in the gender logic of coolness, and that this logic pervades his project overall. While in Tarantino the female is conflated with domesticity and domesticity with the narratively banal, here in Said the domestic is similarly feminized and taken to represent, within an anticolonialist frame-work, the cheerfully colonial.

THE FULLY ACCULTURATED ENGLISHMAN

The cherished axiom of Austen's unworldliness is closely tied to a sense of her polite remove from the contingencies of history. It was Q. D. Leavis (1942) who first pointed out the tendency of scholars to lift Austen out of her social milieu, gallantly allowing her gorgeous sentences to float free, un-tainted by the routines of labor that produced them and deaf to the tumult of current events. Since Leavis, numerous efforts have been made to count-er the patronizing view that Austen, in her fidelity to the local, the surface, the detail, was oblivious to large-scale struggles, to wars and mass move-ments of all kinds. Claudia Johnson (1988), for example, has challenged R. W. Chapman's long-standing edition of Austen for its readiness to illustrate her ballrooms and refusal to gloss her allusions to riots or slaves and has linked Austen to a tradition of frankly political novels by women (xvi–xvii). It is in keeping with such historicizing gestures that Said's *Culture and Im-perialism* insists on *Mansfield Park*'s participation in its moment, pursuing the references to Caribbean slavery that Chapman pointedly ignored. Yet while arguing vigorously for the novel's active role in producing imperialist plots, Said also in effect replays the story of its author's passivity regarding issues in the public sphere. Unconcerned about Sir Thomas Bertram's colo-nial holdings in slaves as well as land and taking for granted their necessity to the good life at home, Said's Austen is a veritable Aunt Jane—naive, complacent, and demurely without overt political opinion.

I will grant that Said's depiction of Austen as unthinking in her references to Antigua fits with his overall contention that nineteenth-century Euro-pean culture, and especially the English novel, unwittingly but systemati-cally helped to gain consent for imperialist policies (*CI* 75). While defend-ing the pleasures of many a specific text, Said agrees with critics such as D. A. Miller and Franco Moretti that the novel as a genre served conservative ends. It was, Said asserts, one of the primary discourses contributing to a "consolidated vision," virtually uncontested, of England's righteous imperi-al prerogative. Austen is no different from Thackeray or Dickens, then, in her implicit loyalty to official Eurocentrism. At the same time, Said's ver-sion of Austen in particular is given a boost by the readily available myth of her "feminine" nearsightedness. The advantage of beginning with Austen is, I have said, to grab us by the collar; but I think its effect is also to ease us into his argument with a female novelist framed in reassuringly familiar ways. Sanctioned in large part by traditional scholarship, this rendering of Austen is further enabled, I would argue, by Said's highly selective materialization of her, in two senses. Whereas in subsequent sections of *Culture and Imperialism Aida* is lovingly embedded within Verdi's corpus and *Kim* within Kipling's, and notwithstanding Said's claim that *Mansfield Park* "carefully defines the moral and social values informing her other novels" (62), this single Austen novel is, in fact, almost completely isolated from the rest of her work. Yet had Said placed Sir Thomas Bertram, for example, in line with the deficient fathers who run unrelentingly from *Northanger Abbey* through *Persuasion*, he might perhaps have paused before assuming that Austen legitimates the master of Mansfield Park. If truth be told, Said's attention even to his chosen text is cursory. Austen's references to Antigua (and India) are mentioned without actually being read, though Said stresses elsewhere the importance of close, specific analysis. Maria Bertram is mistakenly referred to as "Lydia" (87)—confused, presumably, with Lydia Bennet of *Pride and Prejudice*. And these are just a few of the signs that *Mansfield Park*'s particular complexity—including what I see as its moral complexity—has been sacrificed, so ready is Said to offer Austen as "Exhibit A" in the case for culture's endorsement of empire.

The picture of Austen is disembodied in not only a textual but also a larger social sense. Though she is recontextualized as an English national in the period preceding colonial expansion, Austen's more precise status as an unmarried, middle-class, scribbling woman remains wholly unspecified. The failure to consider Austen's gender and the significance of this omission is pointed up by Said's more nuanced treatment of Joseph Conrad. According to Said, Conrad stands out from other colonial writers because, as a Polish expatriate, he possessed "an extraordinarily persistent residual sense of his own exilic marginality" (24). The result is a double view of imperialism that at once refutes and reinforces the West's right to dominate the globe. As Said explains, "Never the wholly incorporated and fully acculturated Englishman, Conrad therefore preserved an ironic distance [from imperial conquest] in each of his works" (25). Of course Austen was not, any more than Conrad, "the wholly incorporated and fully acculturated Englishman." Lacking the franchise, enjoying few property rights (and these because she was single), living as a dependent at the edge of her brother's estate, and publishing her work anonymously, Austen was arguably a kind of exile in her own country. If we follow the logic of Said's own identity politics, Austen too might therefore be suspected of irony toward reigning constructions of citizenship, however much, like Conrad, she may also in many respects have upheld them. The goal of this chapter is to indicate where and, finally, to suggest why Said so entirely misses this irony. My point is not to exonerate Austen of imperialist crimes. Surely Said is right to include her among those who made colonialism thinkable by constructing the West as center, home, and norm, while pushing everything else to the margins. The question I would raise is not whether Austen contributed to English domination abroad, but how her doing so was necessarily inflected and partly disrupted by her position as a bourgeois woman.

THE BEAUTIES OF MANSFIELD

Said's opinion that Austen is culpably indifferent to slavery in Antigua depends on two repeated but questionable assertions: that Mansfield Park epitomizes moral order and right human relations, and that Sir Thomas's colonial endeavors, underwriting this order, must therefore be condoned if not actually applauded. Said is not alone in seeing *Mansfield Park* as a celebration of the real estate named in its title, with all its resonance of tradition, wealth locked up in land, and property passed from father to eldest son. Tony Tanner's 1966 introduction to the Penguin edition is an elegant example of this opinion (7–36); Ruth Bernard Yeazell's attractive 1984 essay borrows from anthropology to reach a similar conclusion about the book's investment in reinforcing the boundaries of the Bertram property. Such "conservative" readings inevitably cite the Portsmouth chapters toward the end of the novel, in which Fanny Price disowns her native city and petit-bourgeois family in favor of Mansfield and its harmonious ways—and Said's is no exception. What all of these overlook, however, is the extreme irony of Fanny's idealizing retrospection:

> At Mansfield [as opposed to Portsmouth], no sounds of contention, no raised voice, no abrupt bursts, no tread of violence was ever heard; . . . every body had their due importance; every body's feelings were consulted. If tenderness could be ever supposed wanting, good sense and good breeding supplied its place; and

as to the little irritations, sometimes introduced by aunt Norris, they were short, they were trifling, they were as a drop of water to the ocean, compared with the ceaseless tumult of her present abode. (*MP* 384)

The confident sequence of negatives breaks down here with the concessionary "if" that allows the occasional absence of tenderness at Mansfield. This is followed by Fanny's unsure approach to an unoriginal metaphor— "as a drop of water to the ocean"—which attempts to discount the quantity of aunt Norris's cruelty. The conspicuous banality of Fanny's idiom sets it off, however, from that of Austen's narrator and underlines the degree of critical distance from Fanny at this point.

But even had this description not unraveled on its own, we need only contrast it with the preceding three hundred pages to grasp its utter implausibility. The Mansfield we have seen has been nothing but contention, jealousy, and insensitivity to others. Fanny herself has been its most frequent victim, though one of Austen's themes is this heroine's readiness to misunderstand her pain. Fanny, like the many critics who stress her passivity, is even less able to acknowledge her own pivotal role in Mansfield's bitter generational conflicts and consuming sexual jealousies. After all, Fanny has been exiled for flatly disobeying Mansfield's patriarch, and she has done so out of passionate illicit love for her cousin Edmund. Portsmouth, I agree with Yeazell, is crowded, chaotic, greasy, and alcoholic—awash with stereotypes of the urban poor. But for all this, it only literalizes what at Mansfield is disorder of a more profound and hypocritical kind. At Portsmouth, two sisters tussle over a silver spoon. At Mansfield they wage an unspoken battle over Henry Crawford, as Mary and Fanny do over Edmund. Portsmouth is dirty. Mansfield is adulterous. Portsmouth's patriarch drinks, curses, and ignores his daughters. The father at Mansfield intimidates, exploits, and also ignores his daughters. Portsmouth is noisy. Mansfield's greatest evil is its dishonest silence.

Said's premise, therefore—that "Jane Austen sees the legitimacy of Sir Thomas Bertram's overseas properties as a natural extension of the calm, the order, the beauties of Mansfield, one central estate validating the economically supportive role of the peripheral other" (79)—is undercut by Austen's own critique of the moral blight underlying Mansfield's beauty, which she achieves not least by blurring the normative class opposition between Mansfield and Portsmouth. What Said calls a validation of the English estate as "home," justifying its subjugation of "abroad," I see as an inquiry into Mansfield's corruption that challenges the ethical basis for its authority both at home and, by implication, overseas. Austen does, it is true, ultimately allow Mansfield and some of its sinning inmates to be redeemed, and to this extent she reaffirms the governance of British landowners. As a crucial qualification, however, she declines to make her heroine the next mistress of Mansfield, though Tom Bertram's illness specifically raises the possibility that Edmund will inherit. Tom's survival, placing Edmund and Fanny temporarily at Thornton Lacey and finally not in Mansfield itself but in its adjacent parsonage, suggests Austen's wish to register, even at the end, some disdain for what Mansfield represents. (There is, from the outset, a slap at primogeniture in the younger son's role as hero and the elder's marked delinquency.) Said's designation of Fanny as Mansfield's heir (84, 89) is therefore inaccurate. In fact, Austen pointedly counters the centrality of Mansfield in Fanny's heart by settling her firmly on its perimeter.

PATRIARCHAL VALUES

The character most closely identified with Mansfield Park and its colonial subsidiaries is, of course, Sir Thomas Bertram. Said thus argues not merely that Austen celebrates Mansfield but more specifically that she backs Sir Thomas in his domestic and colonial ventures. Austen is implicated through a series of equations aligning Fanny with her wealthy uncle, conflating Austen with her diffident heroine, and thereby tying the author herself to slavery, in spite of an ethical outlook that might seem to preclude this. Said remarks, for instance, that Sir Thomas's overseas possessions "give him his wealth, occasion his absences, fix his social status at home and abroad, and make possible his values, to which Fanny Price (and Austen herself) finally subscribes" (62). Said describes Sir Thomas as Fanny's "mentor" (89), and he is not the first critic to link uncle and niece, especially in their view of the young people's rage for home theatricals. I would point out, however, that when Sir Thomas sets sail Fanny grieves not (as her cousins think) for him but, on the contrary, "because she could not grieve" (*MP* 66). Likewise, on his return, she feels only a resurgence of "all her former habitual dread" (193). And though Sir Thomas and Fanny are finally reconciled, the key moral and political confrontation of the book remains, in my opinion, that played out between this nobleman and the timid young woman who, astonishingly, stands up to him by refusing to marry Henry Crawford.

The significance of this confrontation is condensed for me by Fanny's response when asked point-blank if her affections are engaged by another: "[Sir Thomas] saw her lips formed in to a *no*, though the sound was inarticulate, but her face was like scarlet" (*MP* 316–17). Here Fanny does and does not confess her terrible desire for Edmund. She mouths a denial but cannot quite speak it; moreover, the word of disavowal she attempts is countered by the somatic affirmation of her blush. Finally, while her "no" in this immediate context would suppress her longing, Fanny's "no" to Sir Thomas (and Henry) in the scene as a whole tacitly asserts her right to reject and also to love where she will. Turning down Henry, Fanny declares her passion for Edmund against all norms of female modesty. In addition, she condemns Henry's history of carelessness with women and questions the double standard that dooms the fallen woman while promising to reform the rake. Crossing Sir Thomas, she declines to enrich her family by sacrificing herself and so dishonors the ideals of female and filial obedience. Regarding the sexual politics of marriage, therefore, far from sharing Sir Thomas's values, Fanny stages a courageous rebellion against them. Threatened by the givens of gender relations in her day, she murmurs a negative that is only partly muted by her uncle's dread presence.

If Fanny's values, in light of the gender struggle central to *Mansfield Park*, cannot without violence be assimilated to those of Sir Thomas, neither can Austen be simply identified with her characters. The collapsing of author into character would be questionable in any case, but especially so given what I have already suggested is Austen's ironic rendering of Sir Thomas and, at times, of Fanny herself. This brings me to Sir Thomas's Antiguan connection and why his West Indian plantation makes the brief appearance that it does. Said quotes the line about Fanny's inquiry into the slave trade being met with a "dead silence," and seems to suggest that Austen's novel, like the Bertram household, has nothing to say about slavery, when in fact the organization of both is premised upon unfree people (*CI* 96). My view, by contrast, is that Austen deliberately invokes the dumbness of Mansfield Park concerning its own barbarity precisely because she means to rebuke it. The barbarity she has in mind is not literal slavery in the West Indies but a paternal practice she depicts as possibly analogous to it: Sir Thomas's bid (successful in Maria's case if not in

Fanny's) to put female flesh on the auction block in exchange for male status.[3]

For this and other domestic tyrannies, including the casual import and export of Fanny Price, the slave trade offers a convenient metaphor.[4] It is a figure made possible by the confluence of abolitionist and feminist discourses emergent in Austen's day, and it takes for granted—as several scholars have argued Austen did—that slavery is a moral offense. Later writers, notably Charlotte Brontë," would make more conspicuous use of slavery as a metaphor for class and gender wrongs among the gentry, but a rather explicit instance occurs in Austen's own next novel, *Emma* (1816).[5] In a well-known passage (surprisingly unremarked by *Culture and Imperialism*), Jane Fairfax likens the commodification of British women by the "governess-trade" to that of Africans by the "slave-trade," hinting that the sale of "human intellect" is no more tolerable than the sale of "human flesh" (*Emma* 300). From a feminist perspective, it seems all too obvious that in *Mansfield Park* slavery functions similarly—not as a subtext wherein Austen and Sir Thomas converge but, on the contrary, as a trope Austen introduces to argue the essential depravity of Sir Thomas's relations to other people. This is not to say that *Mansfield Park* takes much real interest in Antigua and its laborers per se; I agree with Said that they are largely elided and always subordinated to the English material. The imperialist gesture is to exploit the symbolic value of slavery while ignoring slaves as suffering and resistant historical subjects. As a symbol, however, slavery in *Mansfield Park* is far less incidental and inadvertent than Said suggests. Ideologically, moreover, the implications of its use are mixed: though it evacuates the specific content of slavery in the New World, placing its greatest emphasis elsewhere, this figure also turns on a moment of imagined commonality between English women and African slaves, a potentially radical overlap of outrage.

THE ISLE OF WIGHT

Said makes clear that the defining affect of colonialism is arrogance. I have said that Austen's relation to colonialism may be complicated, though not entirely mitigated, by her protest on behalf of women like herself. As a footnote to this comment, I would like to look briefly at what she says about arrogance as a worldview. I think, for example, of *Persuasion*'s meditation on the arrogant occupation of space: Sir Walter Elliot and his daughter Elizabeth are unable to see beyond the bit of land they happen to inhabit, as if its contours and horizons, its interests and intrigues, were the only thing in the world. Emotionally, a reader of Said would recognize, the stage is set for imperial conquest—for such people go abroad only to discount the significance of other populations and outlooks. Anne Elliot, by contrast, is described as "nobody with either father or sister: her word had no weight; her convenience was always to give way;—she was only Anne" (*Persuasion* 37). With little sense of her significance at home, Anne need not travel very far to have her relative "nobodyness" confirmed and to wince at the solipsism of other Elliots.

> Anne had not wanted this visit to Uppercross, to learn that a removal from one set of people to another, though at a distance of only three miles, will often include a total change of conversation, opinion, and idea. She had never been staying there before, without being struck by it, or without wishing that other Elliots could have her advantage in seeing how unknown, or unconsidered there, were the affairs which at Kellynch-hall were treated as of such general publicity and pervading interest; yet, with all this experience, she believed she must now submit to feel that another lesson, in the art of knowing our own nothingness beyond our own circle, was become necessary for her. (69)

Austen's target here is the dying but still haughty aristocracy. Far from questioning colonialism, *Persuasion* celebrates (as a meritocratic alternative) the British navy that made it possible. Yet I can't help thinking that her text here bears somewhat on Said's project of exposing the provincialism underlying colonialism. There is such sensitivity to the way self-importance manifests itself in space, and such severity about mistaking local agendas for "general" and "pervading" ones. Surely Anne's lesson in her "nothingness beyond [her] own circle" is an implicitly anti-imperialist one. Moreover, it suggests once again the crucial operation of gender in Austen, for Anne is able to learn this lesson—and Austen to teach it—because as an apparently unmarriageable woman she is exiled from power.

Mansfield Park too castigates people who, while pretending to worldliness, see nothing beyond their own noses, and even its upstanding heroine is occasionally blinkered by personal interest. Like *Persuasion*, this novel criticizes solipsism primarily as an aspect of personality, not foreign policy, but there is one conversation in which the limitations of its characters are phrased in explicitly geographical terms. Complaining of their uncouth cousin, Maria and Julia Bertram mock Fanny's inability to "put the map of Europe together" or name the "principal rivers in Russia."[6] They marvel especially at her bad sense of direction:

> "Do you know, we asked her last night, which way she would go to get to Ireland; and she said, she should cross to the Isle of Wight. She thinks of nothing but the Isle of Wight, and she calls it *the Island,* as if there were no other island in the world." (*MP* 54)

Compared to the wealthy Bertrams, and even to her seafaring brother William, poor Fanny is, to be sure, less adept at manipulating nations, less masterful in her relation to the globe. The Bertram sisters are also right to boast of their superior fluency in chronologies of English kings and Roman emperors, for their schooling in hegemonic traditions has been more thorough than Fanny's. On the other hand, Fanny's navigational mode as described in this passage is itself a rather imperialist one, for it begins and ends by fetishizing a single island. This island not only happens to resemble Britain in its ability to eclipse others such as Ireland and Antigua, leaving it the exclusive point of reference, but also bears a name suggesting the pseudo-racial basis for its priority. Austen's major point here is clearly to satirize Maria and Julia's class condescension to their simple cousin, but I believe she also likens all three girls to one another and ridicules them together for their lordly outlook upon the world. I offer this passage as additional evidence that Austen is both more aware and more critical of the imperial mindset than Said appreciates; it catches her, indeed, in an attitude of irony toward "*the Island*" and its loyal subjects that inclines, gently, in the direction of his own.[7]

SENSITIVE BUT NOT MAUDLIN

Mansfield Park as I read it, then, has little patience with high-handed patriarchs, their eldest sons, Regency sexual mores, or traditional marital practices; and even England itself is not above criticism. Its irreverence—bearing out Austen's earliest juvenile sketches, resonating with the other mature novels, and anticipating the final, unfinished *Sanditon*—suggests to me a less complacent view of power relations, especially gender relations, than Said is prepared to acknowledge. His inattention to Austen's feminist critique of authority is both the logical result and an ideological cognate of his failure, similarly, to remark the last two decades of intensive feminist commentary on this writer. Asserting that "the best account" of *Mansfield Park* is Tony Tanner's (*CI* 342)—admirable when first published in 1966 certainly, but hardly definitive in 1993—Said appears curiously unaware of the revolution in Austen scholarship instigated by such figures as Nina Auerbach, Patricia Meyer Spacks, Lillian Robinson, Sandra Gilbert, Susan Gubar, and Rachel Brownstein, among others. He therefore feels free to list Austen among those evincing the conservatism of the novel form, arguing that "the consolidation of authority [in Austen, Balzac, Eliot, and Flaubert] includes, indeed is built into the very fabric of, both private property and marriage, institutions that are only rarely challenged" (77). Feminist accounts, by contrast, have brought out precisely Austen's tactful challenge to the gender injustices of both these institutions. Tying the novel's authorization of empire to the "authority of the author" (77), Said further overlooks what feminist critics since Virginia Woolf have seen as the anxious and impaired authority of the female writer. More disconcerting still than his neglect of revisionary axioms concerning nineteenth-century women writers is that Said makes no mention of Margaret Kirkham (1983) or Moira Ferguson (1991), previous scholars specifically addressing the slavery theme in *Mansfield Park* from a feminist perspective.[8] And though he makes positive passing reference to innovative studies of imperialist discourses by Lisa Lowe (1991) and Sara Suleri (1992), he doesn't specify their chapters mobilizing ideas about gender. Nor is there any dialogue with his student, Suvendrini Perera (1991), whose book on empire and the English novel identifies the feminist Orientalism of texts such as *Persuasion* and *Jane Eyre* while arguing that "home" was a construct policing British women as well as colonial "others." Even Gayatri Spivak, the most celebrated feminist postcolonialist, is altogether absent from *Culture and Imperialism*. The pertinence of these names to Said's project is not, I hasten to say, their simple political correctness as females or feminists, but the way their analyses intersect with and would serve to complicate one that proceeds for the most part along a single axis.[9]

While I am not the first to note the paucity of women and feminist criticism in Said's work, it remains a question how these exclusions can coexist with Said's oft-stated appreciation for feminism's political uses.[10] In a 1989 interview, for example, he described his excitement at feminist works by Joan Scott, Helen Callaway, and Jean Franco (Sprinker 248–49), and in *Culture and Imperialism* he stresses the significance of women's movements

in Egypt, Turkey, Indonesia, China, and Ceylon, whose participation in nationalist struggles, by voicing internal opposition, helped to make these less
monolithic (218, 266). Said's reading of *Kim* as "an overwhelmingly male
novel" (136) is itself, at times, incipiently feminist, and he points out more
than once the masculinism of much nationalist discourse. Of Aimé Cé-
saire's use of "man" in *Cahier d'un retour au pays natal*, he observes paren-
thetically, "the exclusively masculine emphasis is quite striking" (280), and
another parenthesis conscientiously admits that Ali Shariati's alternative to
orthodoxy "speaks only of 'man' and not of 'woman'" (334).

The relegation of such glosses to parentheses is telling, however—they are
safely contained, and in no way reorient Said's line of argument—as is the far
more frequent tendency to quote sexist language without any comment. But
the most obvious testimony to both interest and uncertainty regarding feminist agendas is offered by a passage from the book's introduction. Highlighting feminism's contributions to Middle Eastern and postcolonial studies, Said
cites Lila Abu-Lughod, Leila Ahmed, and Fedwa Malti-Douglas, whose recent books on women have begun to redress what was once "an aggressively
masculine and condescending ethos" (xxiv). Following this, however, his
terms of praise take an ambiguous turn. These works are, he declares, "both
intellectually and politically sophisticated, attuned to the best theoretical and
historical scholarship, engaged but not demagogic, sensitive to but not
maudlin about women's experience" (xxiv). Why the sudden urge to reassure
and qualify here? Why the worry lest scholarship by and about women, as a
function of the more lachrymose sex, turn out to be embarrassingly soft and
weepy? And why, finally, the seeming insecurity about "engaged" scholarship,
the need to disparage the waved fist and tearful face as if they were, or so he
implies, inconsistent with carefully reasoned criticism? Keeping these questions in mind, my next section speculates that the troubling sexual politics of
Culture and Imperialism may be bound up with a largely subliminal strategy
of opposition to imperialism: a gender allegory in which the "feminine," re-
tained as a devalued category, is repudiated and reattributed in order to stig-
matize Europe as irrational, appetitive, and morally corrupt.

LADY BERTRAM'S SHAWL

Poststructuralism would seem to have discredited for good any notion of absolute impartial truth, and feminists have long since dismantled the old, hierarchized dichotomy between male/objective and female/subjective. Never-

theless, the quotation above speaks to the continued stigmatizing of scholarship perceived to be heartfelt and also to the gendering of it as feminine. On the one hand, Said's defense of politically invested work by female scholars against implied charges of emotional excess justifies his own style of impassioned scholarship; on the other hand, by raising these charges specifically in relation to women, it also effectively distances the male author from a denigrated mode. The gender reasoning of this defense is reiterated later in *Culture and Imperialism* by a section devoted to the oppositional writings of four male, Third World intellectuals: C. L. R. James, George Antonius, Ranajit Guha, and S. H. Alatas. Celebrating the political content of their work, Said insists he does not mean "oppositional scholarship must be shrill and unpleasantly insistent" (*CI* 258). Given the strong coding of "shrill" as feminine, this protest seems once again calculated to secure the gender status of work whose "masculinity" is endangered by the depth of its feeling. And it doesn't hurt, of course, that the exemplary four are male to begin with.

The "masculinity" of anti-imperialist projects such as Said's is on the defensive for another reason as well. As many have observed, the tropes Said mapped so unforgettably in *Orientalism* veil the East in a cluster of "female" attributes. It is mysterious, sensual, beckoning, undisciplined, and naturally subordinate to a West imagined in correspondingly "male" terms—and Said notes in *Culture and Imperialism* that Europe makes use of a similar vocabulary to depict Africa, Australia, and other "distant lands" (xi). As Suleri has remarked, this gendering of the colonial encounter persists in counternarratives protesting the "rape" of colonial peoples and places. She argues further that the "colonial gaze" may actually regard the colonized less as female than as effeminate, and the result may therefore be feelings of sexual panic in the male colonizer (*Rhetoric* 16–17).[11] From the perspective of the Third World male, however, to the extent that his resistance is mediated by imperialist frameworks, it hardly matters whether he is constructed as "woman" or "effeminate" man, for in either case his normative masculinity is called into question. One function, then, of Austen's primacy in Said's account of European culture, along with the marked masculinity of the resistance cultures he puts forth in counterpoint, may be to invert the received gendering of the colonial couple: to "remasculinize" the colonized male (and emotional male critic).[12]

This is accomplished most obviously by the predominance of men and male quest plots in Said's discussion of anti- and postcolonial texts—James Ngugi's and Tayeb Salih's rewritings of Conrad's *Heart of Darkness,* for example (*CI* 210–11). But the gesture is completed by Said's more subtle characterization of early imperial culture as "feminine," which helps to explain the paradigmatic status accorded to Austen. For though his book takes on European culture generally and does in fact range widely among genres, nations, and eras, its argument nevertheless implies a kind of synecdoche in which this culture is best represented by the novel, the novel by the English novel, and the English novel by Austen. Said opens his reading of *Mansfield Park* by quoting Raymond Williams on Austen's limited perspective "from inside the houses" as opposed to Cobbett "riding past on the road" (84). While Said wants to go beyond Williams's class analysis, his Austen, too, is tied to and constrained by a domestic purview in a specifically gendered way. Defined thus, her work is offered as "the perfect example" (59) of the hegemonic geography emergent in the preimperialist period, centered on a Eurocentric formulation of the category "home." Positioned at the beginning of his genealogy and at the heart of his argument, Austen's fiction works, at least in part, to characterize as domestic and to sex as feminine the larger body of European culture.

In addition to its science of interiors, *Mansfield Park* as representative text has something else to offer the project of feminizing Europe. Demonstrating the careless, everyday use of colonial materials by Austen and her characters, Said cites Lady Bertram's request that Fanny's brother William sail to India, "that I may have a shawl. I think I will have two shawls" (93). Given that Lady Bertram dozes through *Mansfield Park*, a figure of indolence without a shred of moral credibility, it is risky to assume that her appetite for imported goods is approved by the management. What this passage does reinforce, however, is an image of Europe as the leisured consumer of more than one shawl, kept in luxury by the backbreaking labor of colonial workers. It offers, in other words, an inverted sexual metaphor in which the recumbent, feminized East rises to its feet, and the veil that once symbolized its mysterious allure reappears as a shawl, a figure for the consumerism of a pampered and feminized West.

A TOKEN OF PEACE

The cover of *Culture and Imperialism* features a 1907 painting, *The Representatives of the Foreign Powers Coming to Hail the Republic as a Token of Peace*, which I look to for a final illustration of the gender politics underly-

Painting on the cover of Said's *Culture and Imperialism*. Henri Rousseau, *The Representatives of the Foreign Powers Coming to Hail the Republic as a Token of Peace* (1907). COURTESY GIRAUDON/ART RESOURCE, NY

ing Said's anti-imperialism. The painting shows a phalanx of dignitaries in official dress gathered ceremonially on some outdoor steps. Buildings just visible in the background, a tricolor in each window, suggest Paris. The diplomats face forward, clutching olive branches in gloved hands. Front and center are pink-cheeked men almost uniform in height and dressed in western garb. Peeking from the back row are two ruddier faces and one brown. To the far right are half a dozen miscellaneous figures, with complexions, clothing, and headgear vaguely suggesting eastern and African origins. All of these are shorter than the westerners and, to judge by their irregular positions and unmatched stances, have little sense of military discipline. The uneven outline of their heads makes a jagged falling off from the block of massed westerners. Overhead is an awning topped with flags, but the non-western representatives, exceeding this frame, are exposed to the elements. The most prominent flags, with one exception, are easily recognizable as those of Britain (the naval red ensign), France, and the United States. Those farther back include Italy and Imperial Germany, but seem mostly to have been improvised by the artist. Finally, there are three explicitly symbolic elements. First, receptacles of olive branches bear the labels "Paix," "Travail," "Liberté," and "Fraternité." Second, a small lion sits frowning in the foreground—persuaded, it seems, to lie down at last with the lambs. And third, standing to the left in profile, a larger-than-life woman wearing a flowing red gown extends an olive branch over the heads of the company. She supports a shield which, though partly obscured, appears to read: "Union des Peuples."

It doesn't take long to realize that Said means this painting ironically. In this "union" under French auspices, as in the European novel, Enlightenment rhetoric and good intentions cannot disguise the fact that nonwesterners get left out in the cold. Western flags still get top billing, and if all men are equal, western men are clearly more equal than others—more central, more imposing, and more knowable. This is a crucial political judgment to make, and Said has made it for many years with exceptional brilliance and conviction. Yet I turn, in closing, to the cover of *Culture and Imperialism* because its ironized female icon suggests the problematic status of women and the feminine in Said's text. In this painting, the lone female figure is largely an abstraction, no less than the lion at her feet, the branch in her hand, and the shield at her side. Towering over the heads of European men, she stands for their blond, benevolent patronage—and, from Said's point of view, their hypocritical peace. The effect of the cover, therefore, like the argument inside, is to leave out actual women while feminizing the wiles of imperialist culture, scorning them in a language indebted to conventional views of gender. Women did, of course, help to rationalize imperialism, and Austen is guilty along with the rest. But Said's balance sheet still has her paying more than her share of the bills—in part because, like the angel of false peace, she is made to bear, more than any other single figure, the symbolic burden of empire. No wonder that, when Suleri reviews Said for the *Village Voice*, she uses Austen as shorthand for those texts whose interest in imperialism is hidden from view: "For every Salman Rushdie,

there is a Jane Austen" ("Secret" 31). Moreover, because Austen is abstracted from her specific historical context, her Eurocentrism is uncoupled from
what was for her as a woman her incompletely realized citizenship. Off center in relation to the dominant culture, Austen was no more fully embraced
by official fantasies of democracy than the darker "foreign powers"—a fact
her novels suggest she pondered. In reading Austen thus, it is not my intention to pick up the pieces of a shattered idol; like Said, I am more interested in secularity and imperfection. I offer this complicating view, rather,
as a token of the hope I share with him for a more genuine and just union
of peoples.

4

ANDREW ROSS: THE ROMANCE
OF THE BAD BOY

New intellectuals, in fact, are uneven participants on several fronts. They
are likely to belong to different social groups and have loyalties to different social movements. . . . In the face of today's uneven plurality of often
conflicting radical interests, it is quite possible that they will be leading
spokespersons, diffident supporters, and reactionaries at one and the
same time.

—Andrew Ross, *No Respect* (1989)

How many T. S. Eliot scholars have been demonized in the national press for watching too much TV? How many of us sham-
bling eggheads have been mocked in print for dressing too well? Andrew
Ross, director of New York University's innovative American Studies pro-
gram, could tell us about both. Profiled snidely in glossies from the *New York
Times Magazine* to *New York*, Ross has been poster boy for the new cultural
studies and more than once held personally responsible for everything
"trendy" in today's academy. In the mainstream media, he has been made to
stand for the shocking fact that professors trained as literary critics now write
ethnographic studies of rap music, computer hacking, and daytime talk
shows and that we do so with some candor about our left political sympathies. Liberal colleagues like Richard Rorty, writing skeptically about Ross in
the pages of *Dissent*, have piled on as well. Yet if Ross has been hated, he's
also been courted. Ballantine advanced him six figures for his book on Disney's planned community in central Florida, *The Celebration Chronicles*
(1999). In fact, being targeted by traditionalists in the culture wars has only
helped to confirm Ross's prominence among academic superstars.

What has Andrew Ross done to deserve such attention? For one thing, he
has published widely, brilliantly, and with alarming frequency on topics
ranging from Cold War intellectuals to global warming to tourism in Polynesia. Still in his mid-forties, Ross has written six books since 1986 and edit-

ed almost as many. His latest collection of essays, *Real Love: In Pursuit of Cultural Justice*, came out from New York University Press in 1998. From 1992 to 1997, he had a regular column in *Artforum* but still found time to contribute articles to *The Nation* and *The Village Voice*. Pick up any number of collections on Madonna, Anita Hill, or O. J. Simpson, and you'll find a piece by Ross. Indeed, throughout the early 1990s it was hardly possible to open a top academic journal without encountering his commentary on American culture. Then in 1996, all hell broke loose over the Sokal affair. It began when physicist Alan Sokal published a piece in the "Science Wars" issue Ross edited for *Social Text*, a journal with which he has long-standing ties. When Sokal's essay turned out to be a hoax, intended to ridicule the critique of science elaborated by Ross and others, it was Ross who took most of the heat. Recapitulating the terms of the culture wars, the Sokal debate pitted those who mistrust theory, believe in objective truth, and see class as the only basis for left politics against those who argue that representations of race, gender, and sexuality also play a crucial role in who we are and what we can know. Once again, in newspapers and journals across the country, cultural studies was both decried and defended in the person of Andrew Ross.

I hope it is clear by now that I share Ross's sense of the political stakes of reading popular texts and support his efforts to demystify scientific authority. Of all his work, I am perhaps most moved by those sections of *Strange Weather* (1991) and *The Chicago Gangster Theory of Life* (1994) regarding environmental discourse. Citing the ubiquity of eco-language even among presidents and corporations, Ross has shown me its capacity to rationalize a little tyranny in the name of survival and to abet the very militarism it began by opposing. Yet while siding with Ross against *New York*, Rorty, and Sokal, I have my own bone to pick with him, and like his other detractors I single him out because he continues to be such an influential and even emblematic proponent of cultural studies. In the pages that follow, I will argue that Ross's work over the years—untiring in its appreciation for pop truants from rappers to hackers, and acute about matters of race and especially class—has been oddly incoherent when it comes to gender, and derelict if not actually reactionary concerning women's interests.

It is true that *No Sweat: Fashion, Free Trade, and the Rights of Garment Workers*, edited by Ross in 1997, usefully calls attention to the female and child labor that probably went to produce your favorite pair of jeans. But there is also, just for starters, his 1995 *Artforum* column celebrating the female butt in music videos exclusively by men, a piece that refused to name women like Salt 'n' Pepa who might conceivably shake their thangs in defiance of the black male gaze that Ross here universalizes as "black" ("Back on the Box"). Capable of protesting the garment industry's feminization of labor, Ross has been more often content to leave women on the margins and the categories "masculine" and "feminine" just as he found them. There are even moments in his writing of palpable anxiety and hostility in response to female sexual agency and to feminism. None of this would be surprising at the current moment except from the pen of a smart, hip, and principled critic, who frequently reiterates his commitment to social justice. I respect this commitment but see Ross as a telling example of what he himself describes in my epigraph as the sometimes contradictory loyalties of left intellectuals today. Ultimately, I suggest that the very genealogy of his leftness, from early ties to the *Screen* group of film theorists to a later formation by Birmingham-style cultural studies, encourages an uneasy relationship to feminism, notwithstanding an apparent support for women's rights. As perhaps the "coolest" of my cool scholars, Ross demonstrates my thesis particularly well: though ambivalence toward feminism would seem to be at odds with hipness in a political sense, in terms of reigning cultural narratives about men and mothers, masculinity and femininity, a degree of antifeminism may actually be intrinsic to hipness, a significant part of what constitutes it as such.

INVISIBLE WOMEN

Best known for his readings of Batman or the synthetic glitz of techno club wear, Ross was once a psychoanalytic critic in love with twentieth-century poetry.[1] But while his first book, *The Failure of Modernism: Symptoms of American Poetry* (1986), is anomalously literary, its preoccupation with masculine culture, only lightly thematized as such, anticipates the gender trouble of his subsequent work. *The Failure of Modernism* does discuss T. S. Eliot's hysterical heterosexuality and Charles Olson's obsession with patriliny in ways that might seem to diagnose the modern male. Moreover, its thesis—that modernism failed because it tried not simply to query subjectivism but to empty poetry of subjectivity—looks forward to the critique of scientific objectivism that Ross, in a parallel universe to feminist critics of science, would go on to articulate. *Modernism* even includes a couple of parentheses about Lacan's assumed-to-be-male child (45) and Olson's sexism (141). In the end, however, none of this is sufficient to get Ross critical leverage on the maleness of the modernism he discusses. Women writers are virtually absent from this study, and the use of male pronouns when speaking of the generic poet slips from Ross's source materials into his own text, with the effect of naturalizing this absence. And though *The Failure of Modernism* would challenge critical paradigms (Bloom's and Breslin's) pitting poetic "sons" against precursors metaphorized as "fathers," what Ross resists is the fantasy of a free-standing discourse, successfully severed from the past (215–16)—not the omission of mothers and daughters altogether from this account of poetic influence. Indeed, I will argue below that Ross's approach to cultural studies remains invested in the romance of the artist-critic as rebellious "son."

The unremarked omission of women on the part of a young, revisionary scholar is surprising enough in the mid-1980s—how much more so in a piece appearing first in *The Nation* in the mid-1990s, which likewise obscures, even while hedging and defending, its overwhelming interest in guys.[2] "The Gangsta and the Diva" (1994) is nothing if not politically self-conscious, and its twinning of the maligned gangsta rapper and the black queen as against-the-grain performance artists is at first glance compelling. The article is most persuasive when the swagger of the one and the swish of the other are seen as specifically black male retorts to a history and present of white supremacy. To see them thus is to place white attacks on rap as well as fascination with the diva in the implicating context of white people's age-old ambivalence toward black cultural forms. Ross succeeds in interrogating these attacks (if not this fascination) and makes a good case, here and elsewhere, for hip-hop's dynamism and canniness as political theater. But tying macho rapper Treach and diva RuPaul alike to stylings of black *men* should also raise questions along another axis—about whether these figures have a similar relation to traditional, dominative masculinity—and here Ross bows out in several ways.

First, he provocatively names those rappers most notorious for abusing women onstage and off (Snoop Doggy Dogg and Dr. Dre), only to excuse their abuse on the grounds that it originated elsewhere (i.e., in white patriarchy) (191–92). Ross drives home both this logic of exoneration and his own connection to gangsta maleness in a later paragraph about working-class Scottish gangs—"the gangs I grew up around in the industrial Scottish lowlands"—which again concludes that the sexism of these men, themselves disdained by the London press, "did not belong to them" (192). This leaves us, in my view, with a cultural analysis (careless of recent political imperatives) that refuses to parse the way race, class, gender, sexuality, and, yes, Scottishness necessarily interact with and may contradict one another. Ross declines, in short, to articulate the multiple social framings that enabled Dr. Dre (infamously in 1991) to kick the shit out of TV host Dee Barnes, even as he himself was getting the boot from white America. By blaming only the most powerful men (and how many of these actually are there?) Ross also fails to account for the particularity of sexism in a given social setting, its shaping by local traditions of misogyny. And finally, by neglecting this aspect of the gangsta, Ross misses his chance to tally the very different gender calculations of the queen, who has affinities not only with the feminine but also with the black women missing from this piece.[3] For reasons I speculate about later, he appears to identify more with those males who flee from women and femininity—making a point in this instance of crossing over to contemporary black gangs on the backs of Scottish ruffians recalled from his boyhood.

I begin with these readings of two very different texts to insist, in the first place, that gender is a source of dissonance in Ross. His work is so impressive and right-minded overall that one feels tempted to let the little slips or digs around women's liberation go. Further, the moments when he gets it right and the lip service he pays disorient as well as placate the feminist reader. If this were 1973 instead of 2003, if cultural studies were less important, if Andrew Ross were less influential or less politically earnest, sexism of this relative subtlety might pass. But given Ross's stature as a left cultural critic—himself a standing lesson to the unreconstructed left in valuing political categories beyond class and political agents beyond unions—the shoddiness of his sexual politics ought not to be, as it generally has been, above criticism.[4] Before proposing a narrative that speaks to the origins and implications of Ross's gender views, I want therefore to begin by making them visible. Returning to *The Failure of Modernism* and "The Gangsta and the Diva," I will begin by mentioning two rhetorical strategies that illustrate women's continued status, in much of Ross's work, as the second sex.

First, there is *Modernism*'s naturalized exclusion of women—the kind of idiom, normative before 1975, that treats masculinity as if it were universal and is oblivious to gender bias. This mode makes fleeting appearances even in later pieces otherwise bent on cultural specificity. "Back on the Box"

(1995), as I have already said, cites a "long tradition of *black esthetics* based on the erogenous display of the female buttocks" and claims that "as a result . . . the female butt can signify as a source of authority, if not power, in *black culture*" (112; emphasis added). But whose aesthetic, whose culture, and whose authority are actually at issue here? Though Ross reports that women clamor to shake their butts on camera (112) and that doing so at "near-jackhammer velocity" takes skill (17), the videos he mentions still feature men rapping about, looking at, getting off on "video hos" who are hardly, in this context, sexual subjects, much less taste makers or cultural power brokers. In "The Gangsta and the Diva" too, a fine-tuned appreciation for two specifically male cultures alternates with more sweeping language taking them to represent black culture as a whole. Asserting, for example, that "hardcore" rap is "just about the only medium in which ghetto life attains something approaching authentic recognition" (192) or that gangsta rap is "the most articulate frame for black anger" (193), Ross effectively discounts women's renderings of their lives and rages in non-gangsta rap and other media.[5]

In addition to the naturalized exclusion of women, there is also in Ross a mode of feigned inclusion, which sometimes takes the form of a feminist coda following on enthusiasms and claims that would seem to preclude it. "Ballots, Bullets, or Batmen: Can Cultural Studies Do the Right Thing?" (1990) offers a good example of Ross's recourse to the eleventh-hour reprieve. This *Screen* piece, astute in many ways, reads the movie *Batman* (1989) into relation with Spike Lee's *Do the Right Thing* (1989): the former a bat-masked tribute to the white vigilante, the latter a wake-up call to the embattled black community. Through illuminating analyses of both these films, "Ballots" urges cultural studies to bring popular stories from the margins (whether about race or anything else) into debate with more central ones. At various moments, Ross indicates that the vigilante superhero is not only white but male (33), that the black "youth" targeted in Public Enemy's logo is a boy (35), and that *Do the Right Thing*'s Jade offers a muted alternative to the "masculinist" ethic represented, as we saw in chapter 2, by her brother Mookie (38–39).

With these few exceptions, however, the essay takes for granted a racial imaginary and social reality of white/ethnic men locked in struggle with black men, thus reproducing rather than quizzing this aspect of his two key texts. The swerve into adult comics by the Hernandez Brothers in which "female characters are the primary agents" (44), occurring as it does in the penultimate paragraph, therefore comes as something of a surprise. The two Hernandez series Ross mentions, *Locas Tambien* and *Heartbreak Soup*, help him to reiterate his case for putting center into dialogue with margin (here urban Southwest and provincial Mexico) and to argue for a cultural studies reframed to address the history of North American imperialism. But the main point he makes is that "neither [Hernandez series] is guided in any serious way by the masculinist codes of 'doing what you gotta do' which finally govern the worlds of *Batman* and *Do the Right Thing*, and which (both films share this logic) have ugly consequences for almost all the female characters in these films" (44). If this insight had been integral to Ross's readings of these texts, I would pack my bags and go home. In fact, however, the rather serious charge that both films share a masculinist logic has been held in reserve until the last of nineteen pages—and then it occurs in an impatient, apologetic, parenthetical aside.

Other signs of feigned inclusion are the dutiful but gratuitous addition of women/feminism to lists and the politically corrective parenthesis in the context of arguments otherwise assuming, if not asserting, a male-dominated field. Take, for example, *No Respect: Intellectuals and Popular Culture* (1989), a landmark work both for Ross and for the emergent field of cultural studies in the United States. In "Hip, and the Long Front of Color" (65–101), Ross explores the love affair of white intellectuals with black "folk" music (such as be-bop), to which they ascribe a "purity" and apartness from the commercialized sphere of popular black music. Ross himself makes a recuperative case for the impure pleasures of the latter, in keeping with a pro-dirt politics I will have more to say about shortly. For now I am concerned with Ross's reluctance in this chapter to keep in plain view the maleness of his major players—in this case, "folk" as well as "intellectuals." This slant surfaces briefly when Ross considers Norman Mailer's particularly fervid copping of masculinity from black men (87–89).[6] But it is also obscured by the occasional dropping of female names, as in a list of martyred pop rebels that puts Billie Holliday, Marilyn Monroe, and Janis Joplin alongside Charlie Parker, James Dean, Jim Morrison, and others (79). And just as this line-up implies a female presence that "Hip" never begins to materialize, so the chapter's opening mention of Billie Holliday (in a Frank O'Hara poem) mistakenly tropes the material to come, which details an interracial dynamic primarily and significantly between men. The problem, of course, is not male homosociality as a topic but Ross's failure consistently to identify and scrutinize it as such. Nor do I normally object to women in lists except when they are missing from the rest of the text.

A similar inconsistency occurs in *No Respect*'s chapter on camp ("Uses of Camp," 135–70). Observing from the outset that camp taste means differently depending not only on your historical and social position but also on your gender and sexuality (136–37), Ross later explicitly states his intention to address the relation of gay men—not lesbians—to camp culture (158). I agree that this focus makes historical sense; what bothers me is the earlier token inclusion of women, which effectively masks Ross's choice (only reinforced by the use of Susan Sontag) to assume a male subject throughout this chapter. Following Sontag and Mark Booth, for example, Ross depicts the nineteenth-century camp intellectual as a man whose aristocratic airs parody bourgeois values even while suggesting his own marginality (146–47). "Hitherto associated with the high culture milieu of the theater," Ross goes on, "the camp intellectual becomes an institution, in the twentieth century, within the popular entertainment industries, reviving his (and by now, her) role there as the representative or stand-in for a class that is no longer in a position to exercise its power to define official culture" (147). This passage and its parenthesis represent quite well the way forgetfulness about gender alternates in "Uses of Camp" with bursts of self-consciousness about it that nevertheless continue to bracket women's particular stake in camp culture. For despite the space given over to Sontag (who writes about camp from outside it), Ross's addition of "her" remains largely unjustified by subsequent tours of pop camp as well as gay camp artists ranging from Roy Lichtenstein and David Lynch to Boy George and Andy Warhol. No wonder that, in this context, most of the women mentioned by "Uses of Camp" (Baby Jane Holzer, Joan Crawford, Judy Garland, and even those whose agency Ross underlines, like Bette Davis and Mae West) are of interest insofar as they are used by rather than users of camp.

The half-hearted nod to women in an argument that wants to be and probably should be specifically about men does more than injure Ross's feminist credibility; it also leads him into some questionable claims here and in the book as a whole. The first of these arises, I suggest, from his list of rocker women who, beginning in the late 1970s, appeared in drag: Poly Styrene, Jordan, Wendy O. Williams, Patti Smith, Siouxsie Sioux, Annie Lennox, and Grace Jones (164). Adding emphasis to these few lines, a photo of Lennox as

Elvis is one of only two illustrations accompanying this chapter. Perhaps I should be grateful for Ross's effort to remember women at all in a section monopolized by male drag. But it seems to me that, just as David Bowie looks back to the nineteenth-century dandy, the punk butch answers not only her gender-bending brothers in rock (as Ross suggests) but also the mannish lesbians of Paris and Harlem in the 1920s; the butches who drank, flirted, and fought in 1950s gay bars; second-wave feminists only just (by 1975) disenchanted with "androgyny"; and 1970s dykes who (while repudiating butch-femme roles) articulated their group identity in large part through butch looks.[7] By casually assimilating female cross-dressing to male, Ross uproots it from the distinct and by now well-documented history of masculine women, appending the woman in drag to a genealogy that is not, for the most part, her own. In this sense, token inclusion may be no less distorting than leaving women out altogether.

The fleeting presence of women in both "Hip" and "Camp" becomes even more problematic in relation to Ross's larger argument about "intellectuals" and "popular culture." By capriciously interjecting "her" and by dropping in female names when it suits him, Ross veils what has historically been the distinctly male cast of the category "intellectual" as well as, complementing this, the strong feminization of "popular culture" in the modern period. Though often of necessity implying the gender specificity of its two organizing terms, *No Respect* never directly addresses (and sometimes feels free to ignore) this aspect of the binary set out in its subtitle. As we will see shortly, the failure to specify men's privileged relation to the type of the "intellectual" becomes especially misleading in Ross's chapter on pornography.[8]

Whereas the heedless exclusion of women forcibly degenders the world, their fitful inclusion, though easier on the conscience, runs the risk of misgendering it and consequently getting the power relations wrong. If one chooses to write about male-dominated cultures (and after all, someone's gotta do it), it seems important to begin by recognizing the role of "masculinity" and making it an object of analysis. As we have seen, some of Ross's writing does so only to downplay or even to applaud the machismo of a form like gangsta rap. But the mode of self-conscious exclusion can also, unlike modes that ignore or disguise their bias, be the basis for feminist critique. One chapter of *Strange Weather: Culture, Science and Technology in the Age of Limits* (1991), for example, takes this approach with some success. "Cyberpunk in Boystown" (137–67), as its title indicates, ties the vanguardism and cynicism of cyberpunk directly to white boys' fantasies (145) fanned by Reagan-era male panic (152). Explaining that cyberpunk's vision—"youthful male heroes with working-class chips on their shoulders and postmodern biochips in their brains"—deletes the fact of recent uprisings by blacks and women, among others (152), Ross turns his attention to feminist science fiction as well as to hip-hop for imaginings both more hopeful and more democratic.

DOWN AND DIRTY

I move now to a 1994 piece on soccer published in *Artforum* (14–15). The investment of this short text in soccer as a display of virile discipline, abandon, and collectivity followed by an incongruous closing appeal to women's soccer provides another example of the tokenism described above. I also invoke it to introduce a system of moralized antitheses spanning the range of Ross's work, in which women and feminism are typically aligned with the negative pole. This particular essay finds Ross wondering about the sources and merits of national soccer types—do they arise from or are they projected onto the game?—all the while playing around with some appealing characterizations of his own: the "baroque" Brazilians with their "body swerves from hell"; the stalwart English with their ethic of "honest toil"; the "schizophrenic" because self-colonized Scottish; and finally the Americans with their long-standing "immunity" to soccer's charms. Musing on the constructedness of these types, Ross himself erects an opposition between the passionately rowdy, self-consciously working-class game of soccer played everywhere but in the United States (originating, we are told, as a form of class survival and resistance by nonelite teachers in the English public schools) and the well-policed, "gentrified" game that soccer officials wish would result from its Americanization and subordination to the demands of commercial sponsors.

It doesn't take long to figure out who the good guys and bad guys are in this drama. The group loyalties of soccer and socialism are explicitly paired by Americans' aversion to both, making it clear to any reader on the left that resistance lies in watching soccer uninterrupted by beer ads. I agree, to be sure, with the class politics overtly operating here, their support for unruly working-class fans versus crowd-control measures instituted by Margaret Thatcher. What troubles me, though, is the way righteousness, rebellion, and athletic integrity are tied by this argument to an emphatically all-male sport, while domestication, gentrification, and commercialization are linked to the coeducated game presided over by the United States. Ross writes, for example, that the Fédération Internationale de Football Associations "had hoped that subjecting the game to American sports culture—hooligan free, co-ed, and saturated with commodity values—would defuse its class consciousness, and would exorcise the male aggressivity of fans whose 'love' of a team functions like adulterous devotion to a mistress until late in life." Ross obviously shares this love and decries the corruption of soccer by American mores. In opposing the federation's hopes, however, he apparently agrees with it that women in soccer would serve to police working men's transgressive desires, whether sexual ("adulterous" covering here for what Ross later describes more accurately as homoerotic) or political. Within a cosmology valuing dissent and disorder, Ross thus yokes the female athlete to obedience and surveillance. Within a system valuing the popular and proletarian, he damningly lumps coeducation with the corporate and genteel.

Given the generally positive valence throughout the article of untamed virility over against the cluster of overlapping negatives it associates with sissified American soccer, Ross's move in his last paragraph once again to condemn the "Americanized game of stop-and-start, commercial-friendly play bombarded with the heavy statistical artillery of inane commentators" while suddenly singling out for praise "U.S. soccer as a female sport" is at best confusing. I quote his two final sentences in their entirety, including a suggestive typographical inflection: "The proliferation of U.S. soccer as a female sport— the U.S. won the first women's World Cup—heralds a soccer culture with a different destiny, a different GOOOOOOOOOAAAAAALLLLLLL. After all, if you ask why socialism and soccer haven't existed in the U.S., you're assuming that they developed properly elsewhere." This has been precisely the assumption of the piece hitherto, making it rather late in the day to start saying otherwise. Moreover, the lengthening and capitalizing of "goal," while simulating the pronunciation of South American announcers, can't help but add a touch of irony to this conclusion. Ross has put interpretive pressure on the word "goal" previously, noting that grumbling about the "Brazilian Disease" as "too much self-indulgence, too few goals" sounds suspiciously like remarks about "samba-struck narcissists unable to meet their debt payments." What then is the subtextual message about women conveyed by Ross's own punning allusion to their GOOOOOOOOOAAAAAALLLLLLLS?

To my eye, the graphic (as opposed to spoken) overemphasis on "goal" plus the repetition of "different" gestures satirically in the direction of two gynocentric forms alleged to gush—popular women's magazines and in-a-different-voice feminism—as if to hint that women in sports would put a touchy-feely spin on the manly scrimmage. Moreover, while the low-scoring, "beautiful" Brazilian game engrosses watchers by rationing out the pleasure of the goal, Ross's literal elongation of women's goals seems to suggest a slatternly yawner of a game, cheapened by scores too easily gained. Ross has already complained that American sports consumers like to rack up points the way they do everything else, but here American women in particular are tied to what looks on the page like a wide-open goal. In short, riffing on the erotics put in place by Ross's soccer-as-mistress image, I read the spread-eagling of "goal," with its eight enlarged Os, as not a little pornographic. Would it be too much to add, giving this screw a final turn, that Ross's playful capitalization of the GOOOOOOOOAAAAAALLLLLLL of women's soccer might also (recall Freud's fondness for homonymic associations) once again indict while seeming to salvage this game by reconnecting it to "capitalization" in the suspect economic sense?

The gendering of class and, as we've seen in previous chapters, the moralizing of gender that underwrite this soccer piece—posing a heroic, masculinized working class against a corrupt, feminized middle class—anchors a system of binaries running, as I say, throughout Ross's work. In the introduction by Ross to *Microphone Fiends: Youth Music and Youth Culture* (edited with Tricia Rose, 1994), the positive pole is associated not only with proletarian irreverence and insurgency but also with the down and dirty, the virtuously unwashed, the defiantly polluted and impure, locked in struggle with a bourgeois regime of cleanliness. Often, as we'll see later, these two are split by generation as well as gender—harking back, as it were, to the primal scene of a grimy boy resisting maternal ablutions. Here, however, Ross uses this schema to contrast very different kinds of youth cultures: "the impossibly sanitized, aerobicized world of [*Beverly Hills*] *90210*" (5) versus the "style slumming" of grunge culture, the "aversion to cleanliness" of British rave culture, the principled noise pollution of music genres like thrash, and (several zip codes and many social codes away from Beverly Hills) the outlaw world of L.A. gangsta rap (5–6). Class is again the dominant axis of comparison, the preppies of *90210* outflanked by the declassed middle-class kids of various postpunk cultures and by working-class rappers. And while grunge rebuts the "well-scrubbed" with the deliberately dirty, rap adds race to the mix, countering complacent whiteness with up-in-arms blackness.

The siding with poor over rich, black over white, the besmirched over the respectable would be all very well were it not for an inconsistent sexual politics, just discernible between these lines, celebrating the male over the female. In contrast to other pieces we have seen, here Ross does quote dream hampton on female gangstas like herself who revile the sexism of their male counterparts (6). But her remark comes after Ross has already enthusiastically identified "Compton *attitude*" with macho groups like N.W.A. and patiently explained (as in "The Gangsta and the Diva") that early 1990s gangsta sexism and homophobia were "an intrinsic product of the physically threatened conditions under which black male youth negotiated their social survival" (5). The nod to hardcore women like hampton is quickly followed, moreover, by a passage discussing a category of "black youth" that slides unthinkingly into that of young black males (incarcerated at shockingly high rates, etc.) (7). The result is another version of Ross's soccer hierarchy, in which the word "aerobicized" subtly figures the repressed and repressive middle class as female, while the powerful counterdiscourse of L.A. rap (and to a lesser extent grunge) is rendered as overwhelmingly, impressively male.

When it comes to Madonna, whose serial self-reinventions no cultural studies scholar can resist, Ross manages to affiliate even her bad-girl femininity with the more conventional and less cool. Madonna appears fleetingly in *Microphone*'s remarks on *90210*, which tie her to the vacuous Beverly Hills set through a parody of her famous "vogue" video: "Come on, get vague . . . just be vague, there's nothing to it" (4). Ross again puts hip-hop up against aerobics in "This Bridge Called My Pussy," his contribution to the collection *Madonnarama: Essays on Sex and Popular Culture* (1993). If critics have tirelessly parsed Madonna's wigs and crucifixes, here Ross takes the occasion of her much-hyped book *Sex* to look a little lower. "Bridge" opens with praise for *Sex*'s pleasure in diversity and the consequent decentering of straight masculinity. Heterosexual men (rappers Vanilla Ice and Big Daddy Kane in particular) are laughable in *Sex*. "And why not?" Ross asks good-naturedly (47). A paragraph later, the joke has apparently worn thin, as Ross goes to bat for rap (specifically, homophobic gangsta rap), invoked here as a retort to Madonna's Queer Nation. For although Ross notes that both hip-hop and queer cultures are under siege, the citizens of each fighting quite literally for their lives, he stresses that "the difference between them, as everyone ought to know, lies in the divergent careers of Ice-T and Madonna at Time-Warner" (49). Contrasting Time-Warner's promotion of *Sex* with its behind-the-scenes censorship of Ice-T's controversial song "Cop Killer," Ross illustrates once again his tendency to feminize domination by implying, as in the soccer piece, that women are somehow closer than men to corporate power (49–50).

Despite language complicating any simple opposition between white female insider and black male outsider (50), Ross still essentially stages an unnecessary contest between "sex/gender" and "race" for the category by which folks are "most oppressed" (as if these were easily extricable and mutually exclusive), and does so in order to champion "race." Elaborating on the dichotomy schematized above, Ross pits the white/bourgeois/queer/female against the black/proletarian/straight/male and finds the former not only more complicitous with power but also less popular. The Madonna of *Sex* no longer speaks to the masses of teens, according to Ross; her appeal these days is limited largely to the urban and gay (53–55). And if "thrash, power metal and hardcore rap govern the field," Ross argues that "the black dick, in particular, commands allegiance from audiences that the white pussy cannot" (62). So maybe Madonna is getting old, and maybe *Sex* has its limits. It still strikes me that berating "white pussy" with "black dick" only inverts one of our oldest and ugliest ways of understanding gender and race in the United States: the lynching-for-rape model that, as discussed in chapter 2, calls upon fetishized white female sexuality to demonize black male sexuality (with the effect of legitimating white male violence and excluding black women entirely).[9] Nor am I sure that Ross has earned the right to throw around the word "pussy" as he does. This essay is so little pussy-affirmative that descriptions of Madonna as "the sluttest" (53) and "tart" (61), not to mention the title image of "a bridge called her pussy" (52), fail to wrest these terms from their usual pejorative meanings. Ross's "bridge" supposedly refers to Madonna's use of naughty sex to make political connections, but to me it further suggests a male fantasy of star fucking, in which access to celebrity pussy is at once desired and derided. "You may even get lucky," he winks in his final sentence (64).[10]

But "Bridge" goes beyond the soccer and youth culture texts in disparaging, along with the "white feminine" as a social/moral position, the politics of feminism. It conveys this in part by establishing that Madonna acts up against sex/gender norms—and then trumping her decisively with Ice-T. Within this frame, it manages at the same time to find a Madonna who can, when necessary, be mobilized *against* feminism. "Bridge" does this, first, by upholding *Sex* as a slap in the face to "politically correct anti-porn feminism" (58). "Politically correct" and "anti-porn" are Ross's modifiers of choice when evoking an easily vilified feminism. Here and elsewhere, Ross uses such phrases to conjure up a scowling feminist police, hardly different from the "feminazis" of conservative smear sheets, and linked in his value system to the conspiracy of Thatcherites and girl jocks who would take all the fun out of soccer. In this case the fun at issue is sex as depicted by *Sex*, and feminists are naturally assumed to be against it. As we will see, this is not the only place Ross invokes "anti-porn" feminism as if it were coextensive with feminism generally, though in fact he knows well how sharply feminists have split over porn and how ascendant pro-sex feminism has become especially in the academy (witness many of the other essays in *Madonnarama*). Ross does note later in "Bridge" that some "younger feminists" have developed a postmodern appreciation for Madonna's deconstructed femininity and called on her for "a politics which did not deny itself a life of pleasure and style and bleached eyebrows" (60). Yet his writing far more routinely implies that feminists are not only "older" but stodgily unbleached and constitutionally averse to pleasure.

The other way that Ross uses Madonna to malign feminism is by analyzing *Sex*'s Hitchhiker shot (Madonna thumbing in the nude) as an image primarily of class feeling, all the while denying it has anything to do with being a woman. Ross describes this figure deftly as "a nude study in the psychopathology of economics" (59). She holds her handbag, he says memorably, with a "tenacious, white-knuckled grip . . . defiantly at odds with a genteel culture of property" (59). For some reason, however, this nice reading for class desperation and defiance is used to suppress a reading for gender protest and to exclude the Hitchhiker from the "sequence of public feminist iconography" stretching from the 1968 Miss America protests to "Madonna's own crotch grab for a 1989 cover of *Interview*, Demi Moore's pregnancy portrait for *Vanity Fair*, Linda Hamilton's hardbody in *Terminator 2*, Grace Jones's cyborg body still everywhere, and Annie Lennox's and k.d. lang's panoply of cross-dressings" (57). Dismissing these images as conducive to "the sort of liberal media commentary that registers and acknowledges how far women are going these days" (57), Ross reduces this important

archive to Virginia Slims–style sloganeering and trivializes "politically correct" concerns about the imaging of female agency. Not for the first time, he
appears to set a "liberal," corporatized feminism against a forceful class analysis, here centered on a woman but nonetheless reluctant to take up questions
of gender. A blindly bourgeois, commercial-friendly feminism does exist, of
course, as does an antiporn feminism I like no more than Ross does. The
problem is that he mentions these for the most part in lieu of other feminisms, allows them effectively to stand for feminism, and attacks them from
a standpoint identified as outside of feminism—when such a perspective is
available within and often deeply indebted to feminist analyses.

THIS BRIDGE CALLED MY DICK

We can add, therefore, to the list of qualities typically feminized and dis-
owned by Ross regulation generally and in particular a regulatory, guilt-
inducing view of pleasure, sexual pleasure above all. Associated in the soccer piece with a tidy, bourgeois femininity, these are also continually related
in Ross's work to a policing, puritanical feminism. Thus *No Respect*'s chapter on "The Popularity of Pornography" (171–208), while wavering a good
deal in its thinking about women and sexual representation, argues with
greatest conviction both that female desire is genteel and that feminism is
pedantic and squeamish about sex. This long, dense essay takes numerous
turns and makes, in passing, a number of plausibly feminist points. But its
clearest thesis, and the one congruent with Ross's larger argument, lam-
bastes antiporn feminist "intellectuals" for looking down on a pornographic "popular" that emerges in the course of the chapter (notwithstanding
some phrases to the contrary) as ineluctably male. The feminist critique of
pornography, Ross asserts, "reproduces the same languages of mass manip-
ulation, systematic domination, and victimization which had been the
trademark of the Cold War liberal critique of mass culture" (176); its concern for sex workers smacks of the "bourgeois morality" that moved "social
purity" feminists to patronizing pity for Victorian prostitutes (178–79); and
its embrace of wholesome "erotica" as opposed to seamy porn calls upon the
same class prejudices that were mustered to defend *Lady Chatterley's Lover*
and the like as "art" rather than "obscenity" (179–80). In an all-too-familiar
move, Ross stands up for what he calls the popular, vulgar, and unapologetically obscene, defending it from attack by hoity-toity women who

would banish dirty pictures or, just as bad, clean them up into something arty and tasteful.

What we have not seen before, however, is the alignment of these women, as feminists, not only with the middle class but also with other *intellectuals*—the Cold Warriors, hipsters, pop and camp intellectuals whose wary and finally condescending engagements with the popular are the subject and target of this book overall. Despite my own skepticism about antiporn feminists, I would reiterate that Ross's positioning of them overlooks the traditionally difficult if not oxymoronic relation of women to the category "intellectual." To me it seems all too obvious that the terms of *No Respect*'s subtitle, "Intellectuals and Popular Culture," are both classed and gendered—women and the feminine as thoroughly included in notions of the denigrated "popular" as they have been excluded from the meanings and privileges accruing to "intellectuals." The first chapter of *No Respect* hints as much by offering the petit-bourgeois and also embarrassingly "feminine" literary efforts of Ethel Rosenberg as a figure for the people's culture shunned by anti-Stalinist intellectuals, whose maleness (with very few exceptions) goes without saying (15–41). Yet *No Respect*'s probing analysis of the class dynamic between "high" and "low" cultural forms refuses, as we have seen, to address in any sustained way the inflection of this dynamic by gender. Consequently, when it comes to porn, Ross does not hesitate to slot antiporn feminists into the role of "intellectuals" over against a "popular" that slides again and again into pornography from a straight male perspective. As in the more recent pieces above, he depicts a class struggle in which, illogically, most of the women are elite and most of the "people" are men. The political upshot of his analysis is therefore mixed. By valuing a complicated, contested popular, Ross's version of cultural studies rightly corrects the high-art biases associated with such critical traditions as the Frankfurt School and implicit, I agree, in some critiques of pornography. At the same time, insofar as he regenders the recuperated "low" male and the implicated "high" female, Ross keeps in place the Frankfurt School's negative views of the "feminine" and fails to account for the real sexual as well as class politics of porn.[11]

Ross explicitly, rather outrageously, refuses a gender analysis of pornography on the grounds described above: that feminists by definition scorn pornography and its consumers as vulgar. Assuming that the price of feminism is classism, he stages a showdown between mutually exclusive gender and class critiques and stacks the deck in favor of class. Ross can do this, however, only by putting undue emphasis on antiporn feminism while, as in the Madonna piece, downplaying a pro-sex feminism that simultaneously vibrates to hardcore *and* denounces industry sexism. Fourteen pages in, Ross does give a paragraph to prominent "pleasure and danger" feminists such as Ellen Willis and Ann Snitow (185), and later he rehearses many of the pro-sex/anticensorship arguments they and others have made since the feminist sex wars broke out in the early 1980s (188–92). Nevertheless, by refusing to identify these arguments with "pro-sex feminism," referring exclusively to what he calls instead "anti-antiporn feminism" (after "anti-anticommunism"), Ross mutes their affirmation of woman-centered porn, keeps them in thrall to the antiporn idiom, and maps both sides of this feminist debate onto a Cold War discourse incompetent on questions of gender.

More misleading still, the introduction to *No Respect* alludes only to the "anti-antiporn position" (12) taken by "the recent anti-antiporn movement . . . a movement which contests the antiporn critique of popular pornographic culture on the part of feminist intellectuals" (12). Eliding altogether those feminists primarily responsible for articulating the so-called anti-antiporn position, Ross now locates "feminist intellectuals" only on the other side of this issue—the wrong side, of course. This elision is particularly disturbing given that Ross goes on to privilege the porn chapter as *No Respect*'s last word: to rest his case there, as he puts it, "in the contrast between the tradition of suspicion, recruitism, and disaffiliation" (regarding pop culture) that has just been pinned on "feminist intellectuals" and the "more exemplary model of intellectual engagement and activism" identified here with an anti-antiporn movement forcibly stripped of its ties to feminism (12). Rising to quite a pitch at this point, Ross looks to the anti-antiporn position for a "bill of rights for a new social contract between intellectuals and popular culture" and outlines a stirring set of demands for sexual pleasure, sexual rights, and sexual diversity (12–13). Yet this whole attractive manifesto, this call for a "more popular, less guilt-ridden, cultural politics for our time" (13) is quite pointedly framed over and against feminism, which Ross inexplicably collapses into antiporn feminism. Needless to say, such an anti-antipatriarchal paradigm for cultural studies coexists uneasily both with Ross's otherwise radical politics and with his support elsewhere for new social movements, including the women's movement.

Activist sex workers, campaigning for better working conditions and hotter porn for women, are another group combining vehemently pro-sex views with a feminist critique of pornographic conventions. Here are women who might legitimately break up the maleness of "the people" as Ross usually imagines them, thus challenging his primary class opposition between prissy feminists and your average, porn-loving Joe. Part of Ross knows this and wants to affirm his solidarity with the sex worker, whose lowly status he compares at one point to the "truck driver" consumer of pornography: both "have either been taken for granted, morally patronized, or else consigned to the flames of 'false consciousness' by intellectuals" (175). He opens, moreover, with an epigraph by porn star Nina Hartley, explaining that "today's porno is the only game in town. But it's a game where there is a possibility of the players, over time, getting some of the rules changed" (171). We might guess that Ross means to endorse Hartley's faith in revisionary sex work (especially since his other epigraph cites antiporn crusader Andrea Dworkin); indeed, his first paragraph seems to ironize the video store owner who reassures Ross, "man to man," that the new porn for women "eventually did get down to the real stuff; it just took a little longer, and it was, sort of, different" (171). Unfortunately, however, this "different" erotic idiom—the boldly woman-centered videos made by such stars turned directors as Candida Royalle—is quickly, ominously recast by Ross as a matter of class difference. Innovations by female sex workers involving romance, narrative, and mutuality in the context of hardcore are repudiated as no more than "the latest phase in the history of pornography's bid for respectability" (172)—signs, then, not of gender radicalism but of class reaction.

I agree with Ross that the ideology of the "feminine" coincides at points with "good taste" (172), and it may be that the ideology branding sexual women "whores" may make us more circumspect than men about liking to fuck. But this in no way justifies dismissing as gentrifiers those women, both working- and middle-class, who produce and consume porn addressed specifically to them. Ross's predictable case against these women and their fantasies makes a number of unwarranted assumptions: that female porn (and, by extension, female sexuality) is "tasteful," bourgeois, and thus bad, while male porn is "vulgar," working-class, and thus good; that female porn, because it takes longer and appreciates reciprocity, is somehow timid and euphemistic, while waste-no-time, tell-no-story, take-no-prisoners male porn is genuinely "lustful" (172); that female porn, when it promotes safer sex, as in *The Pick-Up*, is a "turn-off" (199), while the turn-on of male porn lies in accepting current heterosexual practices as functions of an unyielding "psychic reality" (200). This is, for one thing, a rhetoric of class that feels free to ignore self-evident class identities and relations. Sex workers like Nina Hartley, Candida Royalle, and, say, Susie Bright—players in the far from respectable porno game determined to change some of its rules—are disqualified here as "people" and classed instead with those feminist "intellectuals" Ross rejects out of hand. Meanwhile, "straight male intellectuals," made to feel "wrong" about liking traditional porn (193), are wishfully allied with truck drivers on the side of the censored and oppressed.

We have only to ask, however, whose lust, whose turn-off, and whose psychic reality are privileged here to recover the gender judgments underlying Ross's language of class and to realize that this chapter attempts to frame as "left" what is basically a backlash defense of mainstream male desires.[12] Ross does this not only by celebrating heterosexual male porn as the authentic "popular" but also by arguing its inevitability in surprisingly essentialist terms. Ross would say, of course, that sexuality changes over time, and he tries to have it both ways on the issue of whether wet dreams can be reformed: "This is not to say that the unconscious does not *learn*; it just cannot be *taught* in any direct way" (200). Yet overall this chapter makes a point of stressing "our" inability to unlearn the dominant pornographic idiom; more than once it argues "the integral importance of 'regressive' but unreformable fantasies of aggressivity to the construction of sexuality" (188). Whose fantasies are unreformably aggressive? Whose sexuality is thus casually universalized? The answer again and again is straight males, whose taste in porn Ross at once lauds in class terms as politically correct and defends, in quasi-biological terms, as politically incorrigible.

Given how thoroughly "The Popularity of Pornography" repudiates erotica that sets a pretty scene and builds slowly to mutually satisfying sex, its effort much later suddenly to recuperate Harlequin romances as a popular, sensual genre for women, not unlike pornography for men, flounders badly (192–93). As with the faux inclusion of activist sex workers, this brief attempt to coeducate the "popular" by invoking romance readers is undercut by the vehemence with which anything like a "love story" has already been excluded from Ross's sexual imaginary (189). Moreover, Ross accurately summarizes Janice Radway's *Reading the Romance* only, in my view, to misappropriate it, for he goes on to equate romances for women with porn for men as texts similarly redeemed by their immense popularity, "however complicit [their pleasures] with patriarchal logic" (193). Yet Radway and other feminist critics, while noting the complicit aspects of popular romances, have suggested that women readers also value these stories for their subtle defiance or circumvention of patriarchal logic. Whereas Ross uses popularity to apologize for the regressive sexual politics of male porn, Radway takes popularity as a cue to explore the progressive implications of romances for women. To the extent, therefore, that Ross momentarily changes his mind in favor of love stories, he reasons differently if not oppositely from the feminist scholars enlisted to help him.

I want to close my discussion of Ross's male-dominated system of binaries by considering a few paragraphs toward the end of *The Chicago Gangster Theory of Life* (1994) that speak to the gender politics of his work on the discourse of environmentalism.[13] The example I will look at occurs in the context of a brilliant, clinching analysis of the way a Malthusian language is used today to understand and diagnose as "natural" conditions of scarcity that are always, Ross stresses, produced and regulated politically (263–73). He warns in particular against "any discourse of limits that equates an 'excess' of rights and freedoms with the excesses of material growth and development generally held responsible for the ecological crisis" (264). Such an equation, Ross notes, too often implies that a contraction of newly won rights for women and racial/sexual minorities necessarily goes along with reduced consumption (265–66). Yet while Ross's trenchant critique of environmental thinking is thus explicitly concerned to protect women's rights, it ignores for the most part the way this discourse, and his own, are unavoidably gendered. As with the categories "intellectuals" and "popular culture" in *No Respect*, Ross has little sustained to say about how profoundly and pervasively "culture" has been coded male, "nature" female, although the book's polemic hinges on these two categories and the relationship between them. There are moments, consequently, when *Chicago* strikes me as reproducing, in only slightly revised form, not only the traditional gendering of "nature" and "culture" but also the customary devaluation of the feminine term.

Take the passage that occurs at the conclusion of this book in which Ross cites an ad for New Cycle Menstrual Lingerie as a regrettable instance of "persuasion by threat" (269):

> Mother Earth won't swallow this for much longer! 11 billion disposable, chlorine-bleached menstrual pads buried or burned each year. Use cloth for Menstrual

Flow! Confront the Inconvenience! Overcome the Taboo! Beautiful, soft, washable cloth menstrual pads & accessories in organic knit or cotton flannel. Next Time: Tampons as sexual harassment & earth abuse. Stay tuned. Don't stuff it! Reuse it! CALL 1–800–845–FLOW.

"Don't get me wrong about this ad," Ross explains. "I am an advocate of reuse, and share the reservations of many environmentalists about the preference of big business for recycling practices. I submit, however, that people for the most part do not respond favorably to coercive messages of this sort that invoke guilt and self-denial" (269). Reuse versus recycling aside, my problem with Ross's response to this ad lies in its tacit elaboration of the gendered dichotomies we have seen elsewhere. Echoing earlier work, *Chicago* would admonish the tyrannizing, guilt-inducing "asceticism" of much green discourse while calling instead for an emancipatory "hedonism" (273), and as before the repudiated "antipleasure" pole is subtly feminized, here as "Mother Earth." Mother Earth joins, then, a family of women—including soccer coeds, the squeaky-clean aerobicizers of *90210*, and antiporn feminists—on the discredited side of social constraint, gentility, sexual prohibition, moral cleanup, and, now, cleanup as morality.[14] Ross's put-down of Mother Earth is different, of course, from the humbling of Nature by Western Science. Indeed, his antagonist is not Nature herself, but rather the ecological, cultural feminists behind this ad who invoke Mother Earth as a prepatriarchal force to be reckoned with. Not nature, then, but a discourse of nature, not the primeval feminine but a specific kind of popular feminism are targeted by Ross's cultural critique—yet its perspective, no less than that of traditional science, remains un-selfconsciously male just as its demonized object remains female.

From an ecofeminist or simply female point of view, by contrast, the Mother Earth of this ad isn't threatening so much as inviting women to identify with and join her in refusing to be penetrated by high-tech, disposable pads/tampons. ("Mother Earth won't swallow this for much longer. . . . Tampons as sexual harassment & earth abuse. . . . Don't stuff it!") What Ross reads as coercion may also be read as an exhortation to resist coercion. Where he finds self-denial one might also find self-affirmation of a particularly bodily/sexual kind, given the regimes of secrecy and distaste surrounding menstruation. ("Overcome the Taboo!") The message to women between these lines is not, as Ross seems to think, "Deprive yourself in order to be environmentally correct, or Mother Earth will punish you," but rather something like, "Rise up, my daughters, and resist the myth that your bodies are Inconvenient and Taboo. Your Menstrual Flow is not dirty but clean, beautiful, and natural as my own Rushing Rivers." Within an ecofeminist context, therefore, far from invoking guilt, this ad offers freedom from shame. Protesting environmental pollution, it also revises views of the female body as polluted; essentializing women's ties to nature, it refutes views of the female body as unnatural and periodically aberrant. Ross devotes part of a previous chapter to "Eco-Woman" and shows, in spite of much ambivalence, that he sees and can appreciate the ecofeminist logic of celebrating as powerful and wild a Mother Earth whom science has sought to tame (220–30). Nevertheless, when it comes to New Cycle Menstrual Lingerie, Ross not only mistakes an antipuritanical reclaiming of the female body for the imposition of puritanism but also instinctively resents as "coercive" the power attributed by feminists to a maternal force.

NO QUESTION OF FEMINISM

As suggested earlier, then, the split in Ross's work between the negative, "bourgeois" female who stamps out dirt and pleasure where she finds them and the positive, "proletarian" male whose vulgarity and lustiness are signs of subversion is sometimes written as a generational split and family tussle between controlling mother and rebellious son. Environmental cops wear the badge of Mother Earth while defiance is tied to dirty-mouthed, male-dominated youth cultures like gangsta rap. The generational axis appears, indeed, to have special significance for Ross. In *Chicago*'s "Eco-Man Evolves from Eco-Woman," he inserts the following apparently gratuitous and wholly unsubstantiated claim: "Most social theorists trace the origin of status hierarchy in tribal societies to internal tensions resulting from the ascendancy of elders; in other words, men and women dominated other men and women through gerontocratic privilege before men dominated women through the sexual division of labor" (225). What, we might ask, does Ross stand to gain from constituting the young—as opposed to women—as the *ur*-oppressed? Quite possibly a rationale for much of his work, which turns again and again to popular youth cultures for political leverage and inspiration. As I have argued, moreover, Ross's dissident kid cultures are almost invariably male-centered, while women (when not merely incidental) tend to be imagined as "older," authoritarian, and readily punitive. All of which is to say that Ross's political investment in male youth, his romance of the bad boy, may be inextricable from an iconography of tyranny as maternal.

If the oppression of boys by women makes little sense, at least to me, as a political paradigm for our times, it obviously makes far better sense as a psychological paradigm of contemporary male development. In what remains of this chapter, I will gloss Ross's frequent attempts to distance himself from one feminism or another in terms of the modern western developmental narrative stressing the need for sons to separate conclusively from primary maternal figures. I take my cue from "Demonstrating Sexual Difference" and "No Question of Silence," Ross's two contributions to the well-known collection *Men in Feminism* (1987), edited by Alice Jardine and Paul Smith. "Demonstrating" was criticized at the time for attacking radical feminism as "essentialist" in language at once theoretically unoriginal and politically suspect.[15] I am further troubled by the fact that both "Demonstrating" and "No Question" take up the issue of "men in feminism" by means of courtroom dramas: the cases, respectively, of Jack the Ripper and of three women on trial for murdering a man in the Dutch feminist film *A Question of Silence*. Ross quips that his fixation with "trials, defenses, prosecutions," etc. in relation to this topic may be "nothing more than a symptom of my litigious male mind" (91). From where I sit, it seems more obviously the product of a guilty male mind along with a strategy of self-defense that quickly takes the form of a counterattack. For though Ross begins by denying the universality of male violence, he ends by turning the tables altogether and implicitly attributing the use of force not to men but to women.

Ross's feelings about feminism in these pieces remind me of men who respond to concern about sexual harassment by fretting that it makes them vulnerable to false charges, with the result that actual power relations are affectively reversed. On a formal level, Ross enacts such a reversal by beginning in his first essay with the Ripper and then turning, in his second, to *A Question of Silence*, so that the man on trial for murder is replaced by a trio of female defendants. A brilliant and powerful film (with something approaching cult status in feminist circles), *A Question of Silence* exonerates these three females by identifying their violence as a logical and even pleasurable response to the routinized brutalization of women. In "No Question of Silence," Ross opens with a title that resoundingly negates such a view, and goes on to complain that the movie's tale of feminist retaliation works to naturalize male violence and is, moreover, unnerving in its "practical effects" (90). Of course the purview of such fictional representations is not practical so much as theatrical (as Ross well knows when it comes to violent porn and cop-killing rap), but his essay still says a rather hysterical "no" to the way *A Question of Silence* laughingly lets women off the hook for manslaughter.

"No Question of Silence" thus redoubles the efforts of "Demonstrating Sexual Difference" to apologize for male domination by cautioning against "essentialism." Beyond this, having chided women for their revenge fantasies, it further accuses feminism of a deadly prescriptiveness. Trials recur in these pieces, Ross finally decides, less because of his male litigiousness than because "the invitation to talk about *prescriptions* for male feminism . . . inevitably [calls] forth reflections about *prescriptiveness* itself, and the various ways in which the prescriptiveness of sexual politics lives out an uneasy relation to the *proscriptions* of the law *as it exists*" (91). As I understand it, this is just a roundabout, heavily italicized way of once again equating feminism with coercion. Like antiporn- and ecofeminism, "sexual politics" as a general category conjures up for Ross inflexible notions of "correctness," prohibition, even collaboration with "the law as it exists." Having put feminism on trial for murder, now with this last phrase Ross recasts it in a role far worse from a left gangsta perspective: as prosecuting attorney, enforcer of the law, upholder of state power.[16]

Enter Ross's mother. Oddly but ever so tellingly, this quaint figure with her old Scottish saw pops up just as Ross is struggling to elaborate his ambivalence toward the issue of men in feminism. "'There are those and there are such as those,'" Ross quotes his mother as saying (91). But where we might expect deference to the folk wisdom of this lower-class woman, Ross offers her favorite maxim as, on the contrary, the ultimate example of a dangerously double-edged prescription. Though meant as a critique of upper-class pretensions, Ross explains, his mother's words serve nevertheless to "naturalize" class hierarchy. According to him, such a dictum "bristles with contradictions which actually sanction and extend social inequalities even while they promise to eradicate mere pretensions to justice" (91). From this we are to gather that feminism—insofar as it shares with Ross's mother an objection to social relations distinguishing "those" from "such as those," is not simply essentialist but didactic and reductive in a particularly *maternal* way—well-meaning but rigid; fond of certain axioms with a doddering tendency to repeat them; naïve about the actual, barbed complexity of these; and sadly complicitous with the very wrongs it would right.

In tension with this maternalized feminism, "No Question" represents Ross as, above all, *young*. "Too young," he writes in his second sentence, to recall personally the birth of the women's movement (85). "Young enough," he notes later, "for feminism to have been a primary component of my intellectual formation . . . the politics of feminism came first, democratic socialism later" (86). Stressing generational differences among male feminists, Ross sets himself off from those older men "whose personal intellectual history includes a substantial pre-feminist phase" (87). Ross, by contrast, grew up with feminism, took its "facticity" for granted (86), was not made but apparently born a feminist. I take it that Ross's point is to establish his feminist credentials by insisting that, for him, feminism *came first*. Yet the usual story of male development would argue that primary identification with the powerful and feminine becomes at some point problematic for boys and must ever after be continually denied in favor of the masculine. As an account of male intellectual formation, this story suggests that Ross's work may find itself at odds with feminism not in spite but precisely because of his having encountered it first. Ross exemplifies what I mean by "cool" insofar as his politics recapitulate this masculine structure of feeling—in which rebellion needs a mother to push back against, and that mother is identified with feminism.

My notions about Ross's intellectual development do not, I should make clear, aspire to more than rough, biographical plausibility. I am less interested in the "facts" of Ross's history than in the myth of his past intimated by his writing. Ross was, for example, actually about twelve years old in 1968 when women's liberation began to make a name for itself in the international media. I was around the same age, and I remember second-wave feminism as a "happening," an intervention in the countercultural scene—not as an inert "fact" of my youth. More pertinent for my purposes, however, is Ross's felt sense of being too young to remember this beginning, so that he situates feminism not as a sibling formation, coming of age alongside him, but rather as a preexisting, parental and (being first) classically maternal one. I want to elaborate, then, on the family romance made available by Ross's own version of his intellectual *Bildung* in the interview he gave to *The Minnesota Review*, which appeared in 1996.

The story begins in the late 1970s at the University of Kent in England, where Ross completed most of his graduate work. As Ross explains, Kent was then a center for new, densely theoretical approaches to film drawing heavily on Lacanian psychoanalysis and identified closely with the journal *Screen*. Among those important to the *Screen* group, many of whom taught at Kent at the time, were two of the founders of feminist film theory: Claire Johnston, whose "Women's Cinema as Counter-Cinema" appeared in a 1973 *Screen* pamphlet (*Notes on Women's Cinema*, edited by Johnston), and Laura Mulvey, whose ground-breaking "Visual Pleasure and Narrative Cinema" was published by *Screen* in 1975. Ross observes that the *Screen* school, like himself at this stage, was "committed to the avant-garde idea" and therefore "very much at loggerheads with the more populist cultural studies tradition that had been active in Birmingham for some time" (77). He is referring here to Birmingham's Centre for Contemporary Cultural Studies (CCCS), home to Stuart Hall, Dick Hebdige, and other scholars whose pioneering work in Marxist theory and studies of resistance in various British subcultures would lay the foundation for American cultural studies. Distinguishing the high-art emphasis of *Screen* from the pop-cultural emphasis of Birmingham, Ross neglects to note another point of contrast between them: that the centrality of feminism to *Screen*'s project differed sharply from the marginality of female scholars, women's cultures, and feminism to work being done at CCCS during the same era.

In *Resistance Through Rituals: Youth Subcultures in Post-war Britain*, which came out of CCCS in 1975, Angela McRobbie and Jenny Garber contributed the sole piece attempting to theorize "girls and subcultures." "The absence of girls from the whole of the literature in this area [of youth subcultures] is quite striking" (209), they wrote. In its domination by and exclusive attention to men, McRobbie and Garber complained, the new "skeptical" sociology (that helped spawn cultural studies) was no different from the old (212). Contrary to male scholars, they hypothesized that girls may in fact be present in subcultural circles but "invisible because the very term 'subculture' has acquired such strong masculine overtones" (211). Three years later, in 1978, the Women's Studies Group at Birmingham finally convinced CCCS to "let" McRobbie and Garber put together an issue of *Working Papers in Cultural Studies* on women (14). "Ten issues, with only four articles concerning women—it seemed about time," they declared in the introduction to *Women Take Issue: Aspects of Women's Subordination* (7). While the very appearance of this volume indicated that attitudes were beginning to change, it was prompted in the first place by what the editors decried as "the continued absence from CCCS of a visible concern with feminist issues" (15).

Ross himself, ironically enough, would not affiliate with the body of work originating at CCCS until he had traded England for America in the early 1980s. As Reagan settled into office, Ross crossed the Atlantic, finished up his graduate work at Indiana and Berkeley, and took a job teaching at Illinois State University. Only then did he encounter the new American cultural studies beginning to take shape down the road at the University of Illinois at Champaign-Urbana. Out of this would eventually come *No Respect* in 1989, which Ross acknowledged "would not have been written" without the influence of British cultural studies. He was careful to note the "national specificity" of this scholarship and stressed the need to adapt its perceptions for American use (*No Respect* 7). Nevertheless, the approach to cultural studies Ross found in the American Midwest was to a significant extent imported from Birmingham via such figures as communications professor Lawrence Grossberg, who studied at CCCS in the late 1960s and overlapped with Ross in Illinois. And though Grossberg has recalled that CCCS actually did a project on women's magazines while he was there (*We Gotta* 404), Stuart Hall and others in *Culture, Media, and Language* (1980) support the complaint of McRobbie et al. that work at the Centre in Grossberg's day was generally impervious to feminism and would not feel its impact until the 1970s were almost over (38–39, 246–56). Indeed, Grossberg's subsequent work on rock, like Ross's on rap, while transposing cultural studies into an American key, has been largely faithful to Birmingham's originary bias in favor of subcultures centered on boys.

Since McRobbie and Garber first intervened back in 1975, both British and American traditions have, of course, gone on to produce important cultural studies of women and girls as well as feminist studies of men—among them McRobbie's own *Feminism and Youth Culture: From "Jackie" to "Just Seventeen"* (1991). Indeed, by attending to the popular and finding moments of resistance in everyday life, cultural studies has enabled feminist recuperations of such frequently denigrated practices as reading romances, shopping, rapping, stripping, and worshipping female pop stars. It is nonetheless true, as "Girls and Subcultures" observed, that founding ethnographies like those of Dick Hebdige on Rude Boys, Tony Jefferson on Teddy Boys, and John Clarke on Skinheads (all in *Resistance Through Rituals*) effectively gave a masculine turn to the very definition of "subculture."[17] The intellectual legacy

Ross laid claim to in Illinois was, in short, both preoccupied by "youth" and also (especially relative to psychoanalytic film theory) dominated by males. The severing of early ties to *Screen* in favor of a bond with Birmingham-style cultural studies could thus be seen as a kind of intellectual oedipal turning point for Ross—the shift, constitutive of normative masculinity, away from mothers to fathers and sons.

Such a reading of Ross's move from Kent to Illinois, film theory to cultural studies, feminism to masculinism in terms of a boy's separation from the maternal has the merit, at least, of appearing to explain Ross's oft-reiterated discomfort with feminism as well as women. It may, moreover, help to shed some light on his specific repudiation of the single tenet most prominently associated with feminist film theory generally and Laura Mulvey in particular: Mulvey's assertion that cinematic conventions position "woman as image, man as bearer of the look" (*Visual* 19). Popularized with unusual speed and enthusiasm, generalized far beyond its original purview, energetically contested and revised (the author herself has "afterthoughts" in 1981), Mulvey's notion of a dominative "male gaze" occupies a central place in the lexicon not only of film theory but also of feminist theory in disciplines from English to anthropology. The "male gaze" represents, in addition, a place where the idioms of academic and popular feminism come together. Like the activists who picketed the 1968 Miss America Pageant, thereby launching second-wave feminism in the United States, Mulvey began her feminist career by protesting the objectification of women at the 1970 Miss World Pageant (3–5), and her theoretical work is in many respects an elaboration of this stand. Since then, the most vocal heirs to these protests have been antiporn feminists, and we have already seen how vehement Ross can be in discrediting their position, how conscientious in neglecting more complicated, pro-sex versions of their critique. Within this context, Ross's celebration of the spectacle of black women's backsides in videos by men is only the most blatant example of what I see in his work as a running rebuke to a widely shared structure of feminist feeling.

Such a rebuke makes sense within the frame of a family romance designating those feminisms referenced by Mulvey as the mother to be outgrown. Certainly Mulvey plays this role for Ross in "The Everyday Life of Lou Andreas-Salomé: Making Video History" (1989), which, appearing the same year as *No Respect*, coincides with his emergence as a cultural studies critic. Included in a volume on feminism and psychoanalysis, this piece is at once a lingering look back at psychoanalytic film theory and a pointed effort by Ross to distance himself from Mulvey and company. Among other things, it gives a rave review to Steve Fagin's experimental video, *Virtual Play*, for what Ross sees as a liberating portrait of Nietzsche's lover, Lou Andreas-Salomé. Though ostensibly feminist in purport and congruent with Mulvey's appeal to avant-garde visual modes, the would-be feminist salvation Ross offers Salomé via Fagin comes at the expense of—indeed, in direct opposition to—many of the founding notions of feminist film theory.

For while Mulvey urges the destruction, through feminist analysis, of conventional male modes of visual pleasure, Ross applauds *Virtual Play* for reassuring viewers that "there are no easy escapes from this movie-theater-cum-prison-house of the male imaginary" (163). And while Mulvey would "break with normal pleasurable expectations in order to conceive a new language of desire" (*Visual* 16), Ross appreciates that *Virtual Play*, even as it falsifies male fantasies of Salomé, also recognizes their "power and fatal attractiveness" (162). Echoing the fatalism with regard to normative heterosexuality that we encountered in *No Respect*'s chapter on pornography, he closes by praising Fagin for refusing to "repudiate the power of desire" (163). The turn from Mulvey is explicit in a passage asserting that "spectacle and narrative have no meaning in themselves, as forms or discourses" (144). Ross says he wishes to stress this point "especially in the context of the last decade of feminist film theory"—which is to say, as a specific refutation of Mulvey's thesis that Hollywood spectacle and narrative function systematically to neutralize the threat (of castration) posed by images of women for "male" viewers. When Ross goes on to claim Fagin's deconstructing but still desiring male gaze, he therefore does so with the idea of spurning an era of Mulveyan scholarship that also happens to coincide with the preceding decade of his own intellectual life.

"Everyday" is in this sense a pivotal text, in which the move away from Mulvey sets the stage for Ross's move away from psychoanalysis altogether. It anticipates his leaving behind a discourse of dreams, infancy, and subjection to the unconscious that, even in its nonfeminist guises, might be seen as a kind of diva to cultural studies' gangsta. I invoke it to conclude my argument that Ross's ambivalence toward the "feminine" and especially toward "male gaze" feminism may be glossed by the received story of male formation, with feminist film theory in the place of "mother," reviled as well as desired because of its very primaryness.

5

HENRY LOUIS GATES JR.:
FIGURES IN BLACK MASCULINITY

For me, I realized as Hortense Spillers spoke, much of my scholarly and critical work has been an attempt to learn how to speak in the strong, compelling cadences of my mother's voice. . . . And for us as scholar-critics, learning to speak in the voice of the black female is perhaps the ultimate challenge of producing a discourse of the critical Other.

—Henry Louis Gates Jr., "The Master's Pieces" (1990)

Of course, the paradox is that the cultural centrality of the African-American—this is a country where Michael Jordan and Shaquille O'Neal look down from every billboard—coexists with the economic and political marginality of the African-American, most especially of the African-American male.

—Henry Louis Gates Jr., *Thirteen Ways of Looking at a Black Man* (1997)

While all of my "cool" subjects, as both cause and effect of their coolness, are visible outside their immediate professional circles, Henry Louis Gates Jr. is perhaps the most broadly influential. Winner of a MacArthur "genius" award in 1981, he has long been the nation's single most notable scholar of African American studies, and has kept his place at the top even as, over the last twenty years, the roster of leading African Americanists has changed and the discipline itself has turned from recovering literary texts to reading such disparate cultural artifacts as black film, black hair, Mapplethorpe, and Benetton. If Gates's prize-winning second book, *The Signifying Monkey: A Theory of African-American Literary Criticism* (1988), made "signifying" a household word among Americanists, these days the name "Skip Gates" is recognized and deferred to throughout the academy and beyond. It invokes not only a major theorist and historian of black literature but also a formidable institution builder, ubiquitous public intellectual, and canny multimedia pundit. As Chair since 1991 of Harvard's Afro-American Studies Department and Director of its W.E.B. DuBois Institute for Afro-American Research, Gates has assembled a stable of stars al-most as luminous as himself, including sociologist William Julius Wilson and theologian Cornel West; so celebrated is this coterie that the merest rumor of reshuffling among them is enough to make front-page news.[1] In 1996 Gates edited the *Norton Anthology of African American Literature* (with Nellie McKay), and he continues to edit an astonishing number of scholar-ly books and to co-edit the journal *Transition*. Of late, however, many of his most ambitious projects have been for audio-visual as well as print media, and geared toward general audiences, from his collaboration with Microsoft (and K. Anthony Appiah) on *Encarta Africana* (1999), a CD-ROM encyclopedia of "the African and African-American experience," to his six-part television series for BBC/PBS, *Wonders of the African World with Henry Louis Gates, Jr.* (1999).[2] Whether commenting on race, rap, sports, sex, slavery, identity, canonicity, creativity, Booker T., Spike Lee, Hillary C., or the GOP, Henry Louis Gates Jr.—staff writer for *The New Yorker* and frequent contributor to any number of highbrow rags—has the ear not only of his university colleagues but also of the professional-managerial classes in much of the western world.[3]

At first glance, Gates would appear to wield his considerable power on behalf of women's rights and gender equity. Unlike Cornel West, he re-frained from endorsing the 1995 Million Man March and went on record around the same time with his belief that O.J. Simpson was guilty of mur-dering wife Nicole. And unlike fellow critic Houston Baker, he has gener-ally been appreciated by feminists, even while stealing some of their lime-light as the busiest and best-known editor of reprints by black women.[4] While Edward Said and Andrew Ross prefer to steer carefully around women's culture, Henry Louis Gates eagerly uncovers, certifies, circulates, and celebrates female texts. Since the early 1980s, when he rediscovered Harriet E. Wilson's 1859 novel, *Our Nig*, Gates has gone on to edit the thirty-volume *Schomburg Library of Nineteenth-Century Black Women Writers* (1988), the ten-volume *Supplement* to the *Schomburg* (1991), the critical an-thology *Reading Black, Reading Feminist* (1990), and *Afro-American Women Writers* (1998). Add to this Gates's much-publicized purchase and publica-tion of *The Bondswoman's Narrative* (2002)—a neglected, unedited novel, apparently just older than *Our Nig*, by ex-slave Hannah Crafts—and you have a male critic whose investment in women's writing is clear and whose commitment to feminism seems unimpeachable.

Clearly Gates goes further than most left-leaning male intellectuals today by not only espousing enlightened views on gender but also actively and self-consciously contributing to feminist scholarship. It is possible, moreover, to see the marked emphasis on dialogue, community, and familial relationships evident throughout his work as signs of an idiom more conventionally "female" than "male."[5] Gates's notion, for example, that black writers "signify" upon each other, continually revising a trope such as the "talking book," picks up on oedipal models of rivalry between (white male) writers and their precursors, yet stresses relations of homage as well as hostility, repetition as well as difference, commonality as well as originality. Similarly, in *Thirteen Ways of Looking at a Black Man* (1997), Gates depicts individual men primarily by coupling them with other men adduced as foils, brothers, rivals, or partners. To the axiomatic pairings of W.E.B. DuBois and Booker T. Washington, Martin Luther King and Malcolm X, Gates adds Albert Murray and Ralph Ellison, Bill T. Jones and Arnie Zane, Jesse Jackson and Colin Powell, Harry Belafonte and Sidney Poitier. Gates's penchant for connection informs his racial politics as well. Antiseparatist in the tradition of DuBois and King, Gates's first reflex—politically, institutionally, and theoretically—is to mix it up. Chief among his many roles (like that of Belafonte and several others portrayed in *Thirteen Ways*) is that of "bridge Negro—one who serves to connect white and Negro" (*Thirteen* 168). In contrast to Andrew Ross, whose individualist mode so decisively abjects the mother, Gates's style is clearly more relational, more tolerant of intimacies recalling the pre-oedipal, less anxious immediately to eschew the maternal and the feminine.

Indeed, Gates codifies his view of the black mother as a model in the passage from "The Master's Pieces" (1990) that I take for my first epigraph. An impulse to cross to the other side of the gender tracks in alliance with black women is also elaborated in the *Schomburg* volumes, and a specific closeness to his mother occupies a central place in Gates's 1994 memoir, *Colored People*. One might even say that Gates represents himself here and elsewhere as a kind of mama's boy, though usually in a less full-blown autobiographical context than in *Colored People* and always, of course, at some remove from the actual man. If Ross's romance is with the "bad boy," Gates's persona is that of the "good boy," and other points of contrast between the two are consistent with what I see as their different degrees of separation from the maternal. For example, Ross practices historiography but is typically more

drawn to futurology, cutting-edge technologies, experimental cultures se-
ceded from the mainstream, everything young, new, and reimagined. Gates,
on the other hand, is basically loyal to origins, serious about mapping traditions and establishing canons, bent on the work of historical recovery;
even when he talks about "the future of the race" (in a book co-written with
West), he does so by looking back to DuBois for a model of black leadership. Then again, Ross allies himself with the grunged, transgressive, irrev-
erent, and disreputable, while Gates pictures himself as well scrubbed,
punctual, respectful, and respectable. In a similar vein, Ross champions rebellion, rupture, offending the ladies, and shocking the grownups, while
Gates exemplifies consideration, moderation, and conciliation, preferring to
foster rather than to rend ties between people and groups.

In addition to being culturally gendered, these distinctions suggest a di-
vergence less in actual class status (which the two presumably share) than in
class sensibility and class strategy. Ross not only parses but speaks the vernacular, and forcefully defends the "lower" pleasures of the popular and
bodily. Culturally, he aspires downward. Gates, on the other hand, endorses but rarely employs the vernacular, makes forays into the popular while
tending to hook it back into the "high," and polemically claims the intellectual over against the physical for himself and black people generally. In
his critical, journalistic, and autobiographical writing, Gates favors (what he
calls after Robert Stepto) "narratives of ascent" (*Thirteen* xiv). This identification with the "bourgeois" and "female" on Gates's part, and likewise
Ross's with the "proletarian" and "male," is not hard to understand given
the way that masculinities are raced and black men treated in this country.
Thus Ross styles himself a gangsta in opposition to effete, nerdy, and com-
placently privileged white masculinity, while Gates styles himself a highbrow member of the Talented Tenth, an agent of uplift, and a keeper of the
hearth as a counter to criminalized and endangered black masculinity. An-
swering a Willie Hortonism still with us in the twenty-first century, countering stereotypes of the hypermasculine and pathological black male, Gates
understandably finds an effective antidote in the type of the studious and
approval-seeking mama's boy.

This strategy, however, is not without its own difficulties of race, class,
and especially gender. The domesticated son, to begin with, puts at risk a
normative American masculinity that depends fundamentally and regardless of race on a rejection of the mother.[6] As theorists of black macho have

observed, this mandate is all the more pressing for black males "feminized" by the legacy of slavery, who are, to make matters worse, more likely than whites to grow up in female-headed households and with a grateful sense of maternal abilities. For despite (and because of) the fact that mothers enjoy a special status in African American culture, repudiation of the "female" is essential to the heroic type of the "bad" black man, admired by blacks and whites alike for his physical prowess and celebrated within a postnationalist black context for his militancy and racial authenticity. Mapping authentic blackness onto authentic masculinity (recall Spike Lee's *School Daze*), this type goes back to eighteenth-century "scientific" debates about whether blacks were or were not "men." But its contemporary form, as others have noted, owes most to 1960s nationalism—the fist in the air that rebutted white supremacy and black "matriarchy" through an affirmation of blackness as the mark of manhood, manhood as the mark of blackness.[7]

By assuming a persona identified with the mother, with the "female" values she represents, and with ascent into the law-abiding bourgeoisie, Gates not only debunks a pernicious stereotype but also makes vulnerable his very "blackness" along with his masculinity. Given, moreover, the construction of black men as sexual, athletic, laboring *bodies* above all (and notwithstanding the extent to which black women are seen this way as well), Gates's professorial status, his fluency in arcane European theory, and his claim to moral/intellectual rather than physical authority go further still to destabilize both his race and gender identities. This chapter will posit two things. First, because these identities are so thoroughly intertwined by current paradigms, discussion of the one frequently, if covertly, bears on the other. So although Gates's work typically takes race as its primary theme, gender inevitably operates as a less fully acknowledged subtext. It is this half-hidden aspect of his writing that most concerns me here. Second, in spite of the fact that Gates goes out of his way to question the concepts of intrinsic blackness and racial authenticity and, similarly, to divest himself of conventional masculinity and a belief in fixed gender binaries, he finds it difficult to relinquish these commonplace essentialisms altogether. Indeed, it appears to me that Gates repeatedly ties himself to black women only to compensate with a panicked reassertion of the norms of black masculinity. This logic of reaction to male "feminization" with a stern masculinism is one we have, of course, already encountered in the narrative rhythms of Quentin Tarantino's *Pulp Fiction*, in the sexual politics of Edward Said's *Culture and Imperialism*, and in the sequential stages of Andrew Ross's intellectual development.

As with Ross, the assertion of a compensatory masculinity is especially evident in the overall trajectory of Gates's career to date: in the transformation, beginning in the early 1990s (and notwithstanding the recent Hannah Crafts discovery), from Gates the learned curator of women's texts to Gates the born-again journalist and convert to the "crisis of the black male." Epitomized by the *New Yorker* profiles collected in *Thirteen Ways of Looking at a Black Man* (1997), the neomasculinist Gates is also on display in his preface to the Whitney Museum's *Black Male* catalogue (1994), in his *Transition* interview with Cornel West (1995), and in the aforementioned pamphlet on DuBois and black leadership that Gates wrote with West, *The Future of the Race* (1996). It is tempting to imagine that the space between my two epigraphs—between claiming the mother's voice and lamenting the special marginality of men—was bridged by opportunism alone, by a wish to remain in step with a culture whose enthusiasm for black women writers appears to have peaked soon after *Beloved* (1987). I am suggesting, however, that Gates's genteel, mama's-boy image has always put him on the defensive in relation to the type of street-certified black masculinity going back, say, to the Panthers and passing through Superfly on the way to Snoop Doggy Dogg. Mother lover instead of muthafucka, continually at risk of being deraced as well as unsexed, Gates has long been under pressure to reassert the very black maleness that, theoretically, he disowns and deconstructs.

If we see such a reaffirmation diachronically in the shift from reading feminist in the 1980s to looking at black men in the 1990s, this shift was arguably anticipated by Gates's two earliest and densest works of scholarship, *Figures in Black: Words, Signs, and the "Racial" Self* (1987) and *The Signifying Monkey: A Theory of African-American Literary Criticism* (1988). I suggest that the first of these books had a "feminizing" and "whitening" effect, which required of the second a hasty return to true, gritty, black manhood. This return was achieved, we will see, by such authenticating means as the vernacular, the phallic body, the conspicuously heterosexual, and the intensely male homosocial, with particular emphasis on ties between black fathers and sons.[8] Above all, I propose that both books, even as they call attention to women writers, develop paradigms in which the valued terms—poststructuralist theory in the first book, black popular speech in the second—are strongly coded as male. Recalling our other scholars, and despite his support for women's writing and women's rights, Gates asserts his theoretical and political "coolness" in opposition to a theoretical naiveté marked as "feminine" and, as I will show, at the expense of a criticism and politics centered on women.[9]

HIS MOTHER/HIS SELF

I am arguing, then, that the sexual politics even of Gates's first, conspicuous incarnation as a critic and editor of black women's writing are, in fact, fraught with ambiguity. As a trope for this ambiguity, I begin with an anecdote that Gates tells more than once about himself as a child in relation to his mother's voice. The version I will discuss occurs at the end of "The Master's Pieces: On Canon Formation and the African-American Tradition," an essay forcefully defending black canons and culminating in the lines cited by my epigraph (*Loose Canons* 40–42).[10] As Gates would have it, the incident illustrates and explains his sympathy with black feminist agendas. In my reading, by contrast, it dramatizes his highly vexed relation to black women and their words, informed not only by sympathy with women but also by anxiety about masculinity and a consequent desire for mastery.

The final section of "The Master's Pieces" is headed by a quotation from Hortense Spillers's well-known essay, "Mama's Baby, Papa's Maybe." Noting that under slavery the Law of the Father did not recognize black fatherhood as such, Spillers sees the African American mother, despite her own disenfranchisement, as unique in her hold on the black imagination and in her availability as a psychic resource for her sons. "It is the heritage of the *mother*," she concludes, "that the African-American male must regain as an aspect of his own personhood—the power of 'yes' to the 'female' within" (40). Gates glosses this approvingly both as a figure for black men "gaining their voices through the black mother" and as a call for "a revoicing of the 'master's' discourse in the cadences and timbres of the Black Mother's voice" (40–41). He follows up with the story of being "little Skippy," only four years old and commanded to say his first "piece" (religious recitation) before an expectant congregation. Though he knows it perfectly, when the time comes he is struck dumb. After an excruciating silence, his mother rises from the back and sings out the forgotten lines: "Jesus was a boy like me, and like him I want to be." Then comes the clinching paragraph about going on to do the work of canon reformation "in the voice of the black female" (41–42).

My first problem with this parable arises from Spillers's minimizing (in her essay as a whole) the significance of gender difference and inequality within African American culture. She is right, of course, that black paternity was discounted by a system of slavery in which children inherited the mother's status. But agreeing that black men have never shared the prerogatives of white patriarchy, that maternity is inflected by specific racial histories, and that enslaved women and men alike were alienated from their very flesh by whip and by law does not mean, in my opinion, that African American men have either little investment in the "male" or a peculiarly untroubled and inward relation to the "female." It is this latter implication, in any case, that Gates takes away from Spillers: a model in which black men need only murmur "yes" to their inner female before speaking not merely *of* black women's writing but *as* and *for* black women. This move to assume the mother's femininity is so painless, lets the critic-as-son off the hook of male privilege so completely, and finesses so satisfyingly the concerns of more skeptical black feminists, that Michael Awkward does not hesitate simply to copy Gates's use of Spillers in an essay licensing his own work on Hurston, Morrison, and other women writers (14–15).[11]

The story of the speechless child disturbs me as well insofar as it develops the suggestion that black females are in possession of rhetorical opportunities that black males lack. If Ross approaches gender politics from the viewpoint of a sullen male teen, here Gates bases his formulation on the perspective of a barely fluent preschooler. Though he regards the female more warmly than Ross, he too downplays male domination in favor of maternal domination. The "Skippy" narrative not only dramatically overstates female power but also, between the lines, appears to resent it. For the mother's performance, though intended to rescue her son, serves at the same time to highlight the fact of his nonperformance. Gates's final image of the crowd laughing and clapping as the poor child "crawls" back to his seat ("slinks" in the *Colored People* version [117–18]) would seem to indicate feelings on his part less of appreciation than of lasting mortification. While professing to celebrate her, the story actually works to bind the mother who speaks to the son who cannot, to make the black female's eloquence coincide with the black male's relegation to childhood and to silence.

So although this anecdote ostensibly accords with Spillers's vision—a black man gaining his voice through the mother—a second reading suggests to me a boy shamed because spoken for by his mother. It is therefore not, I would argue, the model for a critical practice honoring the mother's voice so much as the motivation, the primal scene if you will, underlying a criticism that returns to the place where women speak in order to master an original trauma. Gates does this by laying professional claim to women's writing—authenticating, framing, and otherwise putting his name to it—in a way that invokes the mother so as to raise *his* voice, this time, on her behalf. Indeed, the final line about "*us* as scholar-critics, *learning* to speak in the voice of the black female" (42; emphasis added) seems to picture the scholar-critic as a young man studying a second language—excluding women, who presumably need less tutoring in this register.[12] What Gates offers as a trope for his feminism, a praise song for women who speak out, I take, on the contrary, as a trope for a son's traumatized and thus at times appropriative relation to black women writers.

The recitation anecdote figures not only the emotional logic but also the method by which attention to black female words may coexist somewhat paradoxically in Gates with the suppression of black femaleness. In viewing the black mother from the perspective of a helpless four-year-old, the tale exaggerates her potency and thereby erases her as a beset social subject. The effect of overrecognizing her is actually, in some sense, to underrecognize her. Thus Gates registers only "strong, compelling cadences," rhythms of invincibility, when in fact his mother's lines point directly to her invisibility as a female in both black and white religious traditions: "Jesus was a *boy* like me, and like him I want to be" (42; emphasis added).[13] In *Colored People*'s lengthier treatment of the mother figure, the disabling aspects of her circumstances as a black female in postwar West Virginia are again almost wholly under erasure. Gates tells us this gifted young woman dropped out of school to put her four brothers through college (32), but it never occurs to him that a pattern of female self-sacrifice might compound her rage over racism and contribute to her later breakdown. One of these brothers told the story of her unsung heroism—how she worked, sent money, did the laundry they mailed home—to a TV show called *The Big Payoff*. Mama is publicly celebrated and officially paid off with gifts of clothes, jewelry, and "a whole set of American Tourister luggage" (33). Touched by his uncle's thoughtfulness, Gates seems to consider the score even at this point. "I used the medium suitcase when I went off to Yale some fifteen years later" (33), he adds—oblivious to the irony of packing up his mother's prize to further his own educational goals. I will argue below that this ability to overlook the subordination and silencing of women within black households makes it easier for Gates to dismiss the feminist anger and misconstrue the feminist analyses of such texts as *Their Eyes Were Watching God* and *The Color Purple*. More than once, it seems to me, he trades on but manages to miss the point of the black woman's story—using her baggage to reach his own destination.

RHETORICAL MAN

Figures in Black: Words, Signs, and the "Racial" Self (1987), Gates's first authored book, consists largely of essays previously published between 1979 and 1984 in a wide range of unrelated venues—one comes, for example, from Gates's edition of Harriet E. Wilson's *Our Nig*, another from *Critical Inquiry*. Strategically juxtaposed in this debut volume, however, their meaning becomes inseparable from the ways in which they interact with one another and with the book as a whole. This interaction is key to my reading. The overall project of *Figures* is to consolidate Gates's case for a new black formalism, challenging the long tradition of reading African American literature primarily for its sociological and political content. As its introduction explains, the book calls for "that which, in the received tradition of Afro-American criticism, has been most repressed: close readings of the text itself" (xix). Endeavoring to recover the "textuality" of black writing, *Figures* also mounts a controversial defense of "theory," by which Gates means the precepts of French deconstruction predominant in the early 1980s, especially at Yale, where he was teaching at the time.

Gates notes the need to adapt this theory, developed by white men vis-à-vis white texts, to the African American idiom: "I have tried to work through contemporary theories of literature," he tells us, "not to apply them to black texts, but to transform these by translating them into a new rhetorical realm" (xx). The last chapter of *Figures*, in formulating a specifically black concept of "Signifyin(g)" inspired by Ishmael Reed's *Mumbo Jumbo*, begins to do this work of translation. Signifyin(g) as a uniquely black vernacular and literary practice (and this same essay on Reed) would become the cornerstone of *The Signifying Monkey*, published the following year.[14] In *Figures*, however, despite some framing language and a final chapter to the contrary, Gates's tendency is really to use rather than to transform Yale-style deconstruction. As the introduction to *Signifying* observes, in this second book poststructuralist theories have finally receded to the status of "analogies," whereas in *Figures*, Gates now admits, those theories were still foregrounded and taken as "points of departure" (xxiv).

If *Figures* sees poststructuralism as the solution, the problem, as I say, is the critical habit of looking to African American literature for its contribution to racial uplift and (especially during the Black Arts movement of the late 1960s and early 1970s) for its fidelity to black experience, all the while neglecting its formal and aesthetic qualities. Drawing on his doctoral thesis, Gates further observes that black writing going back to the eighteenth century was routinely cited as evidence for (or against) the humanity of slaves and their descendants, and it is partly for this reason that the black tradition has come to judge itself in terms less artistic than propagandistic. "I realized," he writes, "that the black tradition's own concern with winning the war against racism had led it not only to accept this arbitrary relationship [between literacy and humanity] but to embrace it" (xxiv). What I seek to demonstrate, however, is that even as *Figures* advocates, above all, a new appreciation of black texts for their rhetorical complexity and wit, the only two chapters addressing women writers—those on Phillis Wheatley and Harriet E. Wilson—identify them both with precisely those theoretically "naïve" paradigms Gates sets out to discredit.[15]

Briefly in chapter 1 and at length in chapter 2, "Phillis Wheatley and the 'Nature of the Negro,'" Gates takes the reception of this poet to represent the troubling treatment of African American writing over the years as a series of documents about the character of "blackness." Indeed, Gates argues that Wheatley's reception has "*largely determined* the theory of the criticism of the creative writings of Afro-Americans from the eighteenth century to the present time" (79; emphasis added). As he recounts in an earlier essay, Wheatley's *Poems on Various Subjects, Religious and Moral* was published in 1773 only after "eighteen of Boston's most notable citizens" had personally interrogated its author and attested to their belief that she was capable of producing such a work (*Loose* 51). Prefaced by these white men's authenticating signatures, *Poems* went on to be similarly (though not always so favorably) reviewed by "literally scores of public figures," including Voltaire, George Washington, and Thomas Jefferson—each of them more concerned to mobilize Wheatley for his own racial theory than to analyze her verse for its poetic style (*Figures* 5). Gates further notes the odd discrepancy, lasting well into the twentieth century, between the amount of commentary on

Wheatley and the amount of her work actually in print: though criticism abounded, there was no complete edition of her poems as of 1975 and, until 1935, only a dozen or so had been anthologized (75). Wheatley is a poet, then, whose specific art has been overwhelmed if not largely obscured by the ideological debates she inspired. As much as it mattered *that* she wrote, it seems to have mattered very little *what* she wrote, leading Gates to remark that "had Phillis Wheatley not published, another African slave's poetry would have served equally well as a refutation of certain commonly repeated assumptions about the nature of the Negro" (71).

Gates cannot, of course, help the way Wheatley's own voice has been drowned out by the conversation surrounding her, and it helps to have his account of this history. As the comment above hints, however, to an unexpected degree Gates not only narrates but also himself perpetuates this pattern of reception. In sharp contrast to other chapters (on Frederick Douglass, Harriet E. Wilson, Jean Toomer, Sterling Brown, and Ishmael Reed as well as on black dialect), where Wheatley is concerned Gates spends very little time on the texts themselves and never even attempts his own close reading of them. Only in the last couple of pages does he hazard any formal observations, and these are almost humorously broad, incurious, and perfunctory: Wheatley imitated Pope's rhythm and meter, used hyperbole along with other neoclassical devices, and favored the elegy (78). In fact, they pass as criticism only within a tradition overly impressed that a black girl could write at all, much less in heroic couplets, suggesting the extent to which Gates fails to imagine his way outside this tradition. The next two paragraphs paraphrase one Gregory Rigsby on Wheatley's adaptation of the "English" and "Puritan" elegy forms (78) and conclude that "the identification of the conventions of her elegies indicates that Wheatley was an imaginative artist to a degree largely unrecognized in critical literature" (78). Yet Gates ends this chapter shortly thereafter without taking us a single step further toward understanding the specific poetic structures wrought by this imagination.

Indeed, while seeming to argue otherwise, he effectively discourages such an understanding in several ways. Reinforcing the example of his own nonreading, there is the unsubstantiated assertion that Wheatley's verse emulates Pope but lacks "the irony," "the contrast," and "the balance" of his work (78). "'Genius' was not her province to occupy," Gates declares. "The formal gap between Milton, Pope, Gray, Addison, Watts, and Wheatley would appear to be profound" (73). My problem here is less with Gates's negative evaluation of Wheatley's work (to which he is certainly entitled) than with the way these breezy dismissals stand in for and would seem to preclude the kind of close attention he says black texts deserve. Still more inconsistent with Gates's brief for formalism, the entire chapter on Wheatley contains only five direct quotations of her work, and most of these go to demonstrate not her rhetorical agility (or lack thereof) but rather her oft-ignored feelings for the enslaved: here she "discusses the horrors of racial slavery and reveals, to a surprising degree, the quality of concern she felt for Africans" (75); there she "demonstrates an uncommon amount of emotion in her 'Afric's blissful plain'" (76); and here again, in a letter published soon after she wrote in it 1774, she is passionate "on the sheer evil of racial slavery" (77). This kind of one-track, purely referential reading for a writer's racial sympathies is precisely what Gates most vehemently decries. As a result, while seeming to protest Wheatley's long-standing fate as a "metonym" for black literary ability (73–74), Gates un-selfconsciously repositions her in his own work as a metonym for black critical limitations that even he cannot transcend.

Taken by itself, Gates's treatment of Wheatley would not be particularly objectionable. Gender trouble arises, however, from the uses to which she is put as one of only two women in the context of this book as a whole. First in a chronological series of African American writers, she functions not so much as a sainted foremother than, in theoretical terms, as a kind of antichrist to the salvific figure of Ishmael Reed. Wheatley's inextricability from what Gates dubs a tradition of reductively political criticism must be understood, I am arguing, in contrast to subsequent analyses of Reed and other male writers, whose works inevitably summon forth all manner of poststructuralist truisms. Thus Jean Toomer (already regarded as "writerly" to a degree unusual for black authors) is described as putting "his Negro ancestry under erasure," a mode "commonly thought to be Heideggerian or Derridian" but which Gates derives from the "x" in James Weldon Johnson's *Autobiography of an Ex-Coloured Man* (202). Rephrasing Toomer's decision to pass as a "rhetorical gesture," Gates goes on to read the novel *Cane* as what Derrida would call the "trace" of difference, here the trace of Toomer's denied blackness (202). Pointing out that Toomer "sought to save his texts from a critical discourse that would delimit them, that would read them as part of the racial problem," Gates says of Toomer's writing after

Cane, "His concerns as a writer are post-modern, as a critic post-structural, anticipatory" (210).[16]

Gates's ultimate example of postmodern writing and poststructuralist criticism comes in his final chapter on Reed's *Mumbo Jumbo*. In addition to "Signifyin(g)" on Hurston, Wright, and Ellison in racially marked ways, *Mumbo Jumbo* is a compendium of familiar postmodern virtues: it is playful, self-reflexive, parodic, deconstructive, a pastiche of other texts, double-voiced; it comments on the act of writing, refuses closure, glorifies indeterminacy, etc. (235–76). Published in 1972, Reed's third novel lends itself readily to such an analysis. But the same cannot be said of *Narrative of the Life of Frederick Douglass, an American Slave, Written by Himself* (1845), which was, like Wheatley's *Poems*, regarded at the time of its publication as a social experiment in the capacities of the "sable mind" (10). Nevertheless, Gates's two chapters on Douglass, rather than belaboring the sometimes sociological terms of his reception, manage with a little fancy footwork to recruit him for *Figures*'s poststructuralist project.[17]

In a chapter on "Binary Oppositions in Chapter One of *Narrative of the Life*," for example, Gates argues that "Douglass's method of complex mediation—and the ironic reversals so peculiar to his text—suggests overwhelmingly the completely arbitrary relationship between description and meaning, between signifier and signified, between sign and referent" (89). Beyond undoing such key oppositions as rational/irrational, human/beastly, and master/slave, Douglass may deserve credit, Gates concludes, for "the first charting of the black hermeneutical circle" (96)—for suspecting that "not only is meaning culture-bound and the reference of all signs an assigned relation . . . but *how* we read determines *what* we read" (97). Once again, taken in isolation, such an essay on Douglass as deconstructionist would be fine with me; nor is my critique aimed either at Douglass or at deconstruction per se. What I resist is the way this particular reading helps, in the context of *Figures*, to gender the dismantling both of nineteenth-century racial discourse and of twentieth-century black critical discourse as *male*, while Wheatley's work remains passively in thrall to the conventions of her time and ours.

Gates's second Douglass chapter, "Frederick Douglass and the Language of the Self," likewise stresses textual rather than political strategies and achievements, the writing rather than the man or, as poststructuralism would have it, the writing *as* the man. Thus Gates says grandly of

Douglass, "He was Representative Man because he was Rhetorical Man, black master of the verbal arts" (108). Arguing that biographers have yet to depict Douglass in all his complexity, Gates concludes: "For the critic, Frederick Douglass does not yet exist as a three-dimensional person; rather, he exists as a rhetorical strategy primarily, as an open-ended system of rhetorical figures and tropes" (108). Here and elsewhere in this chapter, it is true, a lingering empiricism may be discerned—an old-fashioned desire to get the facts right, to know what Douglass was *really* like, to re-create him in the "three-dimensional" flesh. In fact, the essay opens with Douglass's own desperation to pin down his date of birth (99–102), and it closes with praise for historian John Blassingame, who has not only analyzed the orator's "voice" but also confirmed his birth date and may, Gates speculates, one day be the biographer finally to show us Douglass's "face" (124). Despite these humanist lapses, however, the major claim of this chapter remains that Douglass's three, distinctly different autobiographies (1845, 1855, 1881) should be taken as evidence of his canny self-creation and re-creation through language (116).

In Gates's view, then, while Douglass wished to present himself as fully formed from the beginning (and many a biographer has believed him), his multiple texts and their evolving accounts (of his parents, for example) belie the Enlightenment premise of a pre-given, "unified and consistent subject" (112). Still more to my point, the fact that Douglass, no less than Wheatley, was mired in a discourse making "literacy" the condition of black citizenship is referenced here as a bridge not to the old "sociological" criticism but, on the contrary, to the new "theoretical" paradigms Gates so strongly prefers. "In short," Gates remarks, "slaves could inscribe their selves only in language. Ironically, this selfsame notion of people as subjects and as language . . . is the very idea that lay at the core of the major innovations of post-structural analysis in contemporary literary theory" (105). Gates never directly links the poststructuralism he now locates in debates over black literacy with that said to characterize Douglass's own project, but the adjacency within his essay of these "theory" cells makes them, as if through osmosis, mutually reinforcing. Or, to put it another way, in Gates's chapters on Douglass, virtually all roads lead to Derrida. As a result, the same reception history that designates Wheatley the origin of everything wrong with African American criticism serves, in this case, to confirm Douglass's tie to all that is theoretically correct in the mid-1980s.

Following immediately on this chapter, which, by stressing the paper Douglass, would seem to have achieved the desired "death of the author," is one incongruously devoted to the author's revival. Demonstrating once again that *Figures* is apt to project its residual essentialism onto women writers, the text in question is Harriet E. Wilson's *Our Nig*. Gates does, it must be said, take more note of *Our Nig*'s formal qualities and significance than he does of Wheatley's *Poems*. He discusses its generic relationship to sentimental novels by white women and race novels by black men, remarking its originality (137); he admires the bold irony of its title (128); and he even, likening *Our Nig* to Defoe's *Moll Flanders*, goes so far as to call Wilson "the most accomplished and subtle black novelist of the nineteenth century" (143). Notwithstanding the fact that black writers of this period are better known for slave narratives than novels, this boast would seem to register enthusiasm for Wilson's capacities as an artist. I want to argue, however, that where Gates celebrates Frederick Douglass as "Representative Man because he was Rhetorical Man," his Harriet Wilson is finally not Rhetorical so much as Historical Woman.[18]

For despite the intriguing formal claims he tenders on Wilson's behalf, Gates never goes on to support these through any strenuous close reading. Instead, he runs down "the signal elements of the plot" (140–41), fills in a few more details (144–45), and finally offers some very general and peculiarly sophomoric observations: "the betrayal of good faith" is a "leitmotif" of *Our Nig*, and its heroine is a "figure of alienation" (145). Such critical clichés are hardly an advertisement for close textual analysis, and as it turns out, that is not Gates's overriding purpose. Instead, his major claim concerns the relation between Wilson's "novel" and her "biography," which he alleges to be extremely close indeed. And though he refers to them in his chapter title and elsewhere as two "parallel discursive universes," in the course of his discussion these twin systems sift down into the more mundane and theoretically passé categories of Wilson's *writing* and Wilson's *life*. About these, Gates goes on to suggest not that they are parallel, but that the first conforms so closely to the second as to make them significantly coextensive. Thus the "elemental facts" of Wilson's life between 1850 and 1860 are "represented with little emendation in her autobiographical novel, *Our Nig*" (138). Especially in the last part of her novel, Gates asserts, Wilson "writes close to her own experiences of love and betrayal" (141). And even the "leitmotif" point is immediately (though somewhat illogically) tied to

Gates's far more energetic argument for the "truth" of Wilson's novel: "Perhaps because the fiction represents so closely the apparent experiences of Wilson, *Our Nig* is not about anything more or less than the betrayal of certain forms of trust, of belief" (145).

Qualifying "experiences" with "apparent" and referring carefully to Wilson's "biography" (as opposed to "life"), Gates nods toward a poststructuralist sense of history as narrative. It is nonetheless clear, however, as the sentences above suggest, that Gates wishes primarily to make a case for many of the experiences retailed in *Our Nig* as "real." This case is supported by an extensive chart at the end of the chapter mapping the events of *Our Nig* alongside those of Wilson's life, as far as Gates has been able to reconstruct it (150–63). Though much of Wilson's early history is left blank, beginning around 1850 (when Wilson was twenty-two) there is a high degree of correspondence between the column for *Our Nig*'s eponymous heroine and that for Harriet Wilson, neé Harriet Adams. It is instructive, I think, to compare this device to a similar one used later in *Figures*: another two-column chart, this time mapping the plot of Reed's *Mumbo Jumbo* as a complex series of "mysteries within mysteries," alongside a column of commentary by Gates about the narrative function of each mystery and whether or not it is resolved (264–65). Prefacing this second chart, Gates remarks that the account already given of *Mumbo Jumbo*'s *fabula* or "story" (ordering its events as if they had occurred in "real" time) is "misleading somewhat" (263). More important to us as readers, he explains, is Reed's *sjuzet* or "plot": the proliferation of mysteries as we encounter them in the book, obstructing rather than forwarding the plot and scrambling rather than imitating a "natural" chronology.

This familiar Formalist distinction between "story" and "plot"—in Gates's words, "reality represented" versus "the mode of narration, the literary convention and devices, used to represent" (262)—functions at this juncture as one more way of reiterating the organizing opposition in *Figures* between texts read in simple referential terms for their political content or "story" and those valued for their self-conscious, denaturing rhetorical strategies or "plottedness." *Figures*, of course, intervenes earnestly on behalf of the latter, and this chapter lionizes Reed as the ultimate master of intricate plotting. Wilson, by contrast, though given credit for an ironic title, is identified with a straightforward, realist "plot" that corresponds temporally to the "story" of *Our Nig* and furthermore, Gates argues, coincides significantly with the real story of its author's life. Whereas Reed, embedding plots within plots, parodies African American realism and allegorizes the processes of reading and representation (263), Wilson, telling the story of her life, seems hardly a deliberate artist at all, her narrative is so little "worked on" and her text so little aware of itself as a text.[19] In short, while Gates aestheticizes Reed's work, he folds Wilson's into the history of its author and effectively naturalizes it. As a result, though the essay on Wilson makes much of her, within the poststructuralist frame of *Figures* it has the effect of devaluing her novel as a literary construct.

More historicist than poststructuralist, I myself am generally inclined to appreciate the pertinence of a writer's social position, the material conditions under which she wrote, but this is quite different from reading off Wilson's life directly from her novel, whether or not evidence suggests she drew on her own experiences. And slighting the text's mediating role is especially surprising given Gates's theoretical proclivities in this book; by reducing *Our Nig* to a literal transcript of Wilson's history, he not only downplays her imaginative efforts but also reads in reverse the poststructuralist axiom that "life stories" and "life" itself must be understood as fictions. What would motivate Gates to depart in such a way from the overall polemic of *Figures*? Perhaps he does so in this chapter because its real protagonist is neither Wilson nor her heroine but Gates himself (theory hat temporarily askew) in the guise of historian/detective. From the very first sentence, we are caught up in a drama involving not a nineteenth-century black woman at all but a late twentieth-century black man, "browsing at the University Place Bookshop in Manhattan in May 1981," stumbling across *Our Nig*, and managing at length to confirm his hunch that the author was indeed, as she claimed, both black and female (125–29). By documenting her identity, Gates succeeds in establishing Wilson as "the very first Afro-American woman to publish a novel in English" and extends the tradition of black women's writing by more than thirty years (138). The facts of her life overshadow the formal attributes of her writing in part, therefore, because appreciation for the latter is largely contingent on Wilson's historical status, loudly proclaimed by Gates, as America's *first black woman* novelist.

More important, while Gates opens his investigation into Wilson's history with *Our Nig*'s explicitly autobiographical "Preface" and biographical "Appendix" (consisting of three letters by people who knew her), he quickly proceeds to take the novel itself, especially its last chapter, as an archive of information on its author. Asserting the "truth" of *Our Nig* is therefore essential to the process of authenticating Harriet E. Wilson. As Gates explains, "It was the verification of these biographical details of her life [as represented in *Our Nig*] that allowed for the positive identification of Wilson as both the text's thinly veiled subject and its author" (138). Such a move resurrects Wilson only, we have said, to diminish her as a maker of plots. The same cannot be said of Gates, however, who turns out to be the principal purveyor of suspense in this chapter. For embedded within his tale of finding and authenticating *Our Nig* is his telling of Wilson's life. The relative significance of Wilson's literary narrative and Gates's biographical one is suggested by the final chart, in which the events of Wilson's novel (left column) at first predominate but are gradually matched and then overtaken by those of her "life" (right column), so that by the end Gates's account exceeds Wilson's in both abundance and detail. As Gates the theorist would probably agree, we might therefore rephrase his thesis that *Our Nig* collapses into Wilson's life to say that Wilson's narrative, though painstakingly recovered, ultimately collapses into Gates's.

I want to close this section on the disconcerting sexual politics of *Figures* with one more observation, harking back to my discussion of the mother-son relationship in Gates. Gates explains that an important clue to Wilson's identity was the reference, in her preface, to a child for whose sake she was driven to write and publish *Our Nig*. Pursuing this lead, Gates discovered the death certificate of one George Mason Wilson, a black child born to Thomas and Harriet Wilson, who died of "fever" less than a year after his mother's book appeared. "Had it not been for George's death and his death certificate," Gates comments, "it would have proved remarkably difficult to confirm my strong suspicion that his mother was an Afro-American. His mother's concern for her only chlid's [sic] welfare is responsible for her retrieval from literary oblivion. The irony is profound" (128). Gates's vehemence on this point is worth noting, for he goes on immediately to repeat that "George's death certificate made possible the confirmation of a number of details about Wilson" (128). Following this, he stresses again that "George's death serves as a convenient emblem of the tragic irony of his mother's life and subsequent literary reputation" (128). And finally, for the fourth time in the space of five sentences, he reiterates, "The record of [her son's] death alone proved sufficient to demonstrate his mother's racial identity and authorship of *Our Nig*" (128).

What exactly is the "irony" Gates finds here and why does he dwell on it at such length? Initially he speaks of the maternal "concern" expressed by Wilson's preface, but he soon comes to stress its futility—George's death and the record thereof—as the crucial factor in confirming Wilson's race and establishing her importance. The maternal gesture of the preface thus failed to save poor George—and yet, by giving Gates a lead, it managed eventually to save Wilson's own literary reputation. Gates's insistence on this reasoning is all the more strange given that a child's designation as "black" would not necessarily indicate a black mother (as it does not for the protagonist of *Our Nig*) and that Wilson's race would seem to be more directly verified by the 1850 census (listing Harriet E. Adams as a black female) as well as by her 1851 marriage license (138). But Gates fixes nevertheless on what he construes as a mother's literary life secured by the death of her seven-year-old son, his early demise the price of her voice preserved for posterity. What interests me here, of course, is the way this same logic operates within the "Skippy" narrative discussed above, and the way both stories suggest that recovering literary foremothers is underwritten, for Gates, by filial anxiety. If I am right that he sometimes imagines the mother's words as a dire threat to the son, this would help to explain his subtle discrediting and displacing of Wilson even as (or perhaps because) he endeavors to make a place for her in the canon. In these terms, I find it revealing that *Figures* goes out of its way to grant the son, from his grave, the ability to certify his mother's identity; for this, as we have seen, is precisely the kind of authenticating power that Gates, up from muteness, now claims for himself.

Although *Figures in Black* ostensibly touts one kind of *reading* over another and specifically plugs deconstructionist approaches, the *writing* sampled in this context, whether by Wheatley, Wilson, Douglass, or Reed, also gets drawn up into Gates's polemic and is, by implication, valued or devalued according to its poststructuralist appeal. I have observed too that even in this most Derridian of books, we still find backwaters of concern about one black writer's fidelity to her race and another's real-life experiences. Insofar as Gates harbors critical impulses out of keeping with and disapproved by his overall campaign, he indulges them most fully in his two chapters on women, with the inadvertent effect of marking both Phillis Wheatley and Harriet Wilson as somehow less sophisticated, complex, self-aware, and innovative than their fellow writers. As Deborah McDowell has pointed out, the gendering of high-status theory "male" and theoretical backwardness "female" also informs the controversial exchange between Joyce Ann Joyce and Gates/Baker, which appeared in *New Literary History* the same year as *Figures* (*Changing* 165–67). Gates, for example, complains that Joyce ties him to "structuralism," "poststructuralism," and "deconstruction," "even when these terms are not defined at all or, perhaps worse, *not adequately understood*" (346; emphasis added), and Joyce protests in return that Gates has "no hesitation in attempting to make me appear mindless and backwards in the eyes of white society" (382).

Though Gates undoubtedly gets the better of this debate from a Yale-oriented, theory-centered point of view, within the larger cultural context hailing Gates as a black male, Joyce's rebuke may yet have the power to sting. The overt terms of her critique, drawing on the language and sentiments of the Black Arts movement, are racial: she accuses recent critics, especially Gates and Baker, of failing to address African Americans, of using a "distant and sterile" Euro-American jargon meaningless to most black people (338–39). Regarding Gates she says, "It is insidious for the Black literary critic to adopt any kind of strategy that diminishes or in this case . . . negates his blackness" (341). As noted above, however, critics like Phillip Brian Harper have shown Joyce's nationalist standard of authentic "blackness" to be deeply invested in ideas about gender and sexuality as well as race—specifically, the predominance of heterosexual masculinity. So it should come as no surprise that Joyce, while referring carefully to "he or she," continues to generalize about African Americans under the rubric of the "Black Man" (338, 339), or that the scarcely veiled result of her attack on Gates's blackness is also to impugn his maleness. In fact, at the very moment that Gates, pulling out his big theory guns, affirms his masculinity within the white-dominated academy, he actually undercuts it in terms of racial understandings salient beyond ivied walls. For the Afrocentric man or woman in the street, doing an intricate dance with Derrida is not merely a kind of whiteface—it's a kind of drag.

Faced with the sort of objections raised here by Joyce Joyce and directed at instances of black poststructuralism such as *Figures*, Gates reacts by quoting Tina Turner. "What's love got to do, got to do with it?" he asks in the title and epigraph of his response to her excoriation. Later he will answer the question by disagreeing with Joyce that black writers/critics "love" black readers by feeding their racial self-esteem, offering the counterproposition that black readers "love" black writers by doing the difficult, exegetical work necessary to appreciate someone like Baldwin (or Gates): "*That's* what love's got to do, got to do with it, Joyce Joyce" (354–55). But getting down with Tina is good for more than just a catchy phrase in his self-defense. First, as McDowell has suggested, the sultriness of this particular singer/song has the effect of "sexualizing" Gates's encounter with Joyce, while his buddying up with Baker works to situate her between men (*Changing* 166). In other words, Turner conjures an economy of compulsory heterosexuality that heightens Joyce's vulnerability while underlining Gates's masculine advantage. In addition, recruiting such a song from the top ten for the pages of a scholarly journal relocates Gates in the sphere of the popular, pointedly refuting Joyce's claim that he has lost touch with the majority of black people. Finally, because the vernacular functions as a sign of black male authenticity, Turner helps Gates to seem not only more of a race man but also more of a man. In the following section I turn to *The Signifying Monkey*, the book that succeeded *Figures in Black* and that stands as Gates's major scholarly contribution to date, arguing that it accomplishes essentially the same race/gender work as Turner's hit song within Gates's response to Joyce. By choosing a conspicuously phallic trope to describe black ways of speaking, downplaying the explicit role of poststructuralism (which, by another name, continues to underpin his work), and highlighting the role of a vernacular strongly coded as black male, *Signifying* makes a bid to resecure a culturally resonant African American masculinity that *Figures*, aspiring to masculinity in narrowly white professorial terms, rendered especially precarious.

So if the racial politics of *Signifying Monkey*'s move from deconstruction to the dozens are all too self-evident, my goal is to bring out what seem to me the less obvious gender dynamics underlying this development. As I have suggested, *Signifying* accomplishes its shift from a feminizing white masculinity to a refurbished black masculinity in several, closely related ways. First, it asserts a physical and indisputably heterosexual virility through the anatomical attributes and sexual practices of its eponymous Signifying Monkey and his Yoruba precursor, Esu-Elegbara. Second, it transposes poststructuralism into black terms, by rediscovering its tenets within the long-standing linguistic practices and understandings of African Americans going back to the seventeenth century. Gates started down this road with his essay on Reed and has kicked up some dust by the time he sniffs to Joyce, "Only a black person alienated from black language use could fail to understand that we have been deconstructing white people's language—as 'a system of codes or as mere play'—since 1619" (358–59).[20] Accordingly, in *Signifying* the rarified, French-inflected theory talk of his early work reappears almost wholly re-phrased as the earthy folk language artfully and combatively deployed in bar-bershops, on street corners, and in other public spaces, all less accessible to black women than to black men. Finally, the same remasculinizing end is served by Gates's reading of *Their Eyes Were Watching God*, which casually privileges the very heterosexual plot that Hurston so pointedly ironizes—and that her literary daughter Alice Walker, uncomfortable subject of *Signifying*'s last chapter, so emphatically rejects. And in all of these senses, *Signifying Monkey* not only compensates for *Figures* but also continues its pattern of gendering vaunted categories "male," thus anticipating the more explicit masculinism of Gates's work in the 1990s.

DESPITE HIS REMARKABLE PENIS FEATS

The black trickster figure Gates calls Esu is a composite pieced together from various related deities. As Gates explains, he is Esu-Elegbara to the Yoruba in Nigeria, Legba to the Fon in Benin, Exú in Brazil, Papa Legba in Haiti, etc. (4–6). Associated with divination, mediation, and interpretation as well as with indeterminacy and double-voicedness, Esu makes a com-pelling icon, in Gates's reading, for a sense of language as rhetorical con-struct and play that originates in West Africa and extends from there to black diaspora cultures including that of African Americans. Across his many cultural incarnations, three physical traits recur: Esu is small, he is dark, and he is outrageously phallic. By itself, this last fact would not be par-ticularly striking. What is puzzling, misleading, and not a little infuriating, however, is Gates's absolute denial that Esu inclines in any way toward the masculine, notwithstanding an accumulation of evidence suggesting as much. After almost thirty pages of depicting Esu as male, for example, Gates suddenly insists, "Despite the fact that I have referred to him in the masculine, Esu is also genderless, or of dual gender, as recorded Yoruba and Fon myths suggest, despite his remarkable penis feats" (29). Pinned at ei-ther end by "despite" clauses affirming Esu's maleness, Gates's central claim about androgyny has trouble getting off the ground—and no wonder, given how little he goes on to offer by way of substantiation.

The brief case for this figure's transcendence of gender begins by citing a group of women devoted to Esu, who invoke him in the following way:

"Our mothers, witches, homage to you!/If the little child respects its eld-
ers/Clothes will hang comfortably on its back/Our mothers, witches, we respect you./Deference to you, too, Esu/Our mothers, witches!" (29). Gates
means this to show Esu's conflation with mothers/witches, yet the word
"too" would seem, on the contrary, to mark his difference from them. Set
apart, inserted almost as an afterthought, his status appears parenthetical
and hardly identical to that of the honored female ancestors with whom the
prayer opens and to whom it returns. Next Gates mentions images of Esu
as "paired male and female statues . . . or as one bisexual figure" (29). This
would be more convincing were it not undercut by the accompanying pho-
tographic evidence: six different statues of Esu, none of them female, paired,
or bisexual from what I can tell, and one of them (a contemporary Exú) en-
dowed "with both a large erect penis and a long tail" (16). Gates does, somewhat more credibly, quote a Yoruba scholar asserting that "although [Esu's]
masculinity is depicted as visually and graphically overwhelming, his equally expressive femininity renders his enormous sexuality ambiguous, contrary, and genderless" (29). Yet even here Esu's masculinity is described as
visible to an "overwhelming" degree, while his purportedly "expressive femininity" remains unseen and unelaborated. Moreover, at least in a modern
western context, the very notion of "enormous sexuality" is far from "genderless." The assumption that insatiable sexual appetite is, on the contrary,
quite specifically heterosexual and male is evident, for example, in Melville
Herskovits's description of Legba (cited by Gates) as "hugely over-sexed and
therefore not to be trusted with women" (27). A similar view is implicit in
the linking of Esu's sexual enthusiasm to his role as phallic mediator. Here
Gates follows Robert Pelton in seeing Esu as a "perpetually copulating cop-
ula" (26) and quotes Pelton explaining that Esu's "phallus symbolizes his
being the limen" (27).

I see little, in short, to justify Gates's conclusion that "rather than standing as one more form of sexist discourse, then, the female-other is inscribed
in Esu just as it is in Mawu-Lisa. Both are Janus figures. . . . Each time I
have used the masculine pronoun for the referent *Esu*, I could just have
properly used the feminine" (29).[21] Of course Gates *could* have used the female pronoun for Esu—but he hasn't so far and neither have any of his
sources. Quite the opposite, they have time and again specified the trickster's maleness by referring to him not only as "he" but also as "man," "father," "my mother's husband," and "son." Gates concludes by calling on

several more scholars to support his claim that Yoruba metaphysics escapes sexist binaries—by "doubling the double," embracing "unreconciled opposites," and personifying a "wholeness" beyond gender through the figure of Esu (29–30). But as we have seen, this elegant abstraction is strongly countered by Gates's own inventory of erections and sundry accounts celebrating the markedly male exploits and rivalries of Esu and, in the next chapter, of his "cousin" the Signifying Monkey. In fact, the role of the female in this paradigm is more aptly suggested by a Yoruba proverb figuring the problem of interpretation over which Esu presides: "I see the outside appearance,/I cannot see the inside of the womb/If the inside were like a calabash,/One could have opened it [and] seen everything it contains" (36). Comparing Esu's critical project to that of deconstruction, Gates continues: "It is the pleasure of the critic to open the text, even if not quite as readily as one opens a calabash" (36). Needless to say, much as Gates would stress that Esu partakes of the placenta as well as the semen (36), here the woman/womb is clearly identified not with Esu, the critic/subject, but rather with the poor, susceptible calabash, which occupies the place of breached text/object. This suppressed gender coding, implicit throughout *Signifying*, anticipates that explored in my next chapter, in which queer masculinity, valued for its deconstructive agility, trumps a femininity associated with inert embodiment.

The second chapter of *Signifying Monkey* considers the eponymous primate himself, the New World refiguration of Esu that Gates identifies with "the rhetorical principle in Afro-American vernacular discourse" (44), and which sponsors such verbal tropes as loud-talking, testifying, rapping, playing the dozens, etc. (52). Like Esu, the Signifying Monkey stands for an emphasis in black culture on sound over sense, rhetorical play over semantic fixity, the figurative over the literal. In this form too, tales turn on male competition for verbal and sexual mastery. And as in his first chapter, Gates describes the concept and practice of "Signifyin(g)" in specifically masculine ways, only to insist on its gender neutrality. He acknowledges, for example, that "the Monkey tales have generally been recorded from male poets, in predominantly male settings such as barrooms, pool halls, and street corners. Accordingly, given their nature as rituals of insult and naming, recorded versions have a phallocentric bias." Nevertheless, he continues, "Signifyin(g) can be, and is, undertaken with equal facility and effect by women as well as men" (54). Here he includes an asterisk indicating one Gloria Hall, a professional storyteller of the female persuasion who does Monkey poems. This admission of male bias followed by a denial of the same is echoed (in reverse) by the lines Gates takes from H. Rap Brown for his first epigraph. Whereas Brown's first sentence notes that "some of the best dozens players were girls," the last one decides after all that "signifying *at its best* can be heard when the *brothers* are exchanging tales" (44; emphasis added).

Whether because they were recorded or because they are simply the best, most examples of Signifyin(g) in this chapter are by males. Several involve the rituals of insult and naming known as the dozens in which, Gates admits, women typically do not participate. To me, an obvious reason for this may be the conventional reliance on disrespectful if not obscene references to mothers. As Gates explains, "your mama" is so ubiquitous a taunt as to be the humorously "correct" answer to the question, "Who is buried in Grant's tomb?" (66). Apparent non sequitur to white speakers, within the logic of signifying, "your mama" is the ultimate retort and only right answer to all questions. Given the overdetermined function of "your mama" in the dozens, women may abstain less because they would not signify than because they resist this particular idiom, in which the body of the mother is simultaneously idealized and debased from an emphatically male perspective. Who exactly finds sense and pleasure in reciting (or refuting) lines like "I fucked your mama/Till she went blind./Her breath smells bad,/But she sure can grind" (72)? We need hardly consult Freud to recognize the mix of desire, aggression, and protectiveness driving this genre as that of rebellious, reverent, and insecurely powerful sons. No wonder that mothers and even daughters, positioned by these time-honored sentiments as bodies fucked, blinded, and bad-breathed, have difficulty intervening with feelings and fighting words of their own.

Gates attempts to even things up by seeing the dozens as just one "especially compelling subset" (71) of a much wider and less gendered discursive field. Yet he goes on to illustrate other, "more humane" modes of Signifyin(g) with an example from Brown's autobiography consisting of a very long, very funny, and very masculine boast: "I'm the bed tucker the cock plucker the motherfucker/The milkshaker the record breaker the population maker/The gun-slinger the baby bringer/The hum-dinger the pussy ringer/The man with the terrible middle finger" (73). This winning display of verbal as well as sexual prowess may not ignore female pleasure, but it would seem definitively to preclude a female point of view. More disconcerting, when Gates does go out of his way to give a few examples of women

Signifyin(g), drawing on the important work of Claudia Mitchell-Kernan, he refuses to spell out what seem to me the undeniable differences in women's rhetorical strategies.[22] For one thing, all three of the examples Gates takes from Mitchell-Kernan turn on women's bodies and food: on what one woman is serving for dinner and what another likes to eat (82), on how much a woman weighs and how she looks in her clothes (82), on whether a woman's weight gain is due to being pregnant (83).[23] The first and third of these exchanges appear to take place in the home, probably in the kitchen. (The location of the second is unspecified.) In none of them is there a reference to anyone's mama, unless you count the speaker in the last case who is trying to hide her pregnancy. As it happens, neither is there any mention of the sexual exploits or power struggles in the public sphere that are standard fare in the Monkey tales, the dozens, and other forms of male signifying. Interestingly, in the lexicon of both genders, the female body looms large. Yet we have only to contrast Brown's boast about population making with the woman "disgusted" to find herself pregnant for the fifth time (in example 3) to see how differently this theme operates when the speaker and the maternal coincide.

I realize that Gates would probably accuse me of missing the point by attending to the literal as well as figurative aspects of these speech acts. Certainly I agree with him that the first conversation about chit'lins versus prime rib for dinner is a coded debate about cultural nationalism versus assimilation—not finally about food at all (82). I also appreciate that these examples can be formally distinguished from one another (and tied to male instances of the same), the first as "loud-talking," the second as "naming," etc. Nevertheless, though Gates is silent on this point, his own examples go to show that the social context in which signifying occurs, the imagery used, and the ends served are all strongly inflected by gender. The question therefore arises: Do the Signifying Monkey and his precursor Esu have as much explanatory force in glossing the rhetorical practices of black women as they do for black men?

Looking past the rhetoric of gender inclusion, no less misleading in Gates than it was in Ross, I think we must answer this question in the negative. And if Signifyin(g) as a concept is heavily weighted toward male settings, speakers, and strategies, it is hardly surprising that subsequent chapters on Signifyin(g) and African American literature should fail to do justice to women writers. Chapter 3, though it ranges widely over the entire history of African American letters, returns most frequently to Richard Wright and Ralph Ellison for their fictional representations of Signifyin(g), for their Signifyin(g) on earlier writers, and for inspiring later writers to Signify on them. In addition, Charles Chesnutt, Alston Anderson, Paul Laurence Dunbar, W.E.B. DuBois, Langston Hughes, Chester Himes, and Ishmael Reed all get their due with a paragraph or more of critical commentary. Harriet Wilson, Harriet Jacobs, Jessie Fauset, Nella Larson, Lorraine Hansberry, and Gwendolyn Brooks, by contrast, are never even mentioned; nor are most of the women who have made the last thirty years a glorious renaissance in black women's writing. Gates remarks that he *could* turn to Toni Cade Bambara, Sonia Sanchez, and Nikki Giovanni (along with a few other male writers) for further examples of Signifyin(g) rituals (102)—but he never does.

True, Wheatley makes a fleeting appearance as the object of a racist parody (90–91), and Frances Harper gets a few sentences for revising Douglass (122–23). But only Zora Neale Hurston, Alice Walker, and Toni Morrison are included in Gates's schematic representation (Chart 5) of what he calls "the direct relations [of literary influence] most important to my own theory of reading" (111–12).[24] Moreover, while Hurston and Walker will be the subjects of later chapters, Morrison receives no further mention, and Walker receives none in this chapter. This leaves Hurston alone (117–18), among dozens of recent and recently recovered figures, as the only black woman to be quoted and commented on in the whole of Gates's overview of Signifyin(g) and the black literary tradition. The exclusion of women is even more marked when Gates discusses Signifyin(g) practices within jazz. While Coltrane, Charlie Parker, Count Basie, and Oscar Peterson are all celebrated for quoting, revising, and parodying earlier songs and styles (104–5, 123–24), here Gates doesn't so much as gesture toward the Bessie Smiths and Billie Holidays or pause to defend his use of the male pronoun. Despite Gates's highly visible work as an editor of black women's texts, then, and notwithstanding Hurston's walk-on part, women in this central chapter remain a spectral, hypothetical presence: writers Gates could have talked about, writers whose names are floated on a chart but never taken up by the text, musicians cut from the web of male influence and cross-reference.

A female figure does turn up in the discussion of Jean Renoir's film *Sur un air de Charleston*, which Gates praises as "a Signifyin(g) riff of a profound order" (108). "A parody of the literature of discovery so popular in

Renaissance and Enlightenment Europe between 1550 and 1800" (109), this short surrealist narrative features a "scantily clad white Wild Woman" (108) accompanied by a lascivious ape. Amid the ruins of a post-holocaust Paris, she is discovered by an Afro-Astronaut, to whom she can communicate only through her lewd dancing. As Gates explains, "The white Wild Woman is the reversed image of the exotic blacks the Europeans depicted; her fondness for apes is a reversal of common European allegations of the propensity of African women to prefer the company of male apes" (109). What Gates fails to notice, however, is that the *gender* logic of Renoir's scenario does not reverse but only reproduces the original. In both cases, a silent, sexualized woman shakes her booty to embody the allure as well as the debasement of a specifically raced, "primitive" culture, in contrast to a technologically superior and more "civilized" one represented by the male explorer. Like the womb/calabash waiting to be opened, like "your mama" bandied about by the dozens, the discovered Wild Woman is another instance of the objectified feminine in Gates's text—the unspoken correlate of an argument in which Signifyin(g) subjects are almost always male.

Recall that *Figures in Black* opens with what I have seen as an ambiguous discussion of Phillis Wheatley's *Poems* (1773), offering her as origin while tying her firmly to a discredited tradition of valuing black texts in "sociological" rather than aesthetic terms. Chapter 4 of *Signifying Monkey*, "The Trope of the Talking Book," goes one step further by displacing Wheatley's work altogether in favor of five autobiographical texts by black men: James Gronniosaw (1770), John Marrant (1785), Ottobah Cugoano (1787), Olaudah Equiano (1789), and John Jea (1815). Though these are identified by Gates as the earliest examples of African American Signifyin(g) and its "ur-trope" (131), only the first preceded Wheatley, and Gronniosaw's narrative is more properly Anglo-African than African American. Gates would presumably justify his choices in terms of the Talking Book trope, introduced by Gronniosaw and Signified on by the others. Yet Valerie Smith has argued that an emphasis on scenes of reading and literary instruction in black texts may arise from and perpetuate a bias in favor of male writers; the acquisition of literacy that defines Frederick Douglass hardly does so for Harriet Jacobs ("Gender" 60–61). And even if representations of the Talking Book were not inherently gendered, the exemplary texts Gates chooses and his placement of them—between Esu and a preponderance of twentieth-century male writers—would effectively make it so.[25]

This brings me to the final chapters of *Signifying Monkey*: on Hurston's *Their Eyes Were Watching God* (1937), Reed's *Mumbo Jumbo* (1972), and Walker's *The Color Purple* (1982). I have already discussed the (almost identical) version of the *Mumbo Jumbo* essay as it appears in *Figures in Black*, where Gates extols Reed's text for its postmodernity—its revision of black precursors, parody of white signifying systems, and substitution of play and indeterminacy for various essentialisms. As I have noted, Gates credits it above all other works with shaping his theory of Signifyin(g). "*The Signifying Monkey* and *Mumbo Jumbo*," he explains at the beginning of chapter 6, therefore "bear something of a symbiotic relationship" (218). What I want to consider now, as I conclude my discussion of Gates's most important work of scholarship, are the chapters bookending Reed, which take up Hurston and Walker yet seem determined to play down their analyses of black gender practices and the lives of black women.

Hurston and Walker have in common scathing, comprehensive critiques of male domination in African American society of the early twentieth-century rural South. Though racism is a given in their novels, white characters are rare if not invisible. Both books are most concerned with detailing the internal dynamics of the black community, developmental dramas played out within the black family, difficulties encountered by their heroines usually (as critics of Walker never tire of complaining) at the hands of black men. Their depictions of violence against women, expropriation of women's labor and sexuality, limitation of their mobility, and silencing of their voices thus focus specifically on forms of patriarchy within African American and (in *The Color Purple*) West African contexts. Denying that black feminism betrays the cause of antiracism, both writers insist that black women's subordination by black men may coexist with the subordination of African Americans by whites. As Hurston's Nanny famously puts it, "Honey, de white man is de ruler of everything as far as Ah been able tuh find out. . . . So de white man throw down de load and tell de nigger man tuh pick it up. He pick it up because he have to, but he don't tote it. He hand it to his womenfolks. De nigger woman is de mule uh de world so fur as Ah can see" (29). Nor is it individual, anomalous men who are castigated by Hurston and Walker, but views and behaviors shared by men generally, passed from father to son and sanctioned by the community at large. Janie flees not one bad marriage but two, and even Tea Cake, her third, comradely lover, "slapped her around a bit to show he was boss" (218).

Likewise, in *The Color Purple*, Pa's brutality is continued by Celie's husband, Albert, and even the more egalitarian Harpo tries to beat Sophia into submission. (When Sophia fights back, Harpo blames his bruises on a "fractious" mule, a winking reference to Hurston [Walker 43].) For neither of these novels is the project simply to replace a bad man with a good one. Indeed, both quite pointedly leave their heroines economically and emotionally independent of men, and if Hurston troubles the paradigm of black heterosexual romance, Walker moves beyond it altogether.[26]

A few pages from the end of his book, Gates acknowledges this last point, observing that "Celie, Nettie, Shug, and Janie all find a form of freedom in houses in which there are no men. . . . The home that Nettie and Celie inherit will include men, but men respectful of the inherent strength and equality of women" (253). For the most part, however, his readings of Hurston and Walker seem bent on neglecting the womanism of their novels. For one thing, Gates demonizes Janie's grandmother, Nanny, as "the dreaded figure of Medusa" (187). As a result, he feels free to ignore the gender polemic of her slave narrative: a warning to Janie about heterosexual violence ("Ah can't die easy thinkin' maybe de menfolks white or black is makin' a spit cup outa you" [Hurston 37]) and a passing on of her ambition to sermonize on behalf of women ("Ah wanted to preach a great sermon about colored women sittin' on high, but they wasn't no pulpit for me . . . so whilst Ah was tendin' you of nights Ah said Ah'd save de text for you" [Hurston 31–32]).[27] Heedless of these grandmaternal words (a kind of "sermon" after all), Gates maps the novel in terms of Janie's troubled relationships with Nanny, Logan Killicks, and Joe Starks, followed by her discovery of true love with Verigible Tea Cake Woods (*Signifying* 185). According to Gates, the very name "Verigible" (a variant of "veritable") shows that Tea Cake is the real thing (191), their love "true consummation" (193), theirs the perfect "male-female relationship for which Janie had longed so very urgently" (193).

To support this fairy-tale view of the novel, Gates must overlook the fact that, bitten by the mad dog of jealousy, Tea Cake beats Janie—with the result that Janie kills the brutal Tea Cake while keeping alive the tender one in her thoughts and in her story to Phoebe. Furthermore, Gates misreads the celebrated passage in which Janie is described as longing "to be a pear tree—*any* tree in bloom! With kissing bees singing of the beginning of the world! She had glossy leaves and bursting buds and she wanted to struggle with life but it seemed to elude her. Where were the singing bees for her?" (Hurston 25). The pear tree image recurs, as Gates notes, when Janie meets Tea Cake: "He could be a bee to a blossom—a pear tree blossom in the spring" (Hurston 161). Ignoring Hurston's repeated identification of the pear tree with Janie herself, Gates informs us that "Jody is not yet the embodiment of Janie's tree" (188), and that "Tea Cake not only embodies Janie's tree, he is the woods themselves" (191). Of course Tea Cake is an appealing (though not entirely faithful) lover who teaches Janie to drive, fish, shoot, etc., but for all this Hurston images him as an expendable bee to Janie's blossom, one that helps to awaken the pear tree of her *own* sexuality and creativity. Gates, by contrast, installs Tea Cake as the happy ending to what he calls "the tale of Janie Crawford-Killicks-Starks-Woods" (184), thus reframing her quest for an expressive, orgasmic self as a patient wait for the ultimate patronymic.

Idealizing Tea Cake, Gates dilutes Hurston's feminist critique considerably by assuming that its only object is the arrogant Joe Starks. Joe is, to be sure, the book's most unbearable patriarch; jealous of other men's looks, he makes Janie cover her hair in the store and slaps her for burning the dinner one night (Hurston 87, 111). As I have said, however, he is not the only one to be possessive and to hit her, and both incidents of male violence against Janie are met by a chorus of approving voices from the larger community (Hurston 116, 218–19). Gates mentions the conversation between porch-sitters Coker and Joe Lindsay on "the merits of beating women" (*Signifying* 204), but he still sees "Jody's big voice . . . as a synecdoche of oppression, *in opposition to the speech community* of which Janie longs to become an integral part" (200; emphasis added). Though recognizing that when Janie Signifies on Joe it not only kills him but constitutes "the first feminist critique of the fiction of the authority of the male voice, and its sexism, in the Afro-American tradition" (207), Gates insists on identifying Joe, and Joe alone, as "the figure of the male author" (206). Sexism thus appears an individual failing, whereas I believe Hurston shows it to be a pervasive ideology, not opposed to but deeply embedded in the African American speech community.

For while Hurston and Walker criticize many faces of compulsory heterosexuality, from its white beauty standards to its legitimation of male sexual ownership, they are concerned, above all, with protesting its discrediting of women's words. Both novels climax with scenes in which Janie and Celie finally take back the male-dominated conversation, and with it their lives. When Janie retorts to Joe, "Humph! Talkin' 'bout *me* lookin' old! When you pull down yo' britches, you look lak de change uh life" (123), and when Celie calls Mr. _____ a "lowdown dog" before telling him, "It's time to leave you and enter into the Creation. And your dead body just the welcome mat I need" (181), they are not only *playing the dozens* but mutinously *signifying on the dozens* for excluding and demeaning women. The shocking unorthodoxy of their words is registered by the response of onlookers, who gasp and gape in disbelief. Yet Gates, we recall—and this is my principal point here—has all along denied that men have any rhetorical advantage. In this chapter too he cites Hurston's landmark definition of signifying ("showing off") in *Mules and Men* as evidence that "women most certainly can, and do, Signify upon men" (196). A subsequent example from *Mules*, however, would seem to directly undercut his claim. Described blandly by Gates as a case of "classic Signification" between two lovers, the quoted passage features Big Sweet loud-talking about Joe Willard's infidelity—to which Joe responds by questioning her ability and entitlement to speak at all, "Aw, woman, quit tryin' to signify" (197). Convinced that his Monkey is genderless, unaware that his survey of Signifyin(g) from Esu to Reed has slighted and distorted women's voices, Gates cannot possibly do justice to Janie's appropriation of the dozens or to Celie's defiance of the axioms of gendered discourse.[28]

NOT A MINDLESS CHEERLEADER

If *Figures in Black* includes two women writers who are implicitly devalued according to the book's poststructuralist framework, *Signifying Monkey* includes two writers who are not only female but feminist—and refuses to acknowledge the pertinence of their critique to its codification of Signifyin(g). Clearly it is not sufficient to develop over the course of four chapters a model based almost exclusively on men and then blithely tack on a few unsuspecting women. The result, I have argued, is "a theory of African-American Literary Criticism" consistently skewed toward the masculine and committed to denying this fact. Gates would like, it seems, to have his monkey tales and eat the cake of emergent black women's writing too. He satisfies what I have seen as a desire to reestablish his "masculinity" in loosely black nationalist terms, while at the same time positioning himself to capitalize on the late 1980s explosion of interest in Hurston and her literary sisters.[29] Gates was, of course, a key player in this explosion. The publication of *Signifying Monkey* in 1988 coincided with the appearance of the first thirty volumes of the Schomburg series. These were quickly followed by *Reading Black, Reading Feminist* in 1990 and by the next ten volumes of the Schomburg series in 1991. Yet we have already witnessed—in the suppressed gender codings of *Figures in Black* and *Signifying Monkey*, in the contradictory feelings suggested by the recitation anecdote—the ambivalence that accompanied (and may even have motivated) Gates's attraction to and apparent identification with women's voices. The very proliferation of new and recovered books by black women caused many black males considerable anxiety, with Gates's postmodern paragon Ishmael Reed among the most vocal of those protesting the success of sisters like Walker. Taking a page from Deborah McDowell—who singles out, amid a pattern of mischievous reviews by black men in the white media, Darryl Pinckney's 1987 essay pairing Walker with Reed (*Changing* 123–240)—I suggest that by appending Walker immediately after Reed, Gates not only added a woman but necessarily invoked a raging controversy. At the very least, Reed's place in *Signifying Monkey* between Hurston and Walker would seem to code and perhaps to allay male apprehension about the sudden popularity of black female/feminist writers.

I hope my readings of *Figures, Signifying,* and the relation between them have succeeded in showing that Gates's apparently dramatic turn in the last decade from black women to black men is actually consistent with his gender politics in the preceding one. I will close by looking briefly at the way this turn gets played out in *Colored People* (1994), which maps Gates's shift from female to male in autobiographical terms, and in *Thirteen Ways of Looking at a Black Man* (1997), which celebrates the masculinity not only of its subjects but also of its own journalistic voice. In his memoir of growing up in segregated West Virginia, Gates's narrator thinks back, as Virginia Woolf might say, through his mother. His sense of the "colored world of the fifties" comes back to him in his mother's voice (xvi), and his early self overlaps with hers to the extent that, as he puts it, "some of her memories feel like my own" (12). In chapters called "In the Kitchen" and "Love Junkie," we hear, movingly, of a child most at home in his mama's kitchen, basking in the smells and warm tones of women gathered to have their hair done (40), loving the look and feel of the womanly bodies of his mother's friends (103). Gates casts the latter in proto-heterosexual terms, yet the boy protagonist of his tale seems drawn to women in ways suggesting identification as much as desire. He plays with Betsy McCall paper dolls while his mother sews from paper patterns (31) and cooks with her "just to be near her, to be talking with her" (133). Brother Rocky, by contrast, bonds with their father over sports, and the unathletic narrator complains that father and oldest son excluded him, sometimes cruelly, from their "masculine camaraderie" (78–83).

Yet while *Colored People* is thus a passionate tribute to the mother—her elegance and beauty, the "poetry" of the minutes she read as the first black secretary of the PTA, her role in teaching Skippy to read and write in one day in their kitchen (29–33)—its central drama is the narrator's eventual separation from her and his coming of age coincident with her breakdown. He is, to be sure, greatly distressed by the "veil that passed over her life, dimming her radiance" (127) when she was forty-six and he was twelve, and he notes the inadequacy of attributing her "change" to menopause, the only language then available to talk about her depression. As I have noted, however, Gates seems strangely unable to decipher the signs, present in his own telling, of her frustration and despair as a woman who was raised to put men, and even boys, before herself (61–62). Nor does he fully register the significance of ending his story not only with his mother's death in 1987 but also with the act of changing his name from Louis Smith Gates to Henry Louis Gates, after his father. He had always hated the name Smith, he explains, given to him by his mother as a promise to her best friend, Miss Smith; it made him feel "deprived of [his] birthright" (205). Reclaiming his rightful paternal name shortly before getting married, he tells the court he does this "because I love my father and because it is my *true* name" (206; emphasis added).

Colored People, therefore, as much as it pays homage to the mother, finally abandons her in favor of a "true" identity modeled self-consciously after the father's. Gates's story makes clear that his mother was the family's race radical, leading the fight for integration in their town (188), fierce in her racial pride (34–35), and encouraged by the emergence of black nationalism (184), while his father stubbornly lampooned new, more defiant hairstyles and politics (188). It is highly ironic, therefore, that Gates's growing political consciousness as a teenager in the 1960s, the repudiation of his "coloredness" and claiming of his "blackness," is realigned by the end of this account with his father as well as with his male peers (187–88). Disidentifying with his mother, the narrator comes (with little awareness of what he's doing) to subordinate the affective and political logic of his childhood to the larger social logic of the times by which an authentic racial identity can best be affirmed in relation to masculinity.

By the time we get to Gates's preface to the Whitney catalogue *Black Male* (1994), his conversation with Cornel West about "the crisis of the black male" in *Transition* (1995), his coauthorship with West of *The Future of the Race* (1996), and his series of *New Yorker* profiles collected as *Thirteen Ways of Looking at a Black Man* (1997), the affiliation with black men *over* black women is explicit and polemical. The first of these four texts collapses statistics about African American girls as well as boys (born into poverty, dropping out of school) into those specifically about black males (incarcerated, scarce in college) in order to conclude that "the much discussed crisis of the black male is no idle fiction" (13). In the space of a few sentences, black females who are poor and uneducated drop entirely off the screen. In the second text, Gates likewise goads West to explain why racism in America is "worse for men than women" (180). In the third, he unapologetically takes up DuBois's appeal to "exceptional men" to lead black people forward, and in the last he goes to some length to justify his exclusion of black women on the grounds, once again, that they are better off than African American men (v).

Thirteen Ways of Looking at a Black Man, though "relational" in sensibility and secure enough to include the frankly homoerotic stories of James Baldwin and Bill T. Jones alongside the more tamely male homosocial ones of Colin Powell and Louis Farrakhan, clinches the case for abandoning mothers and turning to fathers in order to get leverage on race issues. Not coincidentally, it opens by illustrating what I have seen as Gates's insecurity about his blackness and maleness as a direct result of his class aspirations and success, combined with his penchant for the intellectual and diplomatic over the physical and belligerent. The scene is New Haven in 1969, and the anecdote concerns studious black Yalies accosted on the street by "black revolutionaries of every kind" (xi). Faced with sober Black Muslims and glamorous Black Panthers, Gates recalls feeling at once superior, envious, guilty, and intimidated. The issue, as he recognized vaguely even then, was not only styles of blackness but also styles—and degrees—of masculinity. Gates knows there's something about manhood at stake here, and that's why he uses this tale as a preface to this book. But he can't quite come out and say that the bad-boy, leather-coated Panthers set the standard then and now, and that by this standard, his own kind of on-time-to-class manhood simply doesn't measure up. The essays that follow, earnestly focused on permutations of rivalry and reverence among men and men only, thus serve to stabilize precisely the identity categories figured in the New Haven story as precarious.

I want to conclude this chapter by further suggesting that *Thirteen Ways* does the work of remasculinization not only in its choice of male subjects and celebration of male homosociality but also in its use of the language of journalism. I have already discussed the black masculinizing effect of Gates's turn from the poststructuralist idiom of *Figures* to an identification with, if not use of, the black vernacular in *Signifying*. Gates would, of course, tie himself still more closely and directly to this discourse by means of his much-publicized 1990 testimony defending 2 Live Crew from obscenity charges.[30] Since then, he has continued to distance himself from the high theoretical discourses predominant in today's academy, but less by invoking rap music's black vernacular than by making regular use of the white vernacular in mainstream organs like *The New York Times* and *The New Yorker*. I don't pretend to know exactly why Gates has chosen a popular rather than a scholarly audience for his recent writings. (Even *The Bondswoman's Narrative* is being pitched to airport book buyers.) But given that this is so, I notice some effort being made to mark the journalistic idiom, which might appear a falling off in prestige and "rigor," as nevertheless securely masculine.

Interestingly, when Gates discusses his shift to journalism at the end of *Thirteen Ways*, he contrasts it to a stentorian literary criticism fueled by "a robust, manly emotion like outrage" (216). "Deep down I'm no Stentor," he decides. "I prefer the exploratory to the conclusory mode" (216). This disavowal of manliness is contradicted, however, by the final essay of *Loose Canons* ("Trading on the Margins: Notes on the Culture of Criticism"), in which Gates brings an extended case against the language of current literary criticism through an accretion of images coding the discredited discourse as female. Taking aim at contemporary theory generally, he continually figures this as feminist theory in particular. Consider the following examples. Making the familiar pragmatist complaint that left cultural criticism has little practical effect, he gives the instance of an "Althusserian" film piece that, realistically, does nothing to "bring down the house of patriarchy" (181). Farther down this page, the author killed in the 1970s but revived by "grim-faced" "eighties-style Politics" is referred to as female (181). Things have gotten so bad, Gates continues, that we vie to be the most oppressed and sound like Sally Field ("You like me!") as we accept our "Oppression Emmy" awards (185). We substitute fashion for political substance, he declares, reducing scholarly debate to "what *Women's Wear Daily* would call the 'style wars'" (186). In the same metaphorical vein, Gates likens our arrogance as theory heads to Ethel Merman singing "Anything You Can Do, I Can Do Better" (188). And finally, as the ultimate example of useless though self-important political criticism, Gates offers the work of Luce Irigaray, whose "conception of the amazing fixity of patriarchy . . . is more likely to send us to the margins of Plato, Freud, and Lacan than to encourage anything so vulgar as overt political action" (193). Associated through this series of images with antipatriarchy, female authors, Sally Field, fashionmongers, Ethel Merman, and Luce Irigaray, Gates's shallow, trendy, ineffectual left theory is definitely wearing a skirt.

Speaking of skirts, I am reminded, finally, of a comment Gates makes in his *Transition* exchange with Cornel West, in which he defends humble, practical journalism as nothing so girly as cheerleading. West should be admired, Gates says, as a black intellectual who ranges widely beyond the merely academic, and he adds that such a role "doesn't have to make one a mindless cheerleader . . . there are subtler critical instruments than the pompom and the baton" (173). Renouncing the pom-pom, Gates effectively removes himself along with West from the sidelines of male athletic combat—suggesting to me that, having shifted his allegiance from Saussure to Signifyin(g), from black women in *Crisis* to black men in crisis, he has now, in the persona of the plain-spoken public intellectual, managed at last to bond with his father over sports.

6

QUEER THEORY AND THE SECOND SEX

In what sense does a chapter on queer theory belong in a book about cool men? Aren't gay men (not to mention lesbians) quintessentially uncool: precisely those subjects abjected by conventional masculinity, especially the "bad boy" version of it in which boys will be boys, and gender is tautological? Well, yes. But my topic is not gay men so much as a queer discourse that, while professing to destabilize gender, may still at times have recourse to normative views. Glancing back at academic thinking about sexuality and gender in recent years, I suggest that the demise by 1990 of "difference" feminism—necessary and welcome in many ways—has coincided with a claiming of cool masculinity and of masculinity *as* cool in tandem with a disowning of the feminine. As with my other examples, coolness in this area involves antagonism to a form of constraint figured as maternal. Typically it is first-generation feminist scholarship of the late 1970s and early 1980s that gets thrust into this role, being handily maternalized for semantic as well as structural reasons: because mothers were central to its lexicon, because these scholars have been our teachers and our models, and because they are now, at the dawn of the twenty-first century, the menopausal generation.

The shunning of "mothers" alongside an appeal to "masculinity" for the new, taut, sexy, and smart may be found not only in much queer theory but also in contemporary feminist theory. A shift away from "women" has oc-

curred both because a queer theory skeptical of identity categories has succeeded and in many ways superseded feminist theory and because the
newest generation of feminist theorists has in common with queer theorists
(when, indeed, it can be distinguished from them at all) a particular wariness of 1980s-style "woman-identified" feminism.[1] Of course, one cannot
conflate the feminist and the queer, however intertwined their origins and
concerns—the frequent tension between them is a central theme of the
pages to come. At the same time, insofar as queer theory has now displaced
feminist theory from the position it held around 1981 as the cutting edge of
sex/gender work, I do see this final chapter as partly about a second generation of scholarship developing out of the twentieth-century women's
movement and the rise of lesbian feminism. More than any of the previous
chapters, it is an effort to parse the sexual politics of recent developments
within my own field.

Queer theory has, of course, sponsored important work not only on
women and lesbianism but also on femininity and femme-ness. I'm thinking of writers like Joan Nestle, Arlene Istar, Pat Califia, Jewelle Gomez,
Lynda Hart, Lisa Duggan, and Kathleen McHugh, among others, who have
tried to distinguish and value femme subjectivity both in relation to and
apart from butchness.[2] There are, too, queer texts celebrating male femininity, and all of these may be seen to qualify and complicate my argument
in this chapter.[3] Yet as long as there has been queer theory, there has also
been a strain of internal as well as external feminist critique to the effect
that, notwithstanding its claim to repudiate gender binaries, much of this
discourse is secretly and sometimes quite frankly in love with masculinity.

One of the first and most compelling instances of such a critique came
from Tania Modleski in *Feminism Without Women* (1991)—a title diagnos-
ing what she saw as a disturbing trend beginning in the late 1980s. Her main
targets were studies of masculinity flourishing under the emergent rubric of
"gender studies" (as opposed to "women's studies") and the strict antiessen-
tialism of critics like Judith Butler and Denise Riley, who shun the identities "woman" and "lesbian," however historicized and internally differentiated (3–22). Writing just as queer theory was beginning to be visible as such,
Modleski praised Lee Edelman and others influenced by Sedgwick's *Between Men* (1985). At the same time, she was disappointed by the bracketing of lesbianism in Sedgwick as well as, for example, in the sexuality issue
of *South Atlantic Quarterly* (1989) (12–13).[4] 1991 also saw Blakey Vermeule's

article in *Qui Parle* asking, "Is There a Sedgwick School for Girls?" and shortly thereafter both Terry Castle in *The Apparitional Lesbian* (1993) and Teresa de Lauretis in *The Practice of Love* (1994) would echo and elaborate Vermeule's complaint: that the notion of a "lesbian continuum" as deployed in Sedgwick's *Between Men* served to de-eroticize, despecify, and decenter lesbian sexuality (Vermeule 53–58; Castle 13, 71; de Lauretis 115, 192–93).[5] Biddy Martin, in two brilliant 1994 essays, went further still to parse the subtle gender codings frequently underwriting queer texts; I'll return to Martin shortly as a key inspiration for the readings below.[6] Suzanne Danuta Walters drew on Martin as well as Modleski in a comprehensive 1996 *Signs* piece, which argued that queer theorists from Sedgwick and Butler to Michael Warner and Gayle Rubin have, in various ways, regarded "gay male identity as the site of privileged subjectivity" (836). She was equally concerned about "the implicit and explicit marginalization and demonization of feminism and lesbian-feminism" (837) and, like Modleski, about a fervid poststructuralism inattentive to the material conditions of gender and also race (839–43).

Since Walters there have been, indeed, two entire collections devoted to the tensions between lesbian-feminist and queer paradigms, both published in 1997. *Cross-Purposes: Lesbians, Feminists, and the Limits of Alliance*, edited by Dana Heller and sympathetic to the former perspective, featured essays by old-guard lesbian feminists Bonnie Zimmerman and Lillian Faderman, who angrily defended their work from queer charges of "essentialism, ethnocentrism, separatism, puritanism, political correctness, and so forth" (157–58). Even Sue-Ellen Case, no fan of mainstream lesbian feminism, complained in this volume that "the privileging of gay male culture by queer dykes, along with the . . . mis-remembering of lesbian feminism, has produced the dwindling away of lesbian cultural resources" (211). Ironizing the "new queer dyke" who impersonates gay male styles, Case noted that, if "testosterone is better in the hands of women, appropriating the masculine is not, obviously, beyond gender" (210). *Feminism Meets Queer Theory* (edited by Elizabeth Weed and Naomi Schor), though more balanced overall, reprinted one of the aforementioned articles by Martin ("Extraordinary Homosexuals and the Fear of Being Ordinary") and opened with an essay by Butler herself ("Against Proper Objects") conceding that queer theory had been guilty of mischaracterizing work on gender—erasing radical feminism, antiracist feminism, pro-sex feminism, antiessentialist feminism, and feminist sex radicalism (18–19). Noting that *Gender Trouble* (1990) was written to contest feminist frameworks fixated on the male/female binary, here Butler would temper that challenge by doubting that queer theory's inquiry into sexuality could "ever fully be divorced from questions of gender" (2–3).

Such moments in Butler point to the fact that questions about gender within queer theory have been raised not only by those invested in older feminist paradigms but also by those identified with recent queer ones. Another striking example is de Lauretis, credited with actually coining the term "queer theory" in her 1991 introduction to *differences*. Arguing that so-called "lesbian and gay studies" had frequently elided lesbian difference while seeming to include it, her introduction called on queer theory to address "the enduring silence on the specificity of lesbianism in the contemporary 'gay and lesbian' discourse" (vii). Three years later, however, de Lauretis would criticize Sedgwick along with a general state of queer affairs continuing to prioritize gay men and often dismissive of earlier feminist scholarship. In a paper given at the 1994 MLA and published in *Cross Purposes* ("Fem/Les Scramble"), de Lauretis declared that "queer theory," in failing to differentiate and historicize female as well as male sexualities, had had in practice "the opposite of the effect I had hoped for" (46).[7] All of which is to say that, since 1991, we have seen both the elaboration of an exciting left political practice and body of theory under the rubric of "queer" and the voicing of a complaint from queer as well as lesbian feminists to the effect that queer erotics and politics are made available primarily through masculinity. Among their many charges: as gay male sexualities are glamorized and radicalized, women are left out of major queer texts (which are no less influential for that); "women" is dismissed as a homogenizing identity category (leaving "men" to function as such); lesbianism is untheorized as a discrete desire or theorized in terms derived from models of male sexuality; "masculinity" is fetishized while "femininity" and "maternity" are disparaged, often by queer women as well as men; lesbian scholarship is caricatured, lesbian histories are oversimplified, and lesbian cultures are allowed to dwindle away.[8]

THE SWAMP OF MATERNITY

My project in this final chapter is to build on and develop this critique through readings of queer texts by Lee Edelman and by Judith Halberstam, two scholars linked by their investments in masculinity even while, as we will see, differentiated by Halberstam's specific attention to masculinity in *women*. I take up this critique, like most of the figures above, with a powerful appreciation for the importance of the work I am criticizing; indeed, as I have already suggested, I turn now to the area of scholarship with which I feel the strongest kinship. I will nevertheless argue that queer theory has had several kinds of trouble with women and gender—trouble that is sometimes inadvertent, sometimes by design—beginning with its oft-remarked difficulty in making the vagaries of female desire central to its inquiry. It is an irony evident to all those cited above that, although several of queer theory's "coolest," most influential figures are women, their focus has generally been neither on lesbians nor on female sexuality. Chief among these, as we know, is Eve Sedgwick—who should, however, be given credit for continually pondering her own reasons for bracketing ties between women. *Between Men* has, we have seen, been much criticized for suggesting that homosexuality may be less set apart, and so less stigmatized, for women than it is for men. But Sedgwick would subsequently more candidly trace her relative indifference to female bodies to her interest—both personal and political—in an anal eroticism most visible as a pathologizing figure for male homosexuality ("A Poem is Being Written," 1987). Given this interest, and given the emergence of Sedgwick's work in the Reagan-Bush 1980s, it makes sense that her personal experience of breast cancer would lead her, imaginatively, to men dying of AIDS ("Queer and Now," 1993), and that musings on her own fat would turn quickly to the voluptuous male flesh of Divine and the subject of male drag ("Divinity," 1990–91).[9]

And this is arguably true for queer theory generally—that while the anus might seem to give us an opening for sexuality beyond gender, in academic practice references to rears and behinds are almost always code for scholarship probing the specifically male.[10] There are, as Sedgwick explains, historical reasons for the masculinization of anality, but much queer scholarship assumes and reproduces instead of marking and interrogating this symptom and others of bias toward sexualities imagined as male. Due in part to the accident of Sedgwick's incredibly powerful intellect appearing on the scene in 1985, at a moment when vulnerable gay male bodies were objects of particular pathos and political urgency, an entire field has developed under the influence of her distinct preoccupation with masculinity.

The problem with Sedgwick is that she thinks in such irresistible ways about gay male (and gay male-identified) sexuality, especially in texts by men. If Sedgwick's brilliant example seems to compel inattention to women, Judith Butler has articulated a theoretical position against gender and other identity categories that makes this inattention awkward to talk about.[11] It goes without saying that Butler's wording of identities as performative has helped immeasurably to further denaturalize femininity and to complicate our mappings of sexuality. And if *Gender Trouble* (1990) downplayed dichotomized bodies in favor of fleeting gestures either producing or parodying gender at the level of the symbolic, Butler has since been at pains to counter this apparent antimaterialism, beginning with her very next book, pointedly entitled *Bodies That Matter* (1993).[12] The sexed body, Butler explained, is not static matter but is "forcibly materialized through time," through the reiteration of regulatory norms (1–2). Rosemary Hennessy, however, has noted that "Butler's normative understanding of materiality," stressing the realms of culture and law, neglects economic relations, including divisions of labor based on gender (224–26), and I agree with Hennessy that Butler's work remains, in this sense, insufficiently materialist. More important to my mind, regardless of Butler's efforts to clarify and qualify her claims, is the undeniably deconstructive rather than materialist emphasis of her work, along with its tremendously influential effect on the broader field of queer theory. This effect, in my view, has been to place so much value on instability, fluidity, crossings, and ephemeral surfaces that the stubborn, deep inequity of cultural and social relations organized by gender becomes both less pressing and less recognizable.[13]

We used to think of this particular bag of tricks as "French," and it's always had considerable cachet as well as important deconstructive uses. We've been carrying it around in some form since the 1970s, which is why de Lauretis and others have complained that this aspect of queer theory is not really new so much as preowned. I am arguing, however, that there is something new about how "Butler" functions within feminist and queer discourses today. In left scholarship of the 1970s and 1980s, the strong poststructuralist impulse to destabilize existing paradigms was in continual and sometimes acrimonious tension with the no less compelling impulse to consolidate oppositional identities. There was much discussion about whether poststructuralism served or betrayed political goals formulated by the various new social movements. No one disputed the need to de-essentialize normative categories, but some aspired to theoretical purity while others were convinced that fictions like "women" and "authorship" could, in the right hands, be useful to the work of resistance. Within feminism, this tension was formulated as "theory" versus "practice" and also, in geographical terms, as "Continental" versus "Anglo-American." Today, by contrast, the most vital area of left intellectual inquiry has allowed this tension to go slack. Butler herself, we have said, admits the occasional uses of "identity" labels. But the upshot of her fiercely anti-identitarian work is nevertheless a deep mistrust of identity politics, however strategic, self-conscious, and provisional. Among other things, "the Butler effect" means that, while both sides of the old French/American binary continue to exist, now they are commonly mapped not in *geographical* terms but in heavily moralized *temporal* ones: as "new" versus "old," "hip" versus "passé," "sophisticated" versus "naive," "sexy" versus "disciplinary," "queer" versus "feminist."

I am tempted to quip that this is a poststructuralism reinvented for the Katie Roiphe generation, who came of age the morning after feminism and who fail to appreciate both the intractability of lived gender categories and their practical value in mobilizing on behalf of women. For queer theory's helpful skepticism of identities like "woman" or "lesbian" as apt to be regulatory does not prevent them from continuing to operate—as if they were essential—at every discursive level, including that of queer theory itself. We have already considered the slighting of lesbian specificity. To this I would add what Biddy Martin has boldly shown to be the implicit gender coding of much queer theory, whether the bodies in question are male or female. I return now to the two indispensable articles mentioned above, "Extraordinary Homosexuals and the Fear of Being Ordinary" (1994) and "Sexualities Without Genders and Other Queer Utopias" (1994), in both of which Martin praises the interventions into and deviations from feminist theory made possible by "queerness." At the same time, she goes on to reveal and to question a pattern within queer theory of marking what it values "masculine" and what it repudiates "feminine."

Martin takes queer theory to task for an antifoundationalism in which—what do you know?—the "foundation" is subtly identified with the female, while the debunking power of the "anti" is coded male. "I am worried," Martin writes, "about the occasions when antifoundationalist celebrations of queerness rely on their own projections of fixity, constraint, or subjection onto a fixed ground, often onto feminism or the female body, in relation to which queer sexualities become figural, performative, playful, and fun" (*Femininity* 71). For the "queer" project, focusing on sexuality and its fluidities, is apt to pose itself against the "feminist" one, with its attention to the structures of gender. And while the former is articulated through an emphasis on male sexualities, the burden of gender difference (here as in the dominant culture) is typically borne by women and by feminism. In this context, as in the work of Andrew Ross, the feminist as well as the feminine comes to be derided as what Martin calls "a capitulation, a swamp, something maternal, ensnared and ensnaring" (*Femininity* 72). In other words, within a fiercely poststructuralist schema valuing indeterminacy above all, both femininity and feminism have a tendency to be essentialized. Femininity, unless parodied or renounced, is bound up with conformity to anatomical cues and dutiful, merely procreative sexuality. At the same time, the many convolutions and internal conflicts of feminism—its own antifoundationalism, its pro-sex factions, its struggles with racism, its dissenting leather dykes—are reduced to a simplistic faith in gender "cores." Just as the feminine is troped as biological destiny, so feminism is troped as a quasi-biologist belief system.[14]

There are, then, three senses in which queer theory may be problematic from a feminist point of view. First, it is sometimes a study of men to which women are appended as an afterthought. In this mode, it may slip from seemingly neutral uses of the terms "queer" or "homosexual" to what is then revealed to be male sexuality in particular, only to move back out to ostensibly universal claims, which remain underwritten by masculinity. Second, it favors a poststructuralism so thorough and enthusiastic that the hardening of gender over time, the way its masquerades tend to calcify and continue to matter even in queer contexts, is effectively wished away. Third and most subtly, it tends unconsciously to position women, gender, femininity, and feminism as normative "other" to its antinormative project—and this may occur even when its project centers on female subjectivity—with the result that its own gender codings may be quite conventional.

A central goal of this chapter is to press further on Martin's suggestion that the feminine and feminist are at moments relegated by queer theory to an ensnared and ensnaring "swamp," and that this swamp is somehow "maternal." In fact, I argue that when women occupy the place of "other" within queer discourse it is frequently because they occupy the place of "mother"; and because "mother," in turn, is reduced to biology, heterosexuality, traditional family, coercive normativity. Cherrié Moraga's book claiming queer motherhood is one of several recent challenges to just this set of assumptions.[15] It is nevertheless more often the case that a particular construction of the maternal functions as the means by which women and feminism become negatively charged from a queer point of view. This antagonism toward the maternal contrasts strongly with—indeed, quite pointedly reverses—lesbian feminist paradigms cherishing the mother's body and taking early mother-daughter ties as a trope for lesbian love. De Lauretis, for one, is glad to abandon the "homosexual-maternal metaphor" (see note 183–84n5). As we have seen, however, another effect of the new antimaternalism has been a tendency to disown queer theory's feminist antecedents both for valuing and for being, intellectually speaking, the mother. Given cultural views of mothers and older women generally, it follows easily from such an equation that feminism should be seen as negative about sex and antithetical to sexiness. As for the "feminine," it too is readily conflated with a female embodiment most fully expressed by pregnancy and lactation. Like a textbook illustration of naturalized gender difference, the blissfully pregnant or postpartum woman, whose chromosomes neatly match cultural expectations, is put up against queer theory's transgressive hero, who happens to be biologically male but whose body doesn't line up with either his gender presentation or his sexual practices.

DYING MEN, PREGNANT WOMEN

I see this maternalizing of the female, biologizing of the maternal, and demonizing of both occurring in Lee Edelman's challenging essay, "The Future is Kid Stuff: Queer Theory, Disidentification, and the Death Drive" (1998). In a mode I would describe as incantatory poststructuralism, Edelman analyzes the child as a figure of futurity in political discourse. His target is not simply the conservative uses of sentimentalized innocence and regeneration but the child's indispensability to political thought per se, its deployment as the image of a future on which the very symbolic as well as social order depends. There is much to admire about this bold critique, and certainly I agree that children are typically invoked to legitimate the dominant culture. Yet Edelman's discussion of the trope of the child can't help but offer its own set of tropes, and these not only reflect but also actively reproduce the gender logic above, by which men are tied to a "positive" deconstructive force, women to a "negative" conservative one.[16]

To begin with, Edelman's examples of children are accompanied by other examples, though unremarked as such, of adult females—as if images of children naturally conjure, as an extension of themselves, images of women to care for them. These women are, indeed, so consistently depicted as to give them too an iconic function within the essay. Thus in addition to AIDS poster child Ryan White (25); the waif of the Broadway hit *Les Miz* (21); and Annie, star of her own megamusical (24); we have novelist P. D. James (21); T. S. Eliot's wife, Vivienne (21); the Statue of Liberty (21); and the pregnant women at the wake of Tom Hanks's character, an AIDS-infected lawyer, in the movie *Philadelphia* (24–25). Like the sentimentalized children, all of these women are cited accusingly to illustrate the imperatives of sexual/social reproduction whose effect, indeed whose purpose, is to discipline queerness. Edelman does name several men (Donald Wilmon and Cardinal Bernard Law) who speechify on the importance of "family values" (23, 28–29). But P. D. James's and Vivienne Eliot's poetic utterances (whether as novelist or "character") do not polemically refer to so much as they *imaginatively embody* the ideology of enforced childbearing, supporting my sense that women bear most of the weight, in this piece, of representing heteronormativity. Thus James is mentioned for her dystopian novel, *The Children of Men*, in which social ruin is equated with the failure to reproduce ("less and less in the West we made love and bred children" [21]); Vivienne Eliot is credited with "The Waste Land" line, "What you get married for if you don't want children?" (21); and Delacroix's bare-breasted Liberty is invoked because it hails us (with its promise of freedom) as suckling children (21). Liberty is, in fact, Edelman's very first example of this discourse: "her bare breast making each spectator the unweaned child to whom [a brave new world] belongs." Notice here how the simple fact of the bared female breast "makes" a child, and though topless women are never really simple but always fraught in our cultural imaginary, I do think that Edelman's rhetoric actively works to maternalize this breast, so that it not only nurses but even magically produces a child. The result is that, here and elsewhere, figurations of women's bodies, however islanded, are subtly de-eroticized and assimilated to the figurative child that is this essay's explicit target.

We see this as well in the more extended example of *Philadelphia*'s expectant mothers. With their "reassuringly bulging bellies," they are part of the compound "children and pregnant women," which Edelman reads as an image of futurity working to displace the HIV-positive gay man and his threat to that futurity (24–25). Edelman is undoubtedly right about the creepily consolatory function of multiple pregnancies at the end of *Philadel-phia*; nevertheless, within his own text the cinematic image he offers works alongside Liberty to represent women as lactating breasts and gestating bellies, prostheses to the children they nurse or carry. In an argument against naturalized reproduction—whether of citizens, futures, or meanings—women but not men are silently implicated along with children, just as they are in the culture at large. They are rendered, relative to men, at once closer to children, closer to procreative processes and ideologies, and closer to the policing of sexuality. This is accomplished in part by Edelman's use of the swollen female belly to symbolize a compulsory heterosexuality for which the belly is not, in all fairness, primarily responsible.[17] The effect is that *Philadelphia*'s opposition between dying gay men and pregnant heterosexual women gets redeployed within Edelman's essay to claim death and deconstruction for a queerness coded as masculine in contrast to a straight symbolic order coded as feminine.[18]

The problem with this is not only that it conflates the female body, maternity, and heteronormativity but also that it posits, on the other side, a queerness unpolluted by procreative femininity or, as Edelman says defiantly, "outside the cycles of reproduction" (29). Here Edelman makes use of parallel clauses to underscore the equation between those "choosing to stand" apart from reproduction and those "choosing to stand" by the side of AIDS sufferers (29). Elsewhere in "Kid Stuff" progeny-free queerness is represented by the Tom Hanks character in *Philadelphia* and by the autobiographical gay male "I" who steps forward, momentarily, to gloss a billboard against the grain of its pro-child message (22–23). Observing that the child is tendered in opposition at once to abortion and to queer sexualities, the speaker would refuse "the compulsion to embrace our own futurity in the privileged form of the child and thereby to imagine the present as pregnant with the child of our identification" (23); instead, he challenges us to embrace abortion, to eradicate the poignant optimism of pregnancy. Within such a stark binary schema, what remains unthinkable is queer pregnancy, queerness *within* the cycles of reproduction, queer women with biological children whether from hooking, marriage, or artificial insemination—or, for that matter, queer men with kids genetically their own.[19] The elision of these figures whose depiction would flout the logic of AIDS-versus-pregnancy is evident at two moments in particular, when Edelman acknowledges gay liberal demands for the right to adopt children (in a different register from his own case against the figurative child). In the first instance, he mentions lesbians and gay men working for the right "to adopt and raise children of their own" (25); in the second he invokes "the children we'd as eagerly fly to China or Guatemala in order to adopt" (29). My interest here is not in the merits of campaigns for gay "normalization" and marriage rights but rather in Edelman's suppression of procreative queerness even as he brings up lesbian and gay parenting. By tying this firmly and exclusively to *adoption*, Edelman keeps the category of queerness apart from the feminized, reproductive body, which is imagined as scarcely any closer or more familiar than China or Guatemala.

The split between a heroic gay male sexuality and a maternal body made over entirely to routinized reproduction is further evident in Edelman's book *Homographesis* (1994). In a discussion of James Baldwin, for example, male homosociality is brought out seemingly at the expense of mothers. Here Edelman describes racial domination as a brutal synecdoche, reducing black men to their sexual parts in order to castrate them.[20] In both white and black imaginaries, he argues, race relations are imaged in terms of male homosocial desires and rivalries, bound up with homosexual panic. Citing Toni Morrison's *Beloved* (53), Edelman elucidates the sexual domination of black men by white, completely ignoring the forms that racism might take—and does in this book—when women are involved. Yet surely the most strongly thematized form of racial violence in *Beloved* is the stealing of Sethe's milk and the ghosting of her daughter. To explicate racism in a narrative centered on the black mother without mentioning her appropriated maternity is, in my view, to be guilty of a different synecdoche, the one we encountered in chapters 2 and 5, in which black and white men are taken to stand for the entirety of race relations in the United States.

The privileging of male parts (for the whole) is referenced early on in *Homographesis* by a parenthesis noting apologetically that selfhood is "paradigmatically male in a patriarchally organized social regime" (7). Yet this seems only to license Edelman throughout the book, more often than not, to accept rather than counter the subject's presumed masculinity. Frequently this focus is explicit, and yet, recalling Andrew Ross and Henry Louis Gates Jr., there are also sporadic gestures of gender inclusion, which are then belied by readings either frankly or tacitly exclusive. It is not clear to me, in any case, why *Homographesis* should need, in its central thesis, to privilege the trope of *male* homosexuality as a means of deconstructing stable notions of gender and meaning generally (12), when female homosexuality might, according to his own logic, be said to do similar work.

IN SEARCH OF THE MOTHER'S ANUS

To close my discussion of Edelman, I turn now to another essay, "Seeing Things: Representation, the Scene of Surveillance, and the Spectacle of Gay Male Sex." Originally published in *Inside/Out* (1991) and later reprinted in *Homographesis*, it further illustrates what I see as the problematic posing of maternity over against a celebrated queerness centered on men (and especially young men). "Seeing Things" begins by reinterpreting the primal scene as Freud theorizes it in relation to the Wolf Man. Noting that the Wolf Man "recalls" a sex act in which his father penetrates his mother from behind, Edelman presses Freud on his unelaborated suggestion that this vision of parental heterosex may actually code a fantasy of gay male sex. Edelman's deft analysis allows him to recover in Freud a theory of "the imaginative priority of a sort of proto-homosexuality" (Fuss 101), and to speculate about Freud's evident uneasiness with this idea. But what sort of proto-homosexuality would that be, exactly? The answer, of course, is male homosexuality as observed by a male child. Consequently, the price of Edelman's useful revision, it seems to me, is the mother's desiring body, which is thereby quite casually written out of the sexual imaginary.

Edelman's argument excludes female sexuality, first, by claiming Freud's Wolf Man as his own paradigmatic sexual subject—the one whose erotic development is at issue, the one whose viewpoint structures the scene and whose desires produce its meaning. As Edelman explains in a footnote, he quite pointedly employs the masculine pronoun to indicate that "the gender of the subject in question is male" (115). From this male child's perspective, the adult female is inevitably maternal, and this in and of itself is enough to move her into a putatively asexual space. Surprisingly, however, the maternal object of this particular child's gaze is depicted as few mothers in our cultural archive have been before or since. Eschewing the missionary position in which good wives tolerate sex for strictly reproductive purposes, the Wolf Man's mother does, I agree, certainly invoke (if not necessarily enact) the sodomitical. In a posture suggesting lewd animal display and apparent disregard for family values, she would seem to be, unlike the pregnant women grieving for the Tom Hanks character, highly resistant to either spiritualization or sentimentalization. Indeed, what I see in this scene is a unique opportunity to identify the mother with her own *female anali-ty*—that is, her access *even as a mother* to non-normative, nonprocreative sexuality, to sexuality in excess of the dutifully instrumental.

Edelman's revision does indeed move us in this direction by bringing out the intimations of anality in what Freud describes as a scene of "coitus a tergo" (vaginal penetration from behind). Beginning with Freud's image of doggy-style heterosex, Edelman arrives at that of sodomy between men by implicitly positing, as a fleeting but necessary middle term, the mother's anal eroticism. Regrettably, however, this essay never manages to recognize, much less to value, the queer maternal subject whose pleasure (and ass) would seem to be raised by the primal scene as Edelman reframes it. Granted that sodomy has been, as Sedgwick explains, historically marked as male; all the more reason a contemporary queer reading should recuperate the sodomite as a child-bearing female, precisely because she falls outside stigmatized as well as normative identity categories.[21] Unfortunately, the opposition in Edelman between (male) sexuality and (female) reproduction means that one thing "Seeing Things" cannot see is the staging of sodomitical maternity—any more than "Kid Stuff" can conceive of queer pregnancy.

The second step in erasing maternal desire from the picture is thus to re-place the mother with a male sexual subject. On the one hand, Edelman de-scribes the interest and threat of the primal scene as arising from the infant's identification with *both* actors, who are, moreover, still perceived by him as sexually undifferentiated (101). As a result, this scene serves not only to scramble sex/gender codes but also, more broadly, to challenge basic binary distinctions. At the same time, however, Edelman insists upon the boy's identification less with the mother than with her position, the fantasized substitution of his body for hers as the one being penetrated by the father. Ultimately, then, the gender ambiguity of the one being fucked is resolved in favor of the masculine; and while the figure of a receiving male helps to destabilize such binaries as active/passive, real/imagined, and male/female, it also ties this epistemological work specifically to the spectacle of gay male sex. As Edelman explains, "I would argue that this disorientation of position-ality is bound up with the danger historically associated in Euro-American culture with the spectacle or representation of the sodomitical scene *between men*" (103; my italics). My point, once again, is not to deny that images of male sodomy have been, historically, especially visible, especially dangerous, and especially policed. I would nevertheless ask that a revisionary reading of Freud's primal scene do more than describe this tradition—that it also work against it to give the Wolf Man's mother a queer sexuality of her own. Failing this, the effect of assimilating her scene to an exclusively male homosexual spectacle is to split off and appropriate the mother's voluptuous backside, leaving her coextensive with a "front" fronting only the painful imperatives of heterosexuality. An account that defines her in this way can then celebrate her displacement by the queer son as a triumph for transgressive pleasure. And at that point, the only way for the mother to write herself back in again would be, à la Sedgwick, to route her female anality through the body of a gay man.

A similar rerouting/rewriting of maternal anality occurs in Edelman's subsequent comments on a passage from John Cleland's *Memoirs of a Woman of Pleasure*, in which Fanny spies on two men engaged in a "project of preposterous pleasure" (Cleland 157). Though Fanny is the observer here, unlike the Wolf Man, she embodies not identification with but rather a disavowal of gay male sex, and her role as moralizing observer contrasts sharply with her usual role as shamelessly energetic participant. Edelman fixes in particular on Fanny's observation about one young man: "that if he was like his mother behind [in being penetrated], he was like his father before [in having an erection]." The first clause might, Edelman explains, appear to compare the young man's behind to his mother's behind. And yet, he continues, "most readers of Cleland intuit . . . something else instead: that the man who, from the front, is like his father from the front, is also, from the back, like his mother *from the front*" (105). While Edelman's project is to celebrate this Moebius loop of a man for his "troubling resistance to the binary logic of before and behind," his reading also effectively reinforces the binary logic I have been describing of front/female versus back/male, with the latter preferred as a site of "resistance." Gleaning from this passage Cleland's "metaphoric equation of the young man's anus and the mother's vagina," Edelman seems neither to notice nor to regret that what gets subtracted in such an equation is once again the mother's anus—which I have already suggested might represent the most unthinkable pleasure of all.

The association of asexual reproduction with women and sodomy with men does not, as I have tried to stress, originate with Edelman. To some extent he is simply accounting for the way texts like *Philadelphia* and Freud work—their imaginings of kids and gay men, bellies and behinds, according to a strictly heterosexist and often-misogynist logic. At the same time, by failing consistently to notice and contest the way gender organizes his chosen scenes, he not only relies on but at times regenerates paradigms that disregard or devalue the mother. Like my other cool subjects, then, Edelman has not been singled out for being conspicuously careless of women; a figure like Leo Bersani would more obviously meet this criterion.[22] On the contrary, as with my choice of Henry Louis Gates Jr. over Houston Baker or Andrew Ross over Lawrence Grossberg, I have chosen Edelman precisely because he articulates and intends a solidarity with women that is only sometimes realized in his work—because the pejorative maternal made visible above is at odds with a project that is concertedly progressive, explicitly feminist, and rightly acclaimed for its incisive contributions to the field of queer theory.[23]

*   *   *

Female Masculinity

If I find in Edelman a subtly negative coding of the feminine as fixity and conformity, I turn now to the work of Judith Halberstam, which, in its unapologetic crush on masculinity, also resonates with queer theory's most vaunted paradigms. Significantly, Halberstam differs from all the major figures discussed so far not only in being a woman but also in centering her study on the bodies and subjectivities of women. This closing section of my last chapter—a reading of Halberstam followed by one of Leslie Feinberg's *Stone Butch Blues*—thus marks a shift away from cool men toward a recovery of women and their desires, women and their demands. Halberstam's *Female Masculinity* (1998) initiates this shift by tracing the largely untold story, originating several centuries ago and continuing through the present, of women abjected for their masculinity, whether in books or in films, in the ring or on the stage. As queer/feminist ethnography, it is of immense importance. Masculinity wielded by women is hardly the same as that wielded by men, and I agree with Sue-Ellen Case (see above) that "testosterone is better in the hands of women" (210). Yet I also agree with Case when she goes on to argue that female masculinity does not necessarily get us off the hook of "gender" and its attendant inequities (210). Less satisfying as theory than it is as ethnography, Halberstam's project falters, in my view, when it comes to addressing (or failing to address) the complicated gender politics of its title category.[24] However welcome its focus on women, however distinct from my preceding texts in this regard, Halberstam's book still fits here, I think, at the end of our sequence thematizing cool masculinity, even as it helps to move us toward the butch maternity of Feinberg's novel.

Female Masculinity begins with what I would sympathetically call a second-wave "equality" impulse. Noting the proliferation of conferences and anthologies devoted to analyzing and de-essentializing masculinity, Halberstam points out that few acknowledge the role played by biological women—by female masculinity—in elaborating this construct (13–19). Just as equality feminists complain about women's exclusion from various male bastions (government, business, sports, etc.), so Halberstam complains about women's exclusion from "the privileged reservation" of masculinity itself (xii). And like equality feminists who show that women are worthy by digging up examples of female scientists and women warriors, Halberstam makes a case for women's success at masculinity in part by offering such impressive historical examples as Anne Lister and John Radclyffe Hall. Because the manliness of women like Lister and Hall is more often read as code for their sexuality, we have failed, Halberstam says, to appreciate their contributions to the production of gender: "By making female masculinity equivalent to lesbianism . . . we continue to hold female masculinity apart from the making of modern masculinity itself" (46). As opposed to "difference" feminists, who would value the specificity of women's cultural practices, Halberstam seeks admission for women to the boys' club of modern masculinity.

As I say, I am naturally sympathetic to this desire for women to get credit, for women to gain access. But by bringing out the aspects of Halberstam's project that ally her to the tradition of equality feminism, I mean both to recognize her feminism and to call attention to a key weakness of this often assimilationist strategy: its desire for recognition within established paradigms and its failure therefore to get much critical leverage on them. On the one hand, by claiming for women a category more often understood, even by those who would deconstruct it, as the exclusive birthright of biological men, Halberstam takes the project of denaturalizing masculinity an important step further. Uncoupling "masculinity" from male bodies clinches the point that those qualities clustered under this rubric are no more essential than a swagger or a pair of boxers. Just as drag queens play out the performative character of femininity, so the drag kings Halberstam discusses show that masculinity too is merely masquerade (239).

On the other hand, as I see it, *Female Masculinity* debiologizes masculinity while leaving its *content* more or less intact. This is my main problem with Halberstam: that she legitimates the "masculinity" of a few women without sufficiently interrogating what masculinity means and whether, indeed, it means anything unless opposed to a subordinated "feminine." For although Halberstam rightly notes that butches hardly accede to the privileges of masculine men, she often seems not only to covet these privileges but to covet them *as masculine* (271–72)—marking them as off-limits to those many women (and few men) who remain identified with "femininity." Indeed, within Halberstam's discourse, "masculinity" continues to be characterized by power, aggression, and toughness, while "femininity" continues to be needed as a foil category, understood in relation to a masculine norm as greater passivity, receptivity, and vulnerability. Moreover, if the positive aspect of this masculinity (strength) is still reserved for some and denied to others, the negative aspect (domination) is noted but never definitively discarded.

The key question for me, then, is whether or not Halberstam's female masculinities are substantially different from dominant masculinities in their gender effects. In particular, to what extent can we see them as extricated from masculinist views of women and femininity? At times Halberstam attempts to answer this question, but her formulations tend to waver, and her polemic is pitched in strong opposition to lesbian feminists who accuse manly women of sexism (9). A butch character in *Goldeneye*, for example, who is more masculine but less sexist than James Bond, is celebrated for proving that "sexism and misogyny are not necessarily part and parcel of masculinity." Or are they? Halberstam ends this sentence by hastily adding, "even though historically it has become difficult, if not impossible, to untangle masculinity from the oppression of women" (4). A few pages later, she concedes that "sometimes female masculinity coincides with the excesses of male supremacy, and sometimes it coincides with a unique form of social rebellion" (9). Now this, in my view, is for once a sufficient assessment of the risk involved in recuperating masculinity, however variously embodied by women. It is a risk that should continually inform her subsequent readings of female husbands, inversion discourse, stone butches, transgender butches, butches on film, and drag kings. Halberstam goes on immediately, however, to describe the book as affirming new genders "not by subverting masculine power or taking up a position against masculine power but by turning a blind eye to conventional masculinities and refusing to engage" (9). Such a tactic of disengagement strikes me as evasive and, above all, as untenable. Conventional masculinities engage us whether or not we choose to entertain them; accordingly, what I find in Halberstam, as with my other "cool men," is an ongoing tension between claims to dismantle conventional gender hierarchies and passages that either assume or reaffirm these very hierarchies.

To demonstrate this tension, I begin with Halberstam's critique of a conservative mode of female-to-male transsexuality. In this mode, the transsexual man distinguishes himself from butches and distances himself from homosexuality by avoiding the subcultural markers of jeans, leather, and punk hair in favor of preppiness and heteronormativity. Advice on how to achieve this respectable look circulates on the Internet, and Halberstam remarks that "these tips, obviously, steer the transsexual man away from transgression or alternative masculine styles and toward a conservative masculinity. One wonders whether another list of tips should circulate advising transsexual men of how not to be mistaken for straight, or worse a Republican or a banker" (156–57). Of course, I agree completely with Halberstam on the demerits of this transsexual conservatism; nevertheless, I want to unsettle the easy opposition she sets up between "Republican" and "alternative" masculinities. It seems to me that Halberstam is able to spin female masculinity in a revisionary direction in part because leather-wearing butches evoke a rebellious rather than buttoned-down way of being male. As Jenni Olson writes in the epigraph to Halberstam's chapter 5, "I turned to Marlon Brando and James Dean as my models of butchness" (175). Female masculinity is aligned, in other words, with a specifically *cool* masculinity, and Halberstam's implication in this paragraph is that girls who are boys who are bad boys are self-evidently transgressive— in effect, twice removed from the passing, normalized FTM banker.[25] Yet by now it should be clear that cool masculinity does not necessarily dissent from received gender views and may, on the contrary, be produced by rebellion against a maternalized feminine. In the passage cited above, Halberstam claims as "alternative" a cool male style of defiance by butches, when in fact this style may be quite consonant with "conventional" male contempt for femininity. I realize that Halberstam would caution against equating a girl in rebel drag with the average male teen. But I would caution in turn against simply assuming, as Halberstam does more often than not, that female masculinity—whether in the style of a Brando or a Bush—automatically empties masculinity of its sexism.

Halberstam's last chapter, centered on women and boxing, is called "Raging Bull (Dyke): New Masculinities." Reinforcing the book's major arguments, it illustrates the slippage I see between, on the one hand, Halberstam's desire for masculinities that are fundamentally new in the sense of rejecting male domination and, on the other hand, her willingness to celebrate masculinities designated "new" simply because they are female—however unreconstructed they remain in other respects. As its title suggests, more than any other chapter, this final one advocates the remaking of masculinity by women, asking "not what do female masculinities borrow from male masculinities, but rather what do men borrow from butches?" *Female Masculinities* closes by optimistically suggesting that butches might "transform the mechanisms of masculinity" for men as well as women (276). Using boxing as an example, it speculates that the masculine woman, though formidable in the ring, may serve nonetheless to ironize the masochism of "taking it like a man" (276). Less willing than a man stoically to accept abuse, she may also be less willing to abuse others: "more likely," says Halberstam, "to give than to take" (276). The manly woman may be, in short, a fighter less likely to fight—inclined, rather, to express her rage through "writing and other forms of cultural production" (276).

This critique of male violence, the desire for women to imbue "masculinity" with the ability to "give" or nurture, finds Halberstam gesturing unexpectedly toward the difference feminism popular among an earlier generation of lesbians, and to me it's a compelling gesture. These last few wishful paragraphs are, however, rather inconsistent with the selection of boxing as a figure for female masculinity in the first place. After all, this chapter is not about women who write or paint; it's about women adept at snapping a nose or taking out an eye. In this sense it works better as an "equality" argument, scorning tenderness while claiming physical strength, skill, courage, and even aggression for women; in spite of my ambivalence about boxing, I can definitely appreciate the way professional female fighters deliver a knock-out punch to notions of female fragility. And yet, infuriatingly, when Halberstam champions her boxers for their fierceness, she does so not to explode our limited sense of the "feminine" but rather to reiterate the

usual identification of fierceness with "masculinity." Thus she strongly disagrees with a boxer who—in what might be seen as a bold act of revision—
understands her skills in the ring "as an expression of a true femininity"
(271). Dismissing as simple homophobia this effort to reconceive boxing as
"feminine," Halberstam herself verges on gynophobia in her absolute refusal
to do so. Understandably perhaps, she is most concerned with flagging the
way protestations of "femininity" endeavor to allay homosexual panic in the
sweaty world of women's sports. But surely we do more profound and
longer-term epistemological damage—benefiting women of all genders—
when we admire a mean, hulking, well-muscled fighter not for being like a
man but for being like a woman.

It is one thing to pause over the vindicating moment, whose thrill I share,
when women defy their traditional role and, with the constraints of this role
still fully visible, break out into the more expansive territory of the traditionally masculine. This is the moment when "female masculinity," retain-
ing its oxymoronic force, is usefully disorienting and politically transforma-
tive. "Female masculinity" is also, of course, a place where people live, and
I know that Halberstam means primarily to validate it as such. But I still regret that her analysis tends to get stuck here, refusing the next obvious step
of attacking the binary logic by which "masculinity" is kept afloat.[26] Instead
she argues that attributes such as athleticism—rather than being degendered
and made available to women on that basis—should be extended to women
specifically and only "as masculinity" (272). For me such an unrelenting
emphasis threatens to idealize and even to renaturalize a mode of "masculinity" that remains invested in its own priority and exclusivity.[27] To the
extent that this occurs, "masculinity" slides back into and becomes indis-
tinguishable from an essential notion of "maleness."

Halberstam's comments on "tomboyism" show her once again willing to
demand greater freedom for girls and women only under the sign of masculinity. Of course it is true that the box for "boys" in our culture is far
more spacious than the box for "girls." So it makes sense that girls—
whether in the films Halberstam cites or on the playground—might choose
to resist the constraints of femininity by copping boyness. But if the culture
generally has regarded girls who run, shout, and get dirty as "tomboys," if
such girls are routinely, confusingly, and painfully mistaken for boys (as
Halberstam relates having been) (19), this is only an indication of how crip-
plingly narrow the category of girlness has been. Again, it is one thing for

Image of female masculinity cited by Judith Halberstam. Jeanette Goldstein in James Cameron's *Aliens* (1986).

Halberstam to recuperate these girls and their ambitions, quite another to reproduce rather un-selfconsciously the 1950s logic of "tomboyness," with its redundant insistence on appropriated masculinity, as if second-wave feminism had not begun to give us a language for affirming active, powerful girls as girls. Refusing this language, Halberstam is able to legitimate some girls in the name of boyness but only, as I have said, by calling upon and reinforcing the ideology of male entitlement.

Halberstam says that "tomboys" for her are not male impersonators but members of a "preadolescent gender within which the adult imperatives of binary gender have not yet taken hold" (299)—a statement that would seem to be belied by the very concept of "tomboyism," which so strongly depends on notions of binary gender to identify certain girls as boyish. Yet Halberstam is enabled to make such a claim by her apparent sense that boyness, as opposed to girlness, is somehow untouched by the imperatives of gender— more neutral, natural, free-standing, and normative. She goes so far as to wish that "masculinity were a kind of default category for children," so that girls would be freer to play sports, build things, etc. (269). The problems with this formulation are telling. To see masculinity as a liberating "default category" is, first of all, to ignore its real limitations (love of domination, denial of vulnerability, etc.), which are formative and operative long before adolescence. Second, it offers further evidence that at some level Halberstam regards "masculinity" as *prior* to "femininity," preexisting and fundamental, as if it were not a fraught social construct in its own right so much as a presocial paradise from which girls are unfairly expelled.

I find a similar implication in her use—or nonuse—of denaturalizing quotation marks around "masculinity." After the first sentence of the opening chapter, they drop away almost entirely, with the effect of suggesting, often against the grain of her poststructuralist argument, that masculinity is just out there, knowable and graspable. It is true that "femininity," though referenced far less frequently, also tends to appear uncorseted by quotation marks. But Halberstam's asymmetrical handling of these categories can be seen, for example, in her discussion of the stone butch, who "has made the roughness of gender into a part of her identity." As Halberstam explains, "Where sex and gender, biology and gender presentation, fail to match (female body and masculine self), where appearance and reality collide (appears masculine and constructs a real masculinity where there should be a 'real' femininity), this is where the stone butch emerges as viable, powerful, and affirmative" (126). Note that halfway through the sentence, the opposition between a deep, plausible femininity ("sex," "biology," "female body") and a shallow, implausible masculinity ("gender," "gender presentation," "masculine self") is inverted. The stone butch who only "appears masculine" is suddenly granted a real and viable masculinity, while femininity is not only displaced but also cast into doubt by the quotation marks setting off its "reality." The polemical intervention here, though useful in validating the stone butch, is achieved by asserting the "truth" of "masculinity" over against a more fraudulent "femininity."

In other words, just as Edelman begins by seeing the sexual actors in Freud's primal scene as ambiguously gendered but ultimately rewrites them as male, so Halberstam begins by unmooring masculinity, allowing it to circulate among a few women as well as men, only finally to anchor and recenter it as the real and normative. For a final instance of the way Halberstam's language effects this recentering, we need look no further than the title of her book, in which the noun "masculinity" is modified by the adjective "female," so that the substantive status given over to masculinity is clearly announced. Contrast Halberstam's "female masculinity" to Esther Newton's "mannish lesbian" or Pat Califia's "macho slut," and we see that Halberstam has not only abstracted butchness away from the body of a particular "lesbian" or "slut" but also, at a grammatical level, reversed Newton and Califia by subordinating the "femaleness" of this body to its "masculinity."

We might also compare the stability of Halberstam's "female masculinity" to the ambiguity of "he-she," a term favored by Leslie Feinberg's butch narrator in *Stone Butch Blues*, in which "he" can slip between being the first half of a compound noun and being (especially when spoken) an adjective characterizing "she." Halberstam might have achieved a similar ambiguity with the title of her final chapter, "Raging Bull (Dyke)," which offers to rewrite the noun "bull" (in "raging bull") as a modifier for "dyke" (in "bull dyke"). In fact, however, "dyke" thus bracketed is represented less as the featured subject of this chapter than as a parenthetical add-on. In *Gender Trouble*, Judith Butler famously gives the example of a lesbian femme who, by liking "her boys to be girls," places the "figure" of masculine identity against the "ground" of the female body. Butler observes that this relation between "masculine figure" and "female ground" is readily reversed by women who "prefer that their girls be boys," and the point of her discussion is to stress "the destabilization of both terms as they come into erotic interplay" (123).

Juxtaposed in this way, Butler continues, masculine and feminine, figure and ground, "lose their internal stability and distinctness from each other. . . . Neither can lay claim to 'the real,' although either can qualify as an object of belief" (123). While Halberstam would probably subscribe to this view, in *Female Masculinity*, gender is rarely such a vertiginous Escher print, in which figure can become ground can become figure. Rather, Halberstam likes, quite simply, for her girls to be boys (as the subjects of her book if not the objects of her desire). Female masculinity is so fervently and exclusively believed in that it does indeed lay claim to "the real," as if masculinity were the only possible ground.

As I say, it is not the compromised poststructuralism of this view that bothers me but rather the content of its essentialism, which echoes traditional gender relations by so strongly preferring an athletic, unhampered "masculine" to a clumsy and confined "feminine." Complementing this preference is Halberstam's deliberate choice to ignore female and male femininity, which she argues are already "accorded far more attention today than female masculinity" (273).[28] I hope my chapter so far has succeeded in qualifying this claim, and I would close this section by adding that Halberstam, when she does not ignore the feminine, tends to understand it in relation to procreative norms and obligations. "Presumably," she says in her closing pages, "female masculinity threatens the institution of motherhood: I suppose people think that if female masculinity is widely approved, then no one will want to take responsibility for the trials and pains of reproduction" (273). Like Lee Edelman, Halberstam takes for granted here that *female* femininity means, first and foremost, the purely instrumental, conventional, undesirable, and asexual work of reproduction.

We see this same unexamined view at work when Halberstam discusses the punitive ending of the Robert Aldrich film, *The Killing of Sister George* (1968). Abandoned by her lover, the butch actress George is further humiliated by losing her job and being offered the part of a cow's voice on a children's show. "The final reduction of butch to 'cow' or nonhuman also suggests a gross oversimplification of complex individuality" (183), Halberstam comments. Subsequent sentences stress George's relegation to the "nonhuman and nonverbal," but do nothing to unpack the gender logic of George's debasement, which is not only dehumanizing but also specifically feminizing. Halberstam is right, of course, to protest the homophobia of George's tragic ending, but I wish she had noticed and protested the unspoken equation here between emasculation and animalization not as rutting dog or raging bull but, in keeping with gender conventions, as placidly lactating cow.[29] Declining to take this bull by the horns, Halberstam lets stand the implication that feminine women exist largely at an animal level of reproductive function. As with Edelman, for Halberstam a certain kind of "masculinity" is the space of freedom from such biological imperatives, and we have seen that she is tempted to equate it with freedom from social imperatives as well.

My project has been to document and break up the binary that puts femininity, reproduction, and normativity on one side and masculinity, sexuality, and queer resistance on the other. I have offered the hybrid categories of "queer pregnancy" and "sodomitical maternity," hoping to scramble and confuse these polarities. In my final pages, I'd like to offer a third such notion, closely related to the other two, which I call the "butch maternal." By claiming the "maternal" (as opposed to "parental"), I realize I run the risk of once again naturalizing the tie between women and caretaking, as if men were not obligated and qualified to do this important work (and women could do nothing but). The last thing I want to do is to let men off this particular hook or deprive them of this particular pleasure; nor do I wish to re-sanctify maternity as the highest form of womanhood. But given what I have argued throughout *Cool Men*—that many left aesthetic and academic approaches today assert their oppositional status in relation to a demonized "mother"—I want to close by intervening in this logic and redeeming, for political rather than biological reasons, the specifically female parent. There are, in addition, ethical reasons to affirm, for women and men, the *content* of what Sara Ruddick has called "maternal thinking," in direct contrast to the qualities claimed by Halberstam when she celebrates "masculinity" and its back-slapping approach to parenting (and intimacy generally). At the same time, however, I count on the term "butch" to keep the "maternal" from being reenshrined as simply domestic, emotional, self-sacrificing, asexual, and necessarily biological. Furthermore, I intend for the converse to be true as well: that placing "maternal" in conjunction with "butch" will complicate and critique the female masculinity held up by Halberstam. As we have seen, she underscores masculinity to an extent aptly figured by the term "tomboy," with its twofold referencing of masculinity. I find a similar redundancy in the understanding of "stone butch" elaborated in her chapter on Leslie Feinberg's *Stone Butch Blues* (1993). Whereas Halberstam invokes this novel of transgendered development to privilege and defend the "stoneness" of Feinberg's butch protagonist, I want now to explore the same text for the way it affirms while also interrogating "stone butchness," depicts while also destabilizing the butch-femme opposition; and for the way, through its main character, it juxtaposes the figure of the butch with the figure of the mother.[30]

BUTCH MATERNITY

Feinberg's butch hero, Jess Goldberg, grows up in 1950s working-class Buffalo, New York, stigmatized by her parents and brutalized by her peers. She is mentored by older butches in the 1960s, only to be regarded with suspicion by role-rejecting lesbian feminists of the 1970s. Unable to check the box "woman" in any customary sense of the word, Jess begins to pass as a "man." As a man, she is more accepted on the factory floor, safer on the street, and more at home in her body. She remains uneasy in this identity, however, and pays the high price of losing her lesbian feminist lover, Theresa. By the end of the book, Jess has withstood numerous beatings, rapes, firings, and romantic failures; had breast reduction surgery; moved to New York City; and finally stopped taking hormones. She has also come out as a union organizer and as someone who, supported by the drag queen Ruth, is able to claim her gender ambiguity.

Certainly Feinberg's novel narrates the "hardness" of its hero. From the beginning, Jess describes herself as "stone": not a "soft" or "Saturday night" butch but a through-and-through "granite" butch, attracted to "high femme" (274), desiring to touch without being touched, appearing emotionally as well as physically impenetrable, stone in bed and stonily silent about her innermost loves and fears. The counterpart to her hardness is a nurturing, more vulnerable and expressive "femininity," embodied by figures like Ruth and Theresa, who gently bind Jess's wounds, cook for her, and offer her a refuge from factory and street. Nevertheless, in spite of their domesticity and feminine drag, these characters are also depicted admiringly by Feinberg as bold, worldly, defiant of heterosexism, and scornful of masculine condescension. As Jess remembers, "When the bigots came in [to the bar] it was time to fight, and fight we did. Fought hard—femme and butch, women and men together" (7). Jess's first lover is a sex worker named Angie, who recognizes herself in Jess's stoneness. "Usually it's me who reacts like that," she tells Jess (73). Jess's first girlfriend Milli is another "stone pro," of whom she says, "We were both a couple of tough cookies. . . . We matched each other in nerve" (106). When Jess tries to shelter Milli from the risks of sex work, she is backed up against the sink and informed by her irate lover, "Nobody tells me how to run my life, not you, not anybody" (107). Jess retreats into doing the dishes, but her lingering protectiveness eventually drives Milli away (109–13).

Theresa is not a pro, but like Milli and Angie she is a tough cookie. Soon after she and Jess meet while working at a cannery, Theresa is fired for kicking the boss who tries to harass her (121). Later she and a drag queen face down a cop who has beaten another queen; the butches stand frozen as Theresa and Georgetta wield their stiletto heels and order the cop to "leave her alone" (129). Theresa also educates Jess about the sexism of butches as well as men toward women—and about sexism toward butches as well as femmes (138–39). And finally, she leaves when Jess decides to pass as a man because for her it would mean passing as straight (151–53). Jess's last partner is Ruth, who, for all her talents as a homemaker, further complicates the category of "femme" through her biological maleness, her transgressive, stigmatized womanhood. Holding her, Jess comments, "I'd never held a body larger than mine before" (256). Ruth does not tolerate being patronized any more than Milli or Theresa. "Do I look weak to you?" she snaps, when Jess offers to carry her groceries. Continuing Theresa's lessons in feminism, Ruth adds, "Where I come from . . . men don't reward women for pretending to be helpless" (248). Later she gives Jess books on queer history, just as Theresa gave her books on women's liberation.

If femmes like Theresa and Ruth revise "femininity" by tying it to personal and political fierceness, they further break down the binary logic of butch-femme by bringing out Jess's softer side. Ruth immediately inverts gender norms by bringing our butch hero flowers. "I've brought women flowers," Jess says wonderingly, "but no woman ever gave me flowers before. It's a beautiful thing to do" (252). The two neighbors exchange music as well as flowers, and "after a while," Jess confesses, "we exchanged our tears and our frustrations" (255). Ruth paints a watercolor of Jess's face "filled with emotion" (267), and it seems an apt figure for the way she helps Jess's feelings seep to the surface, making them fluid and visible. Jess is not quite correct, then, when she writes in her unsent letter to Theresa, "only you could melt this stone" (11). While Theresa first enables Jess openly to express her fears, loves, and lusts (130–33), Ruth too causes Jess to thaw and overflow. Of course Theresa and Ruth love Jess's performance of butchness, but my point is also their role in articulating her "femme" emotionality.[31] Interestingly, both women explicitly identify Jess with femaleness as well as masculinity. Theresa does so pointedly as a caution against misogyny ("think about it sweetheart—you are a woman"), whereas Ruth does so inadvertently ("I referred to you as s*he*. I wasn't thinking"), but either way the effect, without canceling her butchness or her stoneness, is to supplement her masculinity (139, 263).

Toward the end of the novel, there is a moving scene between Jess and her butch friend Frankie, which further dramatizes not only Jess's reluctance to be "touched" but also the willingness of both character and author to reimagine the butch ideal of manly stoicism. The very structure of this dialogue challenges butch-femme protocols by invoking the butch-butch erotics of Frankie and her lover, Johnnie: first Frankie admits she had a crush on Jess, then Jess jokes about her discomfort with erotic touch, and finally Jess allows herself the refuge of Frankie's muscular arms. It's a scene in which two butches laugh about butch reticence only to end up crying and confessing a longing for "butch words to talk about butch feelings" (275). Of course the whole book, which opens as a passionate love letter to Theresa, is an intensely rendered diary of butch feelings, positive and negative. Indeed, I would argue that the title itself ends with "blues" as a way of both recognizing and countering "stone butchness." Bluesiness dignifies and aestheticizes the joys and especially sorrows of butch subjectivity, including stoneness. At the same time, it works against the stone persona by allowing and valuing vulnerability, affectivity, expressivity.

In addition to evoking Jess's feelings, Theresa and Ruth serve to locate them in the space of the domestic. Jess's involvement with each of these femmes sends her into a flurry of nesting behavior—cleaning house, buying furniture, arranging flowers, making a home (123, 252). In fact, she does this on her own in New York City as well, sanding the floors of her first apartment, picking out a rug, thick towels, and bath oils. She even "went crazy buying sheets at Macy's" (237). No wonder Annie, the lover who takes Jess for a typical man, is confused. Jess's domestic and maternal competence— her ease with dirty dishes and patience with Annie's daughter—seems even more anomalous than her selflessness in bed (187–93). For all Jess's love of motorcycles and the freedom they give her (52), it's clear to me that *Stone Butch Blues* is not a road story but a domestic one. Its most memorable scenes take place not in the street, a bar, or even the bedroom but rather in the kitchen, where Jess bonds with her lovers at the table or quarrels with them at the sink. Jay Prosser has written movingly about the urgency and difficulty of "home" for Feinberg's narrator—both in the sense of coming home to her body and, more important, in the sense of finding, or at least dreaming, a transgendered community. Agreeing with Prosser that Jess's transgender plot "is informed at all points by a longing for home" (178), I add an understanding of "home" in the most practical, domestic sense—food, flowers, sheets, and towels—and in the primal, emotional sense of relations recalling an original (though not necessarily biological) intimacy.[32]

Jess's butch domesticity brings me, finally, to what I am calling the butch maternal. Shortly after moving to New York, Jess begins to read about feminism and has a sudden realization: "The idea had never occurred to me. What would I have done if I'd gotten pregnant after a rape?" (239–40). Here Feinberg forces us as well as Jess to contemplate the nonidiomatic idea of queer pregnancy, making Jess's deeply felt and fully lived masculinity coincide with the possibility of biological maternity. For the most part, however, what interests me about *Stone Butch Blues* is its juxtaposition of Jess's butchness with maternal structures of feeling that have nothing to do with wombs or genes. We recall that Annie is amazed by Jess's understanding of and interest in her as a mother: "What really blew me away," Annie says about their first night together, "is that you knew I had to take care of my kid and you didn't demand my attention till she went to bed" (192). In fact, Jess helps care for Annie's daughter, Kathy, showing that, if she can do heavy lifting on the factory floor, she is no less skilled at the delicate emotional work, the trivial physical tasks, involved in raising kids.

She patiently gains Kathy's trust, for example, by improvising a dialogue with the child and her stuffed rabbit (187–88). The "maternal" content of their dramatic play is quite complex. As Kathy nurses her ailing rabbit, Jess participates in her world, helps her practice caretaking while, at the same time, gently exhorting Kathy as rabbit/child to get ready for bed. Jess also, in this short dinner scene, grabs a sponge and tells Kathy not to worry about a spill, casually addressing emotional and physical mess in a single gesture. Her response reassures Annie too that Jess doesn't mind eating kid food at the stop-and-go pace dictated by kid ways. The language and actions of the dinner at Annie's may be trite—it's even a bit embarrassing to recount them—but I'm trying to make them visible as part of the texture of Jess's subjectivity, because

I admire the fact that Feinberg does so. Here and elsewhere, she shows Jess in a recognizably "maternal" mode, patented by women though available to men, that involves cycles of feeding, play, interruption, cleaning, consolation, and direction. Jess enters this mode, so easily derided as "uncool," despite having "no relationship to her own uterus" (239) or, for that matter, much of a relationship to Kathy's biological mother. This is mothering outside biological mandates and familial paradigms, including lesbian ones. Nor does it preclude, for Annie or for Jess, the fevered participation in sexual acts that, given the dildo onto which Jess unrolls her condom, mock hetero contraceptive as well as reproductive practices (189–93). Like the Wolf Man's mother and her "unnatural" self-positioning, this maternal butch with her strap-on dick and sensitivity to kids shatters the logic defining queer pleasure and politics in opposition to the mother.

Lest we be tempted to dismiss Jess as merely a "sensitive man," who helps around the house but doesn't define himself through domestic labor or child care, the primacy of "mothering" for her is reiterated more than once. For example, when dreaming of what she would do in an ideal world, Jess tells Ruth: "I think I'd be a gardener in a woods just for children, and when they came by I'd sit and listen to their wonderings" (256). This is clearly not a dream of conceiving or even adopting offspring; but it is a dream of tending and attending to children as well as plants. Though surely sentimental, its picture of adult femaleness in relation to children suggests to me a queered iconography of mothers and kids that would challenge the limits of the discourse Edelman condemns in "Kid Stuff."

I am going to close with what I think of as a more concrete, extended, though finally unrealized version of this dream, a section of the book that crystalizes my sense of the butch maternal. At the center of Feinberg's text, chapter 14 comprises the interlude between Jess's decision to pass as a man and the moment when her body has been redefined by hormones, between butchness and female masculinity on the brink of transsexuality (155–69).[33] During much of this time, Jess stays with her friend Gloria and takes care of Gloria's two children, Kim and Scotty. Even as Jess reads the kids a story, her voice begins to crack and drop (169). As her figure morphs, she flouts the logic of biological ties and becomes passionately involved with someone else's progeny. As with the children in the woods, Jess's "maternal" project in relation to Scotty and Kim is to "listen to their wonderings." Scotty is an independent little soul, who easily accepts Jess's suggestion that girls can marry girls (159–60). For Kim, as an older girl, such issues are both more confusing and more urgent. Not surprisingly, the primary subject of her wonderings is Jess herself; at their first encounter, she stares at Jess as if for dear life. "Kim's face was filled with wonder," Jess remembers, "as though I was a shower of fireworks exploding in a dark sky" (156). The chapter is full of similar moments allegorizing not only the children's flexibility about gender but also, especially in Kim's case, their struggle to discard old axioms in favor of the new knowledge Jess embodies. This knowledge, I suggest, is feminist as well as queer. It involves modeling gender variation and ambiguity; paradoxically, in relation to Kim, it also involves being recognizably *female*, so that the explosive options Jess represents are made available to Kim *as a girl*. It is because she feels this special responsibility to mentor Kim, and because her investment in nurturing is so strongly marked as "feminine," that I see Jess not as a "father" or as a "father/mother," but instead as a masculine "mother."

After Jess's first night on Gloria's couch, she wakes up to Scotty asking, "Is he awake?" Kim answers this question about Jess as I believe she needs to, "Yeah . . . she is" (157). A similar double-take occurs when Jess cooks pancakes, with raisin faces sunk in the batter. "I think I found his smile," Kim says; this time it is Scotty who corrects, "That's her eye" (160). These two instances are followed by several more that likewise bend gender and at the same time—ironically in light of Jess's incipient maleness—move toward affirmations of femaleness. In a way familiar to me as a strategy of feminist parenting, Jess takes every opportunity to keep maleness from being the default category for stuffed animals, wild animals, snow figures, etc. Thus when Kim asks of an eagle at the zoo, "What's he doing?" Jess replies, "She's playing in the snow. . . . That's the girl eagle. . . . The girls are bigger than the boys" (165). Jess tries this again later, telling the kids that she's making a "snowwoman." This time Kim objects. "There's no such thing as a snowwoman," she says, sobbing until Scotty and Jess tactfully switch to the male pronoun (168). Yet later Kim tells Jess, "It's OK about it being a snowwoman," and she nods when Jess suggests they "like him or her the way she is" (168). Notice how these last sentences have it both ways: asserting at once that gender may be unstable ("him or her") if not indeterminate ("it"), and that girls can be anything they want, including snowpeople ("the way she is"). Either way, Feinberg shows us how Jess's awareness of gender performativity causes her mothering to swerve from the usual pieties.

Ironically, butch mothers may of necessity be more frankly vulnerable and fallible. Unlike the idealized mother who embodies fixity and certainty (making it all the easier for sons to rebel), Jess makes it clear that mothers don't have all the answers and can't protect their children or even themselves from all harm. Much as she wishes to, Jess cannot keep Kim and Scotty from witnessing her susceptibility to humiliation each time she crosses a street or enters a store. Breaking the news that she must leave them soon, Jess explains that she's going somewhere in order to be safe (166–67). Having shown them a different way to be gendered as well as the outrage such difference may provoke, now Jess demonstrates the need, at times, for parents to act in the interest of self-preservation. Here is another sense, then, in which butch subjectivity informs Jess's maternity—as the victim of continual violence, she is hardly in a position to sentimentalize self-sacrifice.

Heartbroken and furious, Kim begs Jess to let her come too. Jess responds to the grieving kids with a parable inspired by the eagles they've been watching at the zoo. Threatened with extinction, the world's few remaining eagles fly as high as they can. Kim and Scotty should think of her too as taking refuge in the sky and watching over them (167). Likening herself to eagles on high, Jess also ties herself to the specifically female eagle in the passage mentioned above, the large bird who "hopped down into the snow and unfolded her powerful wings." "She leaped and twirled in the snow," Jess explains. "I remembered the newspaper reported her egg had hatched last week, but the eaglet had died. I wondered if she danced in bitter grief" (165). At the very moment, then, that Jess relinquishes her female embodiment, she is imaged in relation to an eagle suffering a pointedly maternal loss. Invoking a bird and her egg, Feinberg seems to legitimate, by biologizing, Jess's own sorrow at the impending separation from her young. In effect, Jess's leaving Kim and Scotty for a place of "maleness" coincides with the naturalizing of her maternal status, even as Feinberg stresses that hers is a "butch" maternity—vulnerable, self-preserving, and revisionary. Jess promises Kim and Scotty that one day she'll come back to them, and her yearning to do so echoes throughout the last half of the novel. Several times, Jess vows to find them, remembering how "[her] coming had shaken Kim, root and branch, and [her] leaving had hurt her the most" (280). By the end of the book, Jess has accomplished many of the tasks she has set for herself, but still hasn't returned to tend the plant that is Kim. This makes me think that perhaps the "blues" in *Stone Butch Blues* is in part the butch mother's keening for her lost daughter, a narrative Feinberg hardly had to go far in the real world to find. And then again, perhaps the novel itself is a return to the daughter, in the form of a tale both inspiring and cautionary.

In the paragraphs above, I have tried to convey what I see as the maternal affect and practices of a butch protagonist more immediately legible as simply "stone." By claiming her "maternity," I have wanted to complicate an emphasis such as Halberstam's that would tie Jess's butchness primarily to masculinity, butch-femme sexuality, and untouchability. I hope I have shown that Feinberg legitimates while also questioning all of these categories, and that she accomplishes the latter largely by portraying Jess's "femme" investments in expressivity, domesticity, and children. I have also stressed Jess's role as a "mother" to Kim—by which I mean her role in offering the daughter not only transgenderedness but also empowered femaleness. At the same time, I have wanted to make clear that "butchness" crucially transforms the "maternal" as well as vice versa: modifying maternity away from the necessarily biological, away from normative family structures, away from merely instrumental sexuality, away from selflessness to the point of self-sacrifice, away from conventional "certainties" about sex/gender, and aligning it instead with a pedagogy of liking him or her the way she is.

POSTSCRIPT: DOING THE RIGHT THING

Most of these pages have been spent elaborating a hermeneutics of disapproval. Each of my chapters has suggested that second-wave feminist values, theories, and methods have simply not been taken seriously by many of those oppositional scholars and innovative artists of the 1990s who, of all people, might have been expected to seize on and elaborate them. I have written from a pressing concern that U.S. feminism, still emergent as a politics and body of knowledge, is in danger of being suppressed not as the result of disagreement within our ranks or even hostility from outside but rather as the result of systematic neglect by our ostensible allies on the cultural left. I have argued that this neglect may arise in part from a construction of left/bohemian rebellion that presumes masculinity and actually requires distance from the feminine. Now, at the end of this book, it's far too late to apologize for being cranky; too late as well to stress once again my respect for the work I criticize. It might, however, legitimately be asked after so much unhappy diagnosis, "What does this woman want?"

First, in the realm of academia, there is obviously a continued need for cultural studies that prioritize women—their representations in diverse literary and pop cultural forms, their authorial contributions to these forms, their roles in constructing race and in resisting racism, their tense and tender relations to one another—without reducing them to their gender alone or deploying a single, fixed notion of their womanhood. By now we have had not only a plethora of calls for such complex, postidentitarian readings but also many, many feminist works offering flexible, situational, intersectional analyses of gender as it functions in a particular setting. It is my opinion that, while these calls have come from all corners of the academic left, feminist scholars have generally been both more earnest and more successful in heeding them. This book has endeavored to show the difficulty left scholars often have negotiating several ideological axes at once; here I cite just a few (among dozens I could name) who offer, by contrast, models of sustained political and analytical multitasking.

In the area of postcolonial studies, I think of Anne McClintock, who studied with Edward Said. Her *Imperial Leather: Race, Gender and Sexuality in the Colonial Contest* (1995) takes for granted the interpenetration of its title categories and demonstrates, in contexts ranging from Victorian England to modern South Africa, their continual tendency to overlap with and code one another. Angela McRobbie, as I note in my discussion of Andrew Ross, has done a great deal to revise British cultural studies paradigms, contesting definitions of "subculture" that cannot account for the practices of female youth. Her diachronic study of girls' magazines, *Feminism and Youth Culture: From "Jackie" to "Just Seventeen"* (1991), takes off from earlier Birmingham Centre ethnographies, sharing their interest in class while correcting for their focus on boys. Tania Modleski—from her landmark *Loving With a Vengeance* (1982) to her recent collection of essays (1998)—can also be counted on for complex feminist readings of contemporary culture: for a critique of masculinities (including the academic), for insight into movies knotting ideas about race/gender/sexuality, and for a principled focus on women.

When it comes to race studies I look to such figures as Deborah McDowell and to Phillip Brian Harper. McDowell's *"The Changing Same"* (1995) not only recovers and reads black women's writing but also develops a race/gender metacriticism: stringent parsings of commentaries from mainstream reviews to works of high theory. I likewise admire Harper's *Are We Not Men?* (1996) for its bold interrogations of race, gender, and sexuality as normative categories—their interaction with one another and their function together in producing a black masculinity panicked about the "feminine." Harper's book moves us into queer theory, an area in which I have already cited the feminist writings of Teresa de Lauretis and Biddy Martin. De Lauretis, in *The Practice of Love* (1994) and elsewhere, has eloquently protested the erasure of lesbianism within feminist and queer theory alike.

Poststructuralist feminist of long standing, she has elucidated gender as a so-cial "technology," even while refusing to disappear the female body and its same-sex desires. As chapter 6 makes clear, I also value Martin's essays in *Femininity Played Straight* (1996) for their disclosure of the operation of sex-ual difference within queer theory, for their defense, too, of queer invest-ments in interiority, attachment, and sociality. All of these texts find a us-able feminist past while bringing feminism into dialogue with exciting new work in other spheres of left inquiry. It seems to me they are doing the right thing and challenge the rest of us to do likewise.

Finally, a few more general thoughts about what I want as an antidote to coolness. We have seen in chapter after chapter the anxious disavowal of the domestic and maternal: in Tarantino's use of violence to dispel intimacy and debunk a domestic realism; in Said's taking of Austen's domestic novels to stand for European imperialism; in Ross's iconography of the mother as con-ventional and domineering; in Gates's various narratives of mastering and fi-nally rejecting the mother's legacy; and in Edelman's willingness to ignore maternal sexuality. Instead of this contempt for the mother as uncool, I want to question a masculinity overinvested in youth, fearful of the mutable flesh, and on the run from intimacy. I want to claim, in its place, the jouissance of a body that is aging, pulpy, no longer intact. I want to insist on female pleas-ure generally and especially that putative oxymoron, maternal pleasure (sodomitical or otherwise). As my defense of Feinberg's sentimentality sug-gests, I want a subject who is tender-hearted and (disregarding Said) quite possibly maudlin; who is neither too hard nor too fluid for attachment; who does the banal, scarcely narratable, but helpful things that "moms" do. I want an excess of feeling not over the purity of little hothouse children but over the high rate of queer teen suicide. I want the decline of the domestic as a separate, inherently female sphere and the vindication of domesticity as an ethic, an affect, an aesthetic, and a public.

We have also seen the repeated association of masculinity with "true" op-positional politics: in Lee's and Gates's equation of a street-toughened viril-ity with authentic blackness; in Said's choice of male narratives to articulate resistance to colonialism; in Ross's privileging of guys who play soccer or read porn as rebels against bourgeois protocols; in queer theory's identifica-tion of gay male sexuality with the sexily antinormative. In such contexts, women, bizarrely, have been taken to represent the forces of conventionality and conservatism, and of course I want to dispute these gendered political paradigms. In fact, like the bad boy and the good poststructuralist, I too am committed to breaking rules, exploding received categories—but not in a way that amounts to a formalism, transgression for its own sake. I want kids and theorists, rather, to make moral discriminations in their trashings, and to be capable as well of close, unironic engagement with the world. I realize that many of these things—scholarly attention to women and gender; defense of practices and values marked as feminine; political outrage and agency for women—were on our list of feminist demands back in the early 1980s, when we asked for them under the sign of a recuperated "femininity." Perhaps there is less risk of gender essentialism if, reinventing feminist critique for the twenty-first century, we ask for them now under the canceled sign of cool masculinity.

NOTES

PREFACE: THE UNCOOL MOTHER

1. For other recent discussions of coolness, see Thomas Frank's *The Conquest of Cool: Business Culture, Counterculture, and the Rise of Hip Consumerism* (1997), David Pountain and David Robins's *Cool Rules: Anatomy of an Attitude* (2000), and Lewis MacAdams's *The Birth of Cool: Beat, Bebop, and the American Avant-Garde* (2001).

2. But see Kate Weigand's *Red Feminism: American Communism and the Making of Women's Liberation* (2001), which argues that Eleanor Flexner, Gerda Lerner, Susan B. Anthony (grandniece of the nineteenth-century feminist), and others were able to develop feminist views *within* the Communist Party/Old Left of the 1950s. Refusing the term "feminist" (tainted by the middle-class politics of the National Woman's Party), these women nevertheless articulated a critique of male supremacy as well as racism and capitalism, which Weigand sees as having laid the groundwork for second-wave feminism (and, I would add, for what we now call intersectional analysis). In keeping with my own emphasis, however, Weigand admits that "progressive women's struggles of the 1940s and 1950s did not even come close to eradicating gender inequality among American Communists and their supporters. Throughout those decades the Communist Party and the progressive Left continued to perpetuate many of the discriminatory attitudes and policies toward women that Anthony and the others set out to change" (2–3).

3. For an extended critique of Engels and Bebel on women see Lise Vogel, *Marxism and the Oppression of Women: Toward a Unitary Theory* (1983), 73–103.

4. Here I might also mention women's continual difficulty in making their voices heard within the labor movement. On union sexism in the United States,

especially before the 1960s, see Nelson Lichtenstein, *State of the Union: A Century of American Labor* (2002), 88–97; and Elizabeth Faue, *Community of Suffering and Struggle: Women, Men, and the Labor Movement in Minneapolis, 1915–1945* (1991). Two more texts (both products of Thatcher's Britain) are helpful on the masculine bias of socialist iconography. See Julia Swindells and Lisa Jardine, *What's Left? Women in Culture and the Labour Movement* (1990) on the influence, for example, of George Orwell's miners in imaging the heroic worker (and "work" itself) as male (1–23). *Male Order: Unwrapping Masculinity*, ed. Rowena Chapman and Jonathan Rutherford (1988), argues likewise that socialism has been "underpinned by a particular heterosexual masculinity" and goes on to assert: "That man's world, the paternal objective authority of Fabianism and *The New Statesman*, the pub culture of the Working Man, is no longer tenable" (12–13). Rutherford's own essay in this volume names "the clenched fist, the haranguing oration, the rhetoric of fighting and struggling" as other examples of the Left's "strongly masculine tone" (42–46); Rutherford's subsequent discussion of men in flight from the maternal body is relevant here as well (47–52).

5. For more on the relation between mid-century abolitionism and feminism, especially Douglass's shifting views on the woman question, see *Frederick Douglass on Women's Rights*, ed. Philip S. Foner (1976), 3–48.

6. Charles Payne, in *I've Got the Light of Freedom: The Organizing Tradition and the Mississippi Freedom Struggle* (1995), points out that feminist complaints about SNCC in general and Carmichael in particular have recently been contested, or at least qualified (470). Moreover, Payne's own attention to networks of local activists over national leaders, everyday movement work over dramatic public events, underlines the important and even dominant role played by women in organizing the rural South, especially in the early 1960s (265–78). At the same time, Payne's revisionary approach is in part necessitated by the fact that women were far less visible than men in the movement leadership, particularly in the SCLC (Southern Christian Leadership Conference). Noting Dr. King's "inability to treat women as equals," Payne explains that "women within SCLC circles were expected to neither ask nor answer questions" (76). On anxieties about masculinity underpinning Black Nationalism see Michele Wallace, *Black Macho and the Myth of the Superwoman* (1979), and Phillip Brian Harper, *Are We Not Men? Masculine Anxiety and the Problem of African-American Identity* (1996), 39–53.

7. Both Ehrenreich in *The Hearts of Men: American Dreams and the Flight from Commitment* (1983) and Alice Echols in *Shaky Ground: The '60s and Its Aftershocks* (2002) regard men's flight from domesticity in the 1950s and 1960s more positively than I do—as an interrogation, if not of gender inequality, then at least of traditional masculinity. Echols sees the Beats and their New Left successors as "promoting a counterhegemonic (though not feminist) understanding of masculinity." And she adds: "I suspect male new leftists' admiration for the radical

sociologist C. Wright Mills had as much to do with his leather jacket and BMW motorcycle and their evocation of an unfettered, unmanaged masculinity as it did with his excoriation of the white-collar world and his trenchant critiques of functionalism and anti-communism" (*Shaky* 67). Her description of Mills's appeal illustrates nicely what I mean by cool masculinity: the way full rebel drag (leather jacket and motorcycle) is tied up with—and central to the allure of—left politics. Although this "counterhegemonic" masculinity may well protest middle-class mores and sometimes, as in Allen Ginsberg's case, heterosexual ones, I would argue that it does so in part by *feminizing* and *maternalizing* that which it abjects. In this sense, more than merely "not feminist," the Beat/New Left rejection of bourgeois manhood actually reproduces misogynist gender codes.

8.   See also Ann Pellegrini's argument that, while detractors of the star system often accusingly cite Judith Butler, Gayatri Spivak, and Eve Sedgwick, these women are known only to a small coterie. The rare female academic with name recognition beyond the university is more likely to be celebrated for *attacking* these women along with feminist studies—the obvious case in point being Camille Paglia ("Star Gazing" 213). Certainly Paglia supports my point that degree of stardom coincides, in part, with degree of male identification. For Pellegrini's essay and several others mentioned above, see the "Academostars" issue of *The Minnesota Review* (52 [4] [2001]).

1. QUENTIN TARANTINO: ANATOMY OF COOL

1.   Page numbers for *Reservoir Dogs* refer to the Grove Press screenplay (1994); for *Pulp Fiction*, they refer to the Hyperion screenplay (1994).

2.   See Gary Indiana for more on Tarantino himself as a white hipster in love with blackness (64–65); see Sharon Willis on the way white oedipal anxieties in Tarantino's films turn on images of black masculinity (198–216). Critics who have theorized this racial dynamic in more general terms include Andrew Ross in *No Respect: Intellectuals and Popular Culture* (1989), 65–101; Eric Lott in *Love and Theft: Blackface Minstrelsy and the American Working Class* (1993); and Kobena Mercer in *Welcome to the Jungle: New Positions in Black Cultural Studies* (1994), 171–219.

3.   See Gary Indiana, bell hooks, Robin Wood, and especially Jeanne Silverthorne (all in the March 1995 *Artforum*) for incisive comments on Tarantino's typical mistreatment or nontreatment of female characters. Of course Tarantino's 1997 movie *Jackie Brown*, starring blaxploitation star Pam Grier, represents a welcome departure from this pattern. Less anxious than his earlier films to distance and trivialize the feminine, *Jackie Brown* is also a departure in narrative style—without the "adrenaline shot" patterning of violence I discuss here—and this would seem to support my thesis about the emotional work the shot accomplishes for *Pulp Fiction*. I am not surprised that when Tarantino decides to explore female agency he does so through the figure of an African American

woman, since blackness for him so strongly connotes masculinity. Indeed, while *Rum Punch* (the Elmore Leonard novel on which *Jackie Brown* is based) features a white woman named Jackie Burke, Tarantino pointedly darkens her to "Jackie Brown." Given his understanding of race/gender, this revision would go some distance to mitigate and embolden Jackie's femininity. See note 8 below on Bonnie, the only black woman in *Pulp Fiction*, who is similarly masculinized (though only up to a point) by virtue of her race.

4. Tarantino himself speaks lovingly of musical sequences in Godard films that "come out of nowhere," describing them as "so infectious, so friendly." Yet the sweetness for him is explicitly tied to their sudden appearance and, then, disappearance—as if the point were a rehearsal of loss. Recounting his disappointment when the music stops in *Le Petit Soldat*, Tarantino says of *Pulp Fiction*: "I learned that for this film, don't let it linger" (Dargis 18).

5. Charles Deemer, himself a screenwriter, has also noted what he calls the "shock transitions" peculiar to a Tarantino script. Almost always moments of extreme violence, they are heightened by their alternation with "talky" scenes of an interest and length more common to the stage than the screen (61). Deemer's discussion of *Reservoir Dogs*, *True Romance*, and *Natural Born Killers* as well as *Pulp Fiction* suggests that all four of these screenplays share the technique Tarantino introduced with *Dogs*: "a rhythm that fluctuates between shock and leisure, leisure and shock" (63). Though Deemer's interest is primarily formal, he notes in passing that banter in Tarantino is the "playful veneer" of scenes whose "real meaning" lies in their suddenly ensuing violence (63). In other words, he faithfully reproduces what I argue is Tarantino's own implication that intimate small talk is superficial, while violence is the underlying "real."

6. This logic is, of course, even more desperately manifest in the Bonnie and Clyde couples of *True Romance* (1993) and *Natural Born Killers* (1994), suggesting that Tarantino finds it easier to swallow heterosexual love when chased by strong doses of slaughter.

7. Citing their self-conscious haircuts, preppy effeteness, and cohabitation, David Miller suggested to me that the guys behind the closed door may themselves be coded as gay; if so, their murders would be an even more inevitable climax to Vincent's teasing of Jules. Nor is it a coincidence that, in both *Reservoir Dogs* and *Pulp Fiction*, the most over-the-top brutal scenes (Mr. Blond torturing the cop and Zed raping Marsellus) are tied into implied or overt homosexuality, so that violence functions to deny (and, by the perverse logic of *Liebestod*, to effect) an intimacy between men. I discuss this further below. For more on gayness in *Reservoir Dogs* see Robert Hilferty's excellent review; Cynthia Baughman and Richard Moran also comment insightfully on the gay desire behind Butch's story in *Pulp Fiction* (114). Finally, given the frequent association of vampires with both male and female homoeroticism, Tarantino's use of this trope in his screenplay for *From Dusk Till Dawn* (1996) is relevant here as well, especially given the fraternal bonding at the center of this exceptionally violent film.

8. Hooks and Silverthorne both note that Bonnie, the sole black woman in *Pulp Fiction*, "has no face . . . we see her only from the back" (hooks 64). In Silverthorne's fictional conversation, the Patricia Arquette character further speculates, "So you're saying that by making a black woman signify purity and righteous revenge, Quentin is resolving his guilt about his dialogue's disgust with blacks and women?" (108). While I agree entirely with the spirit of these remarks, I would note that being seen from the back typically corresponds to power in *Pulp Fiction*—the face's open expressivity threatening, I suppose, to undermine coolness. Marsellus and The Wolf, for example, are both glimpsed for the first time from the back, and Marsellus doesn't actually show his face until the episode culminating with his rape (119). In fact, Tarantino's equation of facelessness with power may derive from that scene, when the rapist's visible back indicates his dominant position (129). The shot of Zed's thrusting backside also, however, reveals his own (soon-to-be-demonstrated) penetrability—just as the Band-Aid on the back of Marsellus's phallic neck has earlier suggested the ever-present threat of castration. For more on male precariousness, see below. As for Bonnie, the point would therefore be less her facelessness than her unreality—the fact that she appears only as a figment of the men's fears, that her power is never more than hypothetical. Finally, I would recall that, as with Jackie Brown, in Tarantino's imaginary Bonnie's blackness naturally makes her a more "phallic" female than her white counterpart.

9. "Guys look cool in black suits," he explains, "but what's interesting is how they get reconstructed during the course of the movie. . . . Their suits get more and more fucked up until they're stripped off and the two are dressed in the exact antithesis—volleyball wear, which is not cool" (Dargis 17).

10. We do know, however, that Jules will be destitute in his virtue—as Vincent sneers, "You're gonna be like those pieces of shit out there who beg for change" (174)—leading bell hooks to observe that *Pulp Fiction* seems to posit black poverty as the only alternative to black criminality. Jules's fate, she argues, smacks more of racism than redemption (108). A punitive racial politics is still more insistent in Tarantino's finale to *Four Rooms* (1995). Here a black man bets his little finger against a vintage car; when he inevitably loses, the cleaver falls as if to punish him for coveting a white man's wealth. Once again, *Jackie Brown* represents an exception; this time, for a change, the black heroine gets to walk away from her life of petty crime with close to half a million dollars and a ticket to Spain. (Even more surprising and to Tarantino's credit, her triumph could but doesn't turn out to require the clinching of her romance with Max Cherry.)

11. At the beginning of her book on 1940s films, Mary Ann Doane notes the frequent use of Freudian scenarios such as the Fort!/Da! game to talk about film spectatorship and stresses the gender specificity of this seemingly neutral scenario: "The implications are clearly greatest for masculine subjectivity" (14). Tania Modleski (in *The Women Who Knew Too Much: Hitchcock and Feminist Theory*) makes a similar point about Kaja Silverman's use of Fort!/Da!: while

Silverman describes the masochistic pleasure movie viewers—male and female alike—take in experiencing a loss of plenitude "through the agency of the cut," Modleski insists that men respond not simply with pleasure but rather with ambivalence to a dynamic rendering them passive and thus "female" (*Women* 12–13). I follow Modleski in emphasizing what she goes on to call a "dialectic of identification and dread in the male spectator's response to femininity" (13), the upshot of which is reasserted masculinity and reconsolidated gender norms. I also obviously agree with Modleski, Doane, and other feminist film critics that spectatorship as well as the psychoanalytic paradigms used to theorize it are strongly marked by gender.

12. Actually—according to the fawning, semiliterate, and occasionally useful biography by Wensley Clarkson—groupies argue the weapon belongs not to Vincent but to Marsellus, who has gone to get coffee (223).

13. Two biographical anecdotes are irresistible here, for each shows Tarantino quite clearly using narratives of violence to manage anxiety about close ties to women. In the first, he is only nine and ten years old: for two successive Mother's Days, he presents his mother with carefully written, first-person accounts of a character named Quentin whose mother, at the end of the story, dies (Clarkson 24). Gone! The second anecdote involves the adult Tarantino, already an acclaimed writer/director, describing the importance of bringing personal experiences to bear on his work: "If I was writing *The Guns of Navarone*, all right, and then right at the beginning of writing it I break up with my girlfriend, who I'm like madly in love with and then my heart is shattered, all right, that's got to work into it. Now, the story is still about a bunch of commandos going to blow up a couple of cannons, all right, but that pain that I'm feeling has got to find its way into the story or else, what am I doing?" (Clarkson 93). In my view, *Pulp Fiction* is a similar elaboration of the Fort!/Da! scenario, in which dramatized violence offers a version of separation that puts the boy child back in control.

14. Writing about poster boy William Holden and 1950s manhood, Steven Cohan observes that acting itself has been seen as inconsistent with manhood, its artifice at odds with a virility defined as "natural" and straightforward (220–28). For more on acting, scripting, and directing as recurrent points of reference in *Pulp Fiction*, see Baughman and Moran (115–16).

15. Steve Neale, in "Masculinity as Spectacle," also discusses men in cinema "feminized" by being on display. His argument about violence in the Western and epic—which functions to deny the homoerotic implications of bared male bodies—supports my sense that violence does similar work in *Pulp Fiction*. Neale further notes that the musical is "the only genre in which the male body has been unashamedly put on display in mainstream cinema in any consistent way," and he goes on to single out Travolta in *Saturday Night Fever* as a "particularly clear and interesting example" (15). I am arguing that Tarantino's relation to such display is precisely inconsistent: he gives us the dancing Travolta only abruptly to withdraw and counter this image with bloodshed.

16. I am extrapolating here from D. A. Miller's persuasive analysis of Victorian sensation novels, in which he observes that Wilkie Collins's "particular staging of nervousness remains cognate with that of many of our own thrillers, printed or filmed" (149). Like Collins in Miller's reading, Tarantino wishes to unnerve an imagined male audience even while agreeing with his culture that nervousness is "female." Given that gender inversion continues today, as in Collins's time, to code a stigmatized sexuality, a "straight" text like *Pulp Fiction* must struggle no less than *The Woman in White* to reassert compulsory heterosexuality.

17. Sara Blair identifies The Gimp as a figure for the audience's passive, hypnotized pleasure; we too are "bound in the dark," witnessing scenes of power. Taking up this suggestion, I want to question its "we." In my view, The Gimp's pleasure represents, more specifically, that of the male viewer feminized by sensation. Tarantino can imagine this man and this pleasure, but must almost immediately disown them.

18. See Clarkson on Oliver Stone's attempt to insult Tarantino (during their fight over Stone's adaptation of *Natural Born Killers*) by accusing Tarantino of making "movies," not "films." In Clarkson's account, the insult backfires, since Tarantino sees himself as champion of the lowbrow (236–37). There is also the story of Tarantino at an early test screening of *Pulp Fiction*. Quizzing the audience about its tastes, he tells anyone who liked *The Remains of the Day* to "Get the fuck outta this theater" (226).

19. For more on *Pulp Fiction*'s general preoccupation with anality, evacuation, and mess, see Douglas Mao; Sharon Willis's rich chapter on Tarantino also explores the role of soiling/sanitizing in *Pulp Fiction*.

20. Notwithstanding his postmod penchant for scavenging and reusing the "low," Tarantino remains invested in the "high" originality of his work and in himself as a bad-boy genius. Residually modernist in this regard, he has a reputation for citing other work matched only by his reputation for failing to give due credit.

2. SPIKE LEE AND BRIAN DE PALMA: SCENARIOS OF RACE AND RAPE

1. Robyn Wiegman, in "Melville's Geography of Gender" (1989), makes a similar point about Robert Martin's and Joseph Boone's idealizing of male bonding in Melville. According to Wiegman, the myth of male homosocial democracy not only suppresses the feminine but may also deny (and thereby help to maintain) racial and class inequities among men.

2. Elusive until recently, that is. As this book goes to press, the Central Park jogger case has once again made headlines: thanks to new DNA evidence, the teens have been wholly exonerated, and their convictions have been overturned.

3. For more on the popular narratives arising from this case, see Joan Didion's essay for *The New York Review of Books* (Jan. 17, 1991). While offering considerable insight into the way class (if not racial) ideologies circulated in relation to

this case, Didion finally veers away from analyzing the struggle between New York's powerful and powerless into a decrial of Tammanyism seemingly removed from that struggle. See also Valerie Smith, "Split Affinities: The Case of Interracial Rape" (1990).

4. For references to studies suggesting racial bias in the prosecution of rape cases see Susan Brownmiller, *Against Our Will: Men, Women and Rape* (1976), 215–16; Angela Y. Davis, "Rape, Racism and the Myth of the Black Rapist," in *Women, Race and Class* (1983), 172; Jacquelyn Dowd Hall, "'The Mind that Burns in Each Body': Women, Rape, and Racial Violence," in *Powers of Desire: The Politics of Sexuality* (1983), 349; and Susan Estrich, *Real Rape* (1987), 107. For more on the history and politics of race and rape, see (in addition to the above) Ida B. Wells, *On Lynchings: Southern Horrors; A Red Record; Mob Rule in New Orleans* (1969); *Lynching and Rape: An Exchange of Views*, ed. Bettina Aptheker (1977); Jacqueline Dowd Hall, *The Revolt Against Chivalry: Jessie Daniel Ames and the Women's Campaign Against Lynching* (1979); Hazel V. Carby, *Reconstructing Womanhood: The Emergence of the Afro-American Woman Novelist* (1987), 108–14; Valerie Smith, "Split Affinities" (1990); Robyn Wiegman, *American Anatomies: Theorizing Race and Gender* (1995), 81–113; Sandra Gunning, *Race, Rape, and Lynching* (1996); Saidiya V. Hartman, *Scenes of Subjection: Terror, Slavery, and Self-Making in Nineteenth-Century America* (1997), and Marlon Ross, "Race, Rape, Castration: Feminist Theories of Sexual Violence and Masculine Strategies of Black Protest" (2002).

5. See Hall's essay and book on Jessie Daniel Ames (founder of the Association of Southern Women for the Prevention of Lynching), who in 1930 first contested the logic of chivalry as a rationale for white vigilante violence. White women thus belatedly answered a long-standing appeal to join the black women's anti-lynching movement, begun forty years earlier by Ida B. Wells (Davis 195). On the earliest formulations of rape as "a property crime of man against man," see Brownmiller 18.

6. Even *The New York Times* picked up on this; see Don Terry's "A Week of Rapes: The Jogger and 28 Not in the News" (May 29, 1989), 25. Most of the unremarked rape victims were black or Hispanic.

7. On the "covering up" of complex and diverse Islamic histories and subjectivities by the western media, see Edward W. Said, *Covering Islam: How the Media and the Experts Determine How We See the Rest of the World* (1981).

8. It is tempting, since the World Trade Center bombing of Sept. 11, 2001, simply to say "strike all that," as if none of our earlier paradigms for understanding global relations could speak to our current situation. Certainly one cannot, regarding the present "war on terrorism," see our desire for "protection" as mere fantasy. Nor has the language of "rape" been used to describe the attack—the collapse of the twin phalluses seemed less a penetration than an appalling double-castration. Perhaps in this case there's less need for a trope whipping up support for the American military, since a frenzied desire for re-

venge is already in place. What we have seen, however, is the suddenly conjured spectacle of Afghan women oppressed by the Taliban offered, as in 1991, to further justify our military actions. Of course the suffering of these women is very real, as women's rights groups have been insisting for years. If the outcry by Barbara Bush et al. were equally real, why wait until now to express it? Apparently, even in a world order transformed by 9/11, the chivalric and Orientalist narrative in which the West saves women of the East continues to have its uses.

9. De Palma takes his title and plot from Lang's account, *Casualties of War* (1969). Brownmiller treats the incident in her section on Vietnam atrocities involving rape, as most of them did (101–3). On images of Vietnam, see also Susan Jeffords, *The Remasculinization of America: Gender and the Vietnam War* (1989), and Linda Dittmar and Gene Michaud, eds., *From Hanoi to Hollywood: The Vietnam War in American Film* (1990).

10. This chapter is principally concerned with mappings of black-white relationships in America and does not attempt to describe the way racial minorities in the United States are variously constructed. In this case, however, my point is that blacks and Asians are, precisely, conflated in De Palma's white imaginary; if non-Anglo groups are at times distinguished and played off against each other, they may also, as here, be collapsed into the general category of racial/ethnic Other, allowing the displacement of one by another.

11. On the tradition of black men seeking to speak for black interests and dictate the terms of black self-representation, see Deborah E. McDowell's "Reading Family Matters," in *"The Changing Same": Black Women's Literature, Criticism, and Theory* (1995). In this important essay, McDowell discusses the bid by male reviewers in the late 1980s to reclaim a sphere of African American letters and politics perceived to have been usurped by popular women writers like Alice Walker and Toni Morrison. Among Spike Lee's overtly political projects since 1989, his documentary *4 Little Girls* (1997) would seem to redress the gender imbalance produced by *Malcolm X* (1992) and *Get on the Bus* (1996) as well as by the films discussed here. *4 Little Girls* is, indeed, an affecting account of the 1963 bombing of a black Birmingham church that does its best to individuate the girls who died that day, along with the family and friends who mourn them. Yet the nature of such a narrative, with the title characters necessarily represented by photos and testimonials, is once again to hang a political struggle on the bodies of girls who constitute a central absence. And this absence contrasts sharply with the presence of public male figures, from Andrew Young to Walter Cronkite, whose comments serve to place the murdered children in relation to the larger civil rights movement.

12. Michele Wallace also remarks on the marginality if not triviality of black women in *School Daze* and *Do the Right Thing*. In the former, Wannabee women, though criticized, are nonetheless eroticized, while Jigaboo women provoke laughter and discomfort from audiences rather than approval. Both groups "take no apparent

interest in either politics or culture except as passive consumers" (*Invisibility* 104). Wallace further suggests (as I will below) that Jane's rape, however discredited, still seems the end result of a "filmic imperative" (105). As for the latter movie, she likewise notes the slightness of its female characters, the "reification" of Rosie Perez in the opening sequence ("titillating moves coded as androgynous resistance but without the power of an explicit feminist political critique") as well as Lee's failure to examine the effects of gender on racism. The exception, she says, is "that brief moment when Mookie insists that his sister Jade should not return to the pizzeria where he works because Sal is coming on to her. It is almost as if Lee/Mookie were warning Jade (played by Lee's sister in real life), as a representative of black women in general, to stay out of the focus of his film" (*Invisibility* 108–9). Nor is Wallace encouraged by Lee's well-intentioned efforts to make a woman central in *She's Gotta Have It*, which remains marred by a lingering "mistrust of female sexuality" (102).

For another approach to *School Daze* and *Do the Right Thing*, concerned not with gender but with essentialism and notions of race, see Wahneema Lubiano.

13. See Patricia J. Williams, *The Alchemy of Race and Rights* (1991), which argues that newspaper accounts of the case were not about Tawana at all—they increasingly denied the traumatized state in which she was found, and preferred to play out a debate between "black manhood and white justice" (173). In the swirl of discourse, Williams observes, Tawana herself was virtually absent: "a shape, a hollow, an emptiness at the center" (175).

14. I want to differentiate as well as to associate the white woman and the light-skinned black woman as tropes in the black male imaginary—the latter, as Saidiya Hartman observed to me, having to do with *intra*racial attitudes. For this reason, Lee's *Jungle Fever* (1991), featuring the white woman as an emblem of racial temptation and fall, is a more exact recapitulation of Cleaver. Here the white heroine's ultimate rejection by the politically awakened black hero involves his punitive claim never to have loved her, in effect rewriting their sexual encounters as having degraded her. While they are not identical, she and the Jane figure would seem in this respect to occupy a comparable place, their sexual humiliations serving a comparable function, in scenarios of black male revolt. (But note too that from a *white* perspective, the rape of a light-skinned black woman, as opposed to that of a white woman, scarcely merits remark, much less outrage.)

15. For Hunter-Gault's account of the mediating role she played in the struggle to integrate the University of Georgia, see *In My Place* (1992).

16. Susan Brown, Theresa Collier, and Prayon Meade, interview series with Charlayne Hunter-Gault, *MacNeil/Lehrer Newshour* (New York: PBS, 2 Oct. 1990, 16 Jan. 1991, 11 Feb. 1991, 15 May 1991).

17. To be precise, the "maids" in Saudi Arabia are not, in fact, Saudi but foreign workers from such places as Sri Lanka and the Philippines. For more on the

complex and exploitative relations among women arising from the international traffic in domestic servants, see Cynthia Enloe, *Bananas, Beaches and Bases:
Making Feminist Sense of International Politics* (1990), 177–94.

3. EDWARD SAID: GENDER, CULTURE, AND IMPERIALISM

1. Further references to *Mansfield Park* will be abbreviated *MP* and refer to the Penguin edition (1966). *Culture and Imperialism* will be hereafter abbreviated *CI*.
2. For negative reviews featuring Austen see, for example, Rhoda Koenig in *New
   York* as well as unsigned reviews in *The Wilson Quarterly* and *Economist*. For an
   exception, see Michael Wood's "Lost Paradises" in *The New York Review of
   Books*, which endorses Said's thesis while taking issue, as I do, with his reading
   of *Mansfield Park*.
3. Michael Wood points out that the "dead silence" passage follows directly on Edmund's remark to Fanny that she has recently become "worth looking at." His
   sense of the connection thus made between the objectification of women and
   slaves agrees with my own (46).
4. Said himself refers to Fanny at one point as "a kind of transported commodity."
   But he goes on to stress her "future wealth," likening her expansion into Mansfield to Sir Thomas's into Antigua, so that Fanny as commodity becomes Fanny
   as colonialist (*CI* 88–89). I have already noted that Fanny does not, in fact, inherit Mansfield, but should add that, in any case, even the "best" marriages did
   not increase but actually contracted the personal wealth and rights of women in
   Austen's day. See Lee Holcombe, *Wives and Property: Reform of the Married
   Women's Property Law in Nineteenth-Century England* (1983), and Susan Staves,
   Married Women's Separate Property in England, 1660–1833 (1990).
5. See Karen Sánchez-Eppler, *Touching Liberty: Abolition, Feminism, and the Politics of the Body* (1993), which discusses white feminist uses of the slavery
   metaphor in an American context. On Austen's opposition to slavery and on
   slavery's role as a metaphor in *Mansfield Park*, see Margaret Kirkham, *Jane
   Austen, Feminism and Fiction* (1983), 116–19; Claudia Johnson, *Jane Austen:
   Women, Politics, and the Novel* (1988), 106–8; and Moira Ferguson, *Colonialism
   and Gender Relations from Mary Wollstonecraft to Jamaica Kincaid* (1993), 65–89.
   On Brontë's ambiguous use of this metaphor, see Susan Meyer, *Imperialism at
   Home: Race and Victorian Women's Fiction* (1996), 29–95.
6. Said quotes the "map of Europe" line to illustrate Austen's preoccupation with
   spatial issues. My thanks to Scott Fennessey, whose "Conjunctions of Geography and Society in Austen's *Mansfield Park*" (1994) first got me thinking about
   the Isle of Wight.
7. For another instance of Austen's skeptical patriotism, see *Northanger Abbey* (1818),
   in which the hero begins by chiding the heroine, "Remember that we are English,
   that we are Christians," only to end with the ominous picture of England as a

place "where every man is surrounded by a neighbourhood of voluntary spies" (199). Citing this passage and others, Robert Hopkins reads *Northanger Abbey* as, indeed, an extensive critique of British politics during the Regency period. As he shows, this novel targets not only the practices of surveillance and repression associated with the Pitt ministry (especially after the antitreason and seditious meetings acts of 1795) but also the accelerating pace of land enclosure in the late eighteenth century, which benefited large property owners like General Tilney while displacing the rural poor. But cf. Raymond Williams, who sees Austen as more sympathetic to the "improvement" of large estates.

8. Though Ferguson's book on colonialism and gender came out concurrently with Said's in 1993, her analysis of *Mansfield Park* had appeared in 1991 as an article in *Oxford Literary Review*.

9. In addition to those mentioned above, books addressing the nexus of gender and colonialism include: Anne McClintock, *Imperial Leather: Race, Gender, and Sexuality in the Colonial Contest* (1995); Anne McClintock, Aamir Mufti, and Ella Shohat, eds., *Dangerous Liaisons: Gender, Nation, and Postcolonial Perspectives* (1997); and Ruth Roach Pierson and Nupur Chaudhuri, eds., *Nation, Empire, Colony: Historicizing Gender and Race* (1998).

10. Aijaz Ahmad, in his book *In Theory: Classes, Nations, Literatures* (1992), singles out Said's essay on *Mansfield Park* (first published in 1989), noting its failure to recognize upper-class women as "differentially located in mobilities and pedagogies of the class structure" (186). See also Fawzia Afzal-Khan's review of *Culture and Imperialism* for *World Literature Today* (Winter 1994), which laments Said's neglect of work by postcolonial feminist critics. *Cultural Readings of Imperialism: Edward Said and the Gravity of History*, ed. Keith Ansell-Pearson et al. (1997), is a collection celebrating, developing, and engaging critically with Said's work; surprisingly, however, though essays by Laura Chrisman and Moira Ferguson conjoin feminist and postcolonial concerns, no one in this volume speaks of Said's own failure to do so. This is largely true as well of another collection devoted to explicating and elaborating Said, *Edward Said and the Work of the Critic: Speaking Truth to Power* (2000). The two exceptions in *Speaking Truth* are a parenthetical but definitive remark by Gayatri Spivak ("My friend Said routinely invokes feminism. But beyond drawing a dubious parallel with anticolonialism—as in his conversation with Catherine David at *doumenta x* in 1997—he withholds interest" [64]) and a pointed interview question from Jacqueline Rose: "How come there are so few women in your writing?" In response, Said concedes that "it's true, my experiences, those I feel most comfortable with and have written about mostly, are those defined and shaped by men" (23–24).

11. Joseph A. Boone, in "Vacation Cruises; or, The Homoerotics of Orientalism," *PMLA* (1995), elaborates on the West's coding of Arab males as homosexual. Noting that "Said's failure to account for homoerotic elements in orientalist pursuits is a telling omission" (92), Boone reinforces my sense of Said's stake in realigning eastern men with dominant conceptions of manhood.

12. The defensive nature of Said's investment in a superordinate masculinity, as I see it, recalls Tarantino, whose cool maleness functions likewise to allay fears of feminization. This dynamic also looks forward to my discussion of Henry Louis Gates Jr., the only one of my figures to identify actively and positively with femininity. Even Gates, however, seems finally to compensate for this by overwriting the black feminine with the masculine. As I elaborate in chapter 5, Gates's *Colored People* stages this shift in autobiographical terms, recounting the narrator's ultimate realignment with "maleness" after a childhood of exceptional closeness to his mother and distance from his father. For what it's worth, Said's memoir, *Out of Place* (1999), tells a similar story of intense, long-standing identification between mother and son (both more enduring and more ambiguous than in Gates), along with an equally strong and resentful sense of alienation from the father.

4. ANDREW ROSS: THE ROMANCE OF THE BAD BOY

1. See the interview with Ross in *The Minnesota Review* (1996), where he refers to his "earlier career as a poetry critic and as a psychoanalytic critic of sorts" (77).
2. This piece has since been reprinted in Ross's collection of essays, *Real Love: In Pursuit of Cultural Justice* (1998). Although Ross makes a few minor additions and alterations, for my purposes the text is substantially the same.
3. Ross describes only the parodic relation of the diva to "black female assertiveness" (191). But black women have also, less ironically, been models for as well as allies of black queens. In a volume edited by Ross along with Tricia Rose, for example, voguer Willi Ninja discusses gay-bashing in the black community and observes that "generally, black women are a lot less hostile than the men" (*Microphone* 172). He also singles out Queen Latifah for putting homophobia in its place while making the video "Come Into My House." "Of course, there was a little shade on the set," Ninja recalls, "between us voguers and the homeboy rappers, but she set it straight, 'Just watch the boy dance.' They watched, they shut up" (162). If Ross despairs that "the gangsta and the diva will ever make common cause, let alone appear on the same stage" ("Gangsta" 194), it is perhaps because he overlooks the role that black women might play, indeed have played, in making this happen.
4. Only a handful of critics have taken Ross to task for his gender politics, and their remarks, though perceptive, have been brief. See Elizabeth Weed (71–72), Linda Williams (263–64), and Tania Modleski (*Feminism* 135–36, 166–67). Footnote 58 gives the gist of Williams's remarks.
5. There are a few "gangsta women," but Ross means the gangsta specifically as a type of the masculine. In any case, Tricia Rose suggests that women rappers (gangsta or not) tend to thematize urban life and anger in markedly gendered ways: "Although male rappers' social criticism often contests police harassment and other means by which black men are 'policed,' black women rapper's [sic]

central contestation is in the arena of sexual politics" (147). "Revenge fantasies against black men," she adds later (speaking of the female gangsta group Boss), "are as socially relevant as black men's revenge fantasies against the police" (174). I am also interested in Ross's use of the term "hard-core" in relation to male gangsta rap and its alleged ghetto authenticity. This resonates closely with his celebration elsewhere of "hard-core" (straight male) pornography as true working-class culture. By contrast, women's porn (like women's rap) is disparaged as "soft-core," meaning that it tones down or gentrifies the real thing.

6. Ross writes that "Mailer's celebration of virility and ultimate orgasms fed the macho obsession that was later to draw endless fire from the women's movement" (88). But note that, in the middle of a sentence seeming to side with feminist critiques of Mailer, the unexpected adjective "endless" begins to turn the criticism back on women and feminism, by hinting at images of women as nags and feminists as "shrill."

7. For accounts of lesbian cultures at these various moments in the United States, see Lillian Faderman's *Odd Girls and Twilight Lovers: A History of Lesbian Life in Twentieth-Century America* (1991). Leslie Feinberg's novel *Stone Butch Blues* (1993) vividly describes butch-femme bar culture in 1950s working-class Buffalo, New York. Judith Halberstam's *Female Masculinity* (1998) also discusses "inversion" in the 1920s, butchness in the 1950s, and other types of "female masculinity" from pre-twentieth-century "tribades" to contemporary drag kings. For more on Feinberg, on Halberstam, and on disagreements between Faderman and Halberstam, see my final chapter on queer theory.

8. See Rita Felski on the figure of the intellectual as reconceived by contemporary cultural studies. On the way gender/race informs the category of the intellectual, see especially her comments (following Anna Yeatman) on the "contradictory position" of "subaltern intellectuals" (168). For women and people of color, Felski explains, the status of intellectual is only recently and tentatively available; minority professors are thus "both intellectuals *and* members of historically disenfranchised groups" (169).

9. Ross's exclusion of black women is particularly unfortunate in "Bridge" given that he takes his title from the feminist classic, *This Bridge Called My Back: Writings by Radical Women of Color* (1981).

10. Madonna's "pussy" is also the ambiguous subject of a single sentence in "Back on the Box." Following the remark previously discussed about the female butt in black culture, Ross adds: "By contrast, for a bossy white girl like Madonna, the pussy is the place of truth" (112). It may be that "bossy" is meant positively, but for me it also echoes cheap media criticism of Madonna for having a pussy that knows its own mind. Note too that Ross once again plays Madonna off against black (male) sexuality.

11. A useful focus on class to the inexplicable exclusion, however, of similar insights regarding gender likewise mars Laura Kipnis's book, *Bound and Gagged: Pornography and the Politics of Fantasy in America* (1996). A pre-text for both

Kipnis and Ross is arguably a passage from Fiedler's *What Was Literature? Class Culture and Mass Society* (1982). For though *No Respect* criticizes Fiedler on the Rosenbergs, its analysis of porn echoes Fiedler's assertion that "Bible Belt fundamentalists and radical feminists" alike are motivated to attack pornography by "an underlying fear of freedom as well as a contempt for the popular arts" (49).

12. Linda Williams in *Hard Core* argues similarly that male critics who find porn for women too "tame" may do so from a narrowly male perspective, and she offers as an example Ross's criticism of "The Pick Up" (*Hard Core* 263). "Who," she asks, "is getting turned off here, men or women? For female viewers, traditionally less adventurous and exploratory for the reasons outlined above, the mixture of safety with excitement that this scenario offers may be just what is needed *for* excitement" (264).

    Another example from "The Popularity of Pornography" comes to mind, in which women's pleasure is not so much excluded as blithely folded into and subsumed by men's. I am thinking of Ross's apparently favorable view of the porn classic *Deep Throat* for its representation of "the sexual revolution's two newly 'discovered' adventure zones as if they were one and the same—the centrality of the clitoris for women, and the action of fellatio for men" (174). Contrasting this movie's central conceit—a woman with her clitoris in her throat—with the violent misogyny of *Screw* publisher Al Goldstein and with the actual exploitation of *Deep Throat*'s star Linda Lovelace, Ross seems to agree with those who have praised the film as "the spectacle of a woman actively seeking sexual pleasure" (174). Yet one has only to try reversing this conceit—a man with a penis for a tongue, conveniently driven wild by cunnilingus—to realize how much *Deep Throat* is a male fantasy, and a rather selfish one at that. From a woman's point of view, sexual revolution as well as sexual pleasure requires not only knowing the clitoris is "central" but also knowing where it is.

13. In addition to the example below, I would also note *Chicago*'s long opening chapter on Polynesia (21–98). Here the gender politics of travel to places like Hawaii—always a kind of (male) sex tourism in imagination if not in fact—are mentioned in passing but never seriously taken up. Choosing to ignore the all too obvious metaphorics explored, for instance, by Judith Williamson's "Woman Is an Island: Femininity and Colonization," Ross offers instead an unlikely counterimage of his own, in which the native is a male worker and the exploitative tourists are packs of "little old ladies" with "blue hair rinses" traveling on their life insurance money (90). In my view this passage throws up a kind of screen image (black widows with blue hair and white mobility) eclipsing more evident and salient gender relations. Little old ladies do, I am sure, rinse their hair and fly to Polynesia, causing class as well as gender dynamics to come into play, but as an explanatory trope Ross's image says less, I warrant, about jet-age Orientalism than it does about older women in his own imaginary. See my final section.

14. Ross further feminizes the language of scarcity/abundance and the ethic of austerity by referring several times (including in his final paragraph) to pathological "cycles of binge and purge" (17, 273). Given bulimia's association with women and girls, this metaphor confirms my sense that Ross's critique of environmentalism identifies asceticism/guilt/discipline with the "female."

15. Regarding Ross's emphasis on the social, not biological, construction of gender, Alice Jardine observes, "Feminists have been saying nothing else for years" (58); Judith Mayne suggests that the continual castigation of "radical feminism" and "essentialism" by critics such as Ross abstracts these positions from their historical, "narrative" context, obscuring both their strategic value and their theoretical complexity (62–63, 69–70); and Elizabeth Weed notes that Ross's parenthetical attack on "certain" feminists is a way of "indirectly implicating the victim" (72) and may be a displacement of more general anger concerning the men and feminism question (76).

16. See Cary Nelson's effective reply in his own "Men in Feminism" essay, to the effect that "feminist critiques of feminist practice have been a part of feminism from the outset. They are not merely a matter, as Andrew Ross seems to argue in 'No Question of Silence,' of policing violations of law, of obliterating difference; they are part of a struggle to shape the social formation of the future" (163). Moreover, he continues, though no one can be entirely correct, "taking on the burden of correctness . . . is part of what feminism is about for men" (164).

17. For other, more recent efforts to critique and correct the male bias of cultural studies, see Julia Swindells and Lisa Jardine, *What's Left? Women in Culture and the Labour Movement* (1990); Ann Wilson, "Cautious Optimism: The Alliance of Women's Studies and Cultural Studies" (1996); and Annette Henry, "Stuart Hall, Cultural Studies: Theory Letting You off the Hook?" (2001).

5. HENRY LOUIS GATES JR.: FIGURES IN BLACK MASCULINITY

1. In 2002, West left Harvard and, in a much-publicized move, returned to Princeton.

2. Though pitched to your average PBS viewer, Gates's series became the object of heated debate among scholars, with Africanists from Ali Mazrui to Wole Soyinka flaming or defending the show and each other. The controversy centered primarily on whether issues that might reflect negatively on Africa—female circumcision, African participation in the slave trade, etc.—were presented by the series in ways that pandered to Eurocentric views. For comments on both sides of this debate, see the Web site www.westafricareview.com/war/.

3. Gates's publications over the last decade include, for example: "Delusions of Grandeur: Young Blacks Must be Taught that Sports are Not the Only Avenues of Opportunity" (*Sports Illustrated* 1991); "Just Whose 'Malcolm' Is It, Anyway:

Spike Lee's New Film Biography of Malcolm X" (*NYT* 1992); "Words that Wound: Critical Race Theory, Assaultive Speech and the First Amendment" (*New Republic* 1993); "Black Creativity: On the Cutting Edge" (*Time* 1994); *The Dictionary of Global Culture* (edited with Anthony Appiah; Knopf, 1995); "Hating Hillary" (*The New Yorker* 1996); "Dole 2000: The G.O.P.'s Best Hope for the White House is an Un-Republican Named Elizabeth Dole" (*The New Yorker* 1997); "The White Negro: in *Bulworth* Warren Beatty Puts his Career on the Color Line" (*The New Yorker* 1998); *Black Imagination and the Middle Passage* (ed. with Maria Diedrich and Carl Pederson; Oxford, 1999); *The African-American Century: How Blacks Have Shaped Our Country* (with Cornel West; Free Press, 2000). This highly selective list only begins to suggest the wide range of topics broached and venues graced by Gates's work.

4. Gates asserts his belief in O.J.'s guilt in "Thirteen Ways" (*Thirteen* 119), which originally ran in *The New Yorker* (1995). For the most extensive feminist response to Houston Baker, see two forceful pieces by Ann duCille: "'Who Reads Here?': Back Talking with Houston Baker" (1992) and "The Occult of True Black Womanhood: Critical Demeanor and Black Feminist Studies" (1994).

5. To some extent this may be generally true of African American texts, which tend to understand individual destinies and agendas in relation to those of the larger community. Of course, in formal terms too, black texts are heavily influenced by such dialogic genres as the slave narrative (black narrative in tension with white, authenticating frame), the blues, the dozens, liturgical call-and-response, etc. It is nevertheless the case that conventions of gender and genre opposing isolate males to relational females have a certain hegemonic hold over black as well as white Americans.

6. See Nancy Chodorow, *The Reproduction of Mothering* (1978), and Olga Silverstein and Beth Rashbaum, *The Courage to Raise Good Men* (1994). There is, to be sure, also a sense in which mothers are particularly revered in African American culture; yet this does not preclude (and may even require) a dominant mode of masculinity that strongly repudiates the female. A literary case in point is Toni Morrison's character Ajax (Sula's lover) who is no less sexist for idolizing his mother (duCille, "'Who Reads Here?'" 103–4).

7. Though I generally share duCille's reservations about Houston Baker's gender politics, I appreciate his use of the unspaced "blackmale" to stress the mutual engagement of these two terms in contemporary American culture. For an utterly compelling and unrelenting critique of the compound "blackmale," see Phillip Brian Harper's *Are We Not Men? Masculine Anxiety and the Problem of African-American Identity* (1996). I am suggesting that Gates, by contrast, while urging black "youth" to study as well as play sports, continues to feel the pull of black macho and, unlike Harper, never confronts this ideology head on. Earlier critiques of the tie between black masculinity and notions of racial authenticity include: Michele Wallace, *Black Macho and the Myth of the Superwoman* (1979);

Calvin Hernton, *The Sexual Mountain and Black Women Writers* (1987); bell hooks, *Black Looks: Race and Representation* (1992), 98–101; and Kobena Mercer, *Welcome to the Jungle* (1994), 131–70.

8. The opening of J. Martin Favor's *Authentic Blackness: The Folk in the New Negro Renaissance* (1999) includes a discussion of Gates and the black vernacular—privileged in Gates's work, Favor says, as a site of racial authenticity (5–6). Also relevant here is Favor's citing of Marlon Riggs. As Favor explains, Riggs's documentary *Black Is, Black Ain't* (1995) compares gay filmmakers, "feminist scholars, Ivy League graduates, and members of the middle class," all of whom—if they are "phenotypically black"—may be charged for reasons of class/gender/sexuality with not being "truly" so (Favor 2). Note that Gates falls into not one but three of the four categories named by Riggs as producing "a crisis of authenticity." For more on the role of the vernacular generally in certifying racial/gender authenticity, see Harper (11, 64–67).

9. Although, as I say, Gates has been far less criticized by feminists than Houston Baker and others, a few reviewers have made some rather pointed remarks about his sexual politics. See, for example, Hazel Carby's complaint in *TLS* that *The Signifying Monkey* ignores the work of black feminists and Nell Painter's disagreement in *The Nation* with what she identifies as the masculine bias of *The Future of the Race*. Carby's *Race Men* also notes the masculine anxiety about intellectual reproduction underlying *The Future of the Race*. "It is reproduction without women," Carby argues, citing Gates's lament for the premature deaths of DeChabert and Robinson as evidence of his focus (after DuBois) on intellectual fathers and sons—mothers, by contrast, reproduce only poverty (*Race* 25–27). When Harper poses his "critique of masculinism in African-American culture" against those who persist in calling for "a proper affirmation of black male authority," he, too, includes among them "scholars Cornel West and Henry Louis Gates, Jr., on the role of the African-American intellectual" (ix–x). Valerie Smith's analysis of sexism in African American scholarship actually singles out for praise a review by Gates of Mary Helen Washington ("Gender" 66); on the other hand, her criticism of Robert Stepto—that he unknowingly privileges male texts by taking "the quest for freedom and literacy" as black writing's key theme ("Gender" 60–61)—might equally well apply to Gates. As we will see, his *Signifying Monkey* draws similarly on texts by men in arguing the centrality to nineteenth-century black writing of scenes of literary instruction. Michele Wallace, finally, shares my concern (below) about Gates's appropriation of black women writers: "Having established himself as the father of Afro-American Literary Studies, with the help of *The New York Times Book Review*, he now proposes to become the phallic mother of a newly depoliticized, mainstreamed and commodified black feminist literary criticism" (*Invisibility* 251).

10. Originally published in the *South Atlantic Quarterly* (1990), "The Master's Pieces" was reprinted in *Loose Canons: Notes on the Culture Wars* (1992). The recitation anecdote with which it concludes is repeated almost word for word

but without the critical framing in Gates's 1994 memoir *Colored People* (117–18). It also appeared as the opening to an earlier essay for *The New York Times Book Review*, "Whose Canon Is It, Anyway?" (1989). I myself first heard Gates tell this story as part of an MLA presentation sometime in the late 1980s.

11. Examples of skepticism regarding the appropriation of black women's work by black/white men as well as white women include Wallace (see note 72) and duCille ("The Occult of True Black Womanhood"). DuCille sums up my own feelings about Gates's work when she describes Baker's *Workings of the Spirit* as "least successful and most troubling where maleness and male privilege are placed under the erasure of race and community, where the 'blackmale' scholar labors to be one of the girls or at least a kindred, sympathetic, understanding spirit" (104).

12. The implication that scholar-critics of African American writing are naturally male is reinforced by another essay in this volume entitled "Tell Me, Sir, . . . What *Is* 'Black' Literature?" The title comes from the challenge issued to Gates by one of his tutors at Cambridge upon hearing that Gates planned to write his thesis on black literature (*Loose* 88). By taking the tutor's words as the catalyst not only for his essay but for the project of African American studies overall, Gates frames this project as a black male answer to a white male question.

13. Wallace offers a similar reading of this anecdote in "Negative Images: Towards a Black Feminist Cultural Criticism" (*Invisibility* 251).

14. As Gates explains in *Signifying Monkey*, "Reed's text is the text-specific element from which my theory arose. . . . *The Signifying Monkey* and *Mumbo Jumbo* bear something of a symbiotic relationship" (218).

15. In the brilliant last chapter of *"The Changing Same,"* Deborah McDowell observes that contemporary criticism routinely identifies black women and black feminist thinking negatively with "practice" or "politics" over against the positive association of white women and black men with "theory." The argument I develop below about Gates's alignment of theoretical naiveté with Phillis Wheatley and Harriet Wilson appears to offer further support for McDowell's claims.

16. Here I should note that Toomer occasions some more obviously troubling observations about sex as figure for race. In these terms, Gates writes, his passing amounts to a racial "castration," changing his "deep black bass" to a "false soprano" (208). According to this metaphor, as Gates seems only to half realize, "blackness" and "truth" as well as "beauty" are gendered male, while mutilated blackness and falsity in both aesthetic and epistemological senses is gendered female.

17. On the gender politics of Douglass's primacy in African American studies, see McDowell's critique in "In the First Place: Making Frederick Douglass and the Afro-American Narrative Tradition."

18. Interestingly, the earlier version of this essay, written as the introduction to Gates's 1983 edition of *Our Nig*, includes a lengthy, formal analysis of Wilson's book, in relation, for example, to Nina Baym's "overplot" of sentimental novels written by contemporaneous white women (xxxiv–lv). The novel's autobiographical aspect is mentioned but never assumes the centrality it has in the later

version. The version in *Figures* thus appears to be quite pointedly revised so as to downplay the rhetorical and highlight the historical Harriet Wilson.

19. Cf. Priscilla Wald, who stresses the difference between Wilson's autobiographical persona, "Our Nig," and the author herself; if the former tells her story, the latter reflects upon this telling. Unlike Gates, then (and giving Wilson a good deal more credit), Wald sees *Our Nig* as a self-reflexive text: "This narrative is not finally just an autobiography. It is instead a *narrative about* autobiography, *about* what writing for a particular market does to this African-American woman in pre-Civil War New England—and, more generally, *about* cultural identity" (169).

20. For more on Gates's transformation of poststructuralism to treat African American texts, see Diana Fuss in her chapter on "Poststructuralist Afro-American Literary Theory" (81–86). Defending Gates (as well as Anthony Appiah and Houston Baker) from the backlash against theory by such black critics as Joyce Joyce, Fuss does not remark on what I see as the gender bias of Gates's black formalism. Toward the end of this chapter she does, however, note the "relative absence of Afro-American *feminist* poststructuralism" (94), a remark that begins to suggest the genderedness of Gates et al.

21. Indeed, this assertion itself is inconsistent with what Gates has already told us; Mawu-Lisa, the female-male deity of the Fon, is a version not of Esu but of his *parent*. It is Mawu-Lisa's seventh *son*, Legba, who represents Esu in Fon culture, and Legba's unambiguous masculinity is suggested not least by the myth Gates cites explaining why he always has an erection (27). I would note, moreover, that in Figures 9, 10, and 11, which Gates describes as depicting a "Janus-figure Esu-Elegbara," two heads are visible, but there is little indication (at least in the photos) of two genders.

22. Gates also takes specific issue with Roger D. Abrahams, who argues that black women and children signify more indirectly than black men. "I have found that black men and women use indirection with each other to the same degree" (77), Gates insists. Yet if signifying is motivated in part by the need of subordinate groups to speak obliquely, would it not follow that black women and children, relative to black men, should do so even more markedly?

23. For an incisive and comprehensive exploration of black women's relation to food as a trope in the history of black representation, see Doris Witt's *Black Hunger: Food and the Politics of U.S. Identity* (1999).

24. In fact, Gates's Chart 5 corresponds but loosely to his verbal description of these relations. The "direct black line" he mentions as connecting Hurston and Morrison (111) doesn't appear in the picture (112), and there are other signs he has neither fully realized nor committed himself to this seemingly inclusive model.

25. That Gates is at some level defensive about displacing Wheatley with Gronniosaw et al. may be hinted by three brief references clustered early in this chapter. First, he invokes the authenticating prefaces of Wheatley's *Poems* and Ann Plato's 1841 work to argue, as in *Figures*, that black literacy has long been bound

up with a polemical affirmation of black humanity (130). This sets up his claim about the Talking Book as a trope negotiating "between the black vernacular and literate white text, between the spoken and the written word" (131). Wheatley surfaces for a sentence—uncanny reminder of accounts featuring her more prominently—only to be definitively written over by The Talking Book Five.

The second telling reference also involves the historical significance of black literacy. "If blacks could write and publish imaginative literature," Gates explains, "then they could, in effect, take a few giant steps up the Great Chain of Being, in a pernicious game of 'Mother, May I?'" (130) Blacks were, of course, infantilized when they were not dehumanized throughout the eighteenth and nineteenth centuries, so it makes sense to picture them as twice removed from full citizenship, petitioning children within a child's game. But though mistresses had power over if not direct ownership of slaves, and though female abolitionists spoke out on the question of slavery, it was not generally white *mothers* adjudicating either the value of black literary texts or the status of black people. Needless to say, all eighteen of "the most respectable characters in Boston" who cross-examined Wheatley were white *fathers*. As with Andrew Ross, Gates's imaging of discursive authority as maternal would seem to stem less from gender/race relations in Wheatley's period (or ours) than from Gates's own anxieties about maternal power, whether black or white. In the context of this chapter, I believe the negative maternal trope lines up with and helps to rationalize Wheatley's suppression as literary foremother.

The final salient reference, farther down this same page, is to Rebecca Jackson's autobiographical writings of the early 1830s (unpublished until 1981). According to Gates, Jackson, a contemporary of John Jea, not only makes use of the Talking Book but also "refigures the trope in terms of male domination of a female's voice and her quest for literacy" (130). Yet instead of treating her alongside his other figures—in which case her feminist revision would be the chronological and ideological endpoint of the series—he devotes but two sentences of this chapter to her, explaining in parentheses, "I analyze Jackson's revision in Chapter 7" (130). Like Wheatley, Jackson pops up only to be immediately bracketed in favor of those male antecedents she takes to task, and the effect is not to include her so much as, somewhat guiltily, to mark her exclusion and that of black women generally.

26. On this paradigm in the work of post-Reconstruction women writers as a figure for black political desires, see Claudia Tate's *Domestic Allegories of Political Desire: The Black Heroine's Text at the Turn of the Century* (1992).

27. Though Nanny is obviously wrong to marry Janie off for the sake of "protection," her warnings about the dangers of "love" ("de very prong all us black women gits hung on" [Hurston 41]) are consistently borne out by the rest of the narrative.

28. Gates is further enabled to discount the feminist content of Hurston's and Walker's novels (as he discounts the gender specificity of signifying) by means

of his rigorous formalism. For though Gates describes Janie's story as a romantic quest for a man/tree or, elsewhere, as a gender-neutral quest for "consciousness" (196), he finally argues that "the very subject of this text would appear to be not primarily Janie's quest but the emulation of the phonetic, grammatical, and lexical structures of actual speech, an emulation designed to produce the illusion of oral narration" (196). Hurston, he says, employs a mode of free indirect discourse that blends the black speech of her characters with the literary voice of her early narrator. The result is a book speaking the black vernacular and tying Hurston, through the Talking Book trope, to writers from Gronniosaw to Ellison (192). Though Gates eventually links Hurston to Walker as well, he does so primarily by extending this formalist line of thought. Setting aside the shared gender protest of their novels, Gates contends that Walker's use of epistolary, turning black dialect into letters, echoes Hurston's transfiguration of a written text into a "speakerly" one (251). Persuasive in their own right, such arguments are in keeping with Gates's larger formalist project. Yet I would still ask—how satisfied would we be by a reading of *Invisible Man* that failed to tie its discussion of form to Ellison's concerns about race?

29. See Michele Wallace on the racial and sexual politics of Hurston criticism in "Who Owns Zora Neale Hurston? Critics Carve Up the Legend." Originally published in *The Village Voice Literary Supplement* (April 1988), this essay is reprinted in *Invisibility Blues* (172–86).

30. For a wonderfully thorough and complex reading of the racial and sexual politics of this case, see Kimberle Crenshaw. Crenshaw agrees with Gates that 2 Live Crew's lyrics, drawing on the dozens and other black cultural traditions, have artistic value mitigating their "obscenity" according to legal definitions. At the same time, she continues, "acknowledging this fact [of participation in a Black oral tradition] does not eliminate the need to interrogate either the sexism within that tradition or the objectives to which that tradition has been pressed."

6. QUEER THEORY AND THE SECOND SEX

1. I am speaking here primarily of academic feminism, especially in the humanities. By contrast, much feminist scholarship in the social sciences continues to explore women's "difference," while a highly visible strain of third-wave feminism in the popular sphere is "Girlie," which finds girl power in defiant bonding over Barbies, fashion, and other aspects of traditional girl culture. Though claiming the feminine, this form of youth feminism nevertheless resembles queer theory in tending to reject the "maternal" generation of feminists. For more on Girlie see Baumgardner's and Richards's *Manifesta: Young Women, Feminism, and the Future* (126–66).

2. Nestle is the editor of *The Persistent Desire: A Femme-Butch Reader* (1992), whose subtitle pointedly revises the convention of putting "butch" first. Such a revision is key to her own essay in this volume, "The Femme Question"

(138–46), and to Arlene Istar's essay "Femme-dyke" (378–83). See also, among other femme texts in *Persistent*, Pat Califia's three poems, which both claim and complicate femme desires. Lisa Duggan and Kathleen McHugh are the authors of "A fem(me)inist manifesto," published in the "Queer Acts" issue of *Women and Performance* (1996). Jewelle Gomez's "Femme Erotic Independence" (101–8) and Lynda Hart's "Living Under the Sign of the Cross: Some Speculations on Femme Femininity" (214–23) are two of several such pieces in Sally Munt's *Butch/Femme: Inside Lesbian Gender* (1998).

3. See, for example, Matthew Rottnek's collection, *Sissies and Tomboys* (1999), and Eve Sedgwick's essay "How to Bring Your Kids Up Gay: The War on Effeminate Boys" (*Tendencies* 154–64). Note, however, that Sedgwick is urgent about defending "sissy boys" precisely because, even within the gay community, male femininity has often been stigmatized, in part to counter the traditional view of homosexuality as inversion (157–58). In "Boys Will Be Girls: The Politics of Gay Drag," Carole-Anne Tyler speaks similarly of the misogyny "haunting" many discussions of gay male camp, and goes on to instance Leo Bersani's well-known essay "Is the Rectum a Grave?" (Tyler 38).

   Sedgwick hopes the effect of "queer" on "gay" politics will be a warmer embrace of male femininity, but I agree with Biddy Martin (see below) that queer theory, if not drag culture itself, typically seizes on male drag less to affirm than to parody and disown the feminine. I would, finally, observe that Sedgwick's essay on "bringing your *kids* up gay" (my emphasis) is actually about effeminate *boys*. Though I admire this piece a great deal, I do think it illustrates the tendency for "gay," "homosexual," and even "queer" to function—if only in the brief space between title and subtitle—as false universals within texts concertedly devoted to males (whether feminine or not). Such a slippage results all too easily from the practice Sedgwick elsewhere describes, with characteristic self-awareness, as using "gay" to reference desire "treated as indicatively but not exclusively male" (*Epistemology* 18).

4. In *A Lure of Knowledge* (1991), Judith Roof makes a similar observation about this *SAQ* issue, called *Displacing Homophobia*, in which twelve of thirteen articles are "written by men, mainly about men. Somehow in displacing homophobia," Roof writes, "the editors have also displaced lesbians, manifesting a kind of sapphophobia" (213). Around the same time, Lisa Duggan's essay "Making It Perfectly Queer" (1992) mentions, as a commonplace, that "within the field defined by queer literary theory, lesbian visions remain profoundly ghettoized" (168). Sedgwick's work, Duggan notes, while legitimating queer readings, does so "primarily for the benefit of gay male readers and readings" (168). (In contrast to Modleski and to my own analysis below, Duggan looks to Judith Butler as well as Teresa de Lauretis to produce queer analyses from a feminist standpoint.)

5. The idea of a "lesbian continuum" (on which all women can be located somewhere) originates with Rich's "Compulsory Heterosexuality and Lesbian Existence" (1980), an essay that also stresses the historical particularity and difficulty

of "lesbian existence." While Rich would call attention to this discrete *existence*, Sedgwick cites only the *continuum* to explain her focus not on female but on male homoeroticism, which she sees as more severely proscribed. Castle, however, denies that "women who have sex with each other" blend easily into the crowd of straight women helping each other. Disagreeing with Sedgwick, she insists that the panic caused by lesbianism is "as virulent as that inspired by male homosexuality, if not more so" (71–72). De Lauretis also contests the folding of lesbianism into every woman's experience of female bonding, and traces the source of this impulse back to feminism's fondness for the "homosexual-maternal metaphor": its habit of troping lesbianism in terms of preoedipal ties between mother and daughter. For still another complaint about Sedgwick's bracketing of lesbianism in *Epistemology of the Closet* as well as in *Between Men*, see Carolyn Dever's helpful essay in *Cross-Purposes* (33–39). Like de Lauretis, Dever criticizes feminism as well as queer theory for ignoring specific lesbian histories (even while claiming lesbianism as a principle).

6. "Sexualities Without Genders and Other Queer Utopias" originally appeared in *diacritics*, "Extraordinary Homosexuals and the Fear of Being Ordinary" in *differences*. Both are reprinted in Martin's book *Femininity Played Straight* (1996).

7. Citing Robyn Wiegman in *The Lesbian Postmodern* (1994), de Lauretis agrees with Wiegman that in much recent work the queer rubric "actually neutralizes differences" between lesbian and gay sexualities ("Fem/Les" 46). On another note regarding *The Lesbian Postmodern*, de Lauretis questions this volume's implication that her generation of scholars is pre-postmodern; by 1994, she observes, poststructuralist feminists had been using a PoMo critical vocabulary of "excess" and "contradiction" for several decades (45). De Lauretis concludes "Fem/Les Scramble" by referring to Judith Halberstam's essay "F2M" (1994), in which Halberstam claims for postmodern lesbian desire "the spectacle of *the female body becoming male.*" De Lauretis regards this claim as dismaying evidence of a "new imaginary . . . developed out of the progressive repudiation of femininity and, now, also the repudiation of the female body," and she is baffled by a lesbian desire that no longer takes some version of this body, whether "real or fantasmatic," as its object (47).

8. Other assorted examples of this critique over the years include Julie Abraham's 1992 *Village Voice* essay,"I Know What Boys Like: Tales from the Dyke Side" and her introduction to *Are Girls Necessary? Lesbian Writing and Modern Histories* (1996); Sheila Jeffreys's "The Queer Disappearance of Lesbians: Sexuality in the Academy" (1994); Elizabeth Weed's essay, "The More Things Change," in *Feminism Meets Queer Theory*; and Linda Garber's *Identity Poetics: Race, Class and the Lesbian-Feminist Roots of Queer Theory* (2001), especially the final chapter (176–208).

9. These three essays appear in Sedgwick's *Tendencies* (1993): "A Poem" (177–214); "Queer and Now" (1–20); and "Divinity" (215–51). Sedgwick also theorizes her focus on male over female sexuality (and on sexuality over gender) in the im-

portant, codifying introduction to *Epistemology of the Closet* (1990); see especially Axiom 3, which considers the relevance, or not, to understanding lesbianism of an admittedly gay male-centered study such as *Epistemology* (36–39).

10. D. A. Miller's "Anal *Rope*" and Bersani's "Is the Rectum a Grave?" are classic instances. Another might be Lee Edelman's "Seeing Things," which I discuss below.

11. Generally speaking, Butler develops the attack on identity (as stable and coherent) initiated by Derrida and other poststructuralists in the mid-1960s. A more specific basis for Butler's view (and for queer theory generally) is, of course, Michel Foucault's assertion that homosexuality became more stringently regulated with the shift from a paradigm of homosexual *acts* to one of homosexual *identity* (*History of Sexuality* 42–43). Butler also gives another turn of the screw to Monique Wittig's famous repudiation of the category "women": "It would be incorrect to say that lesbians associate, make love, live with women, for 'woman' has meaning only in heterosexual systems of thought and heterosexual economic systems. Lesbians are not women" ("The Straight Mind" 110).

12. I have already mentioned the concessions to "gender" in "Against Proper Objects"; "Contingent Foundations" (1993) also insists that deconstructing the concepts of "women," "matter," and "bodies" does not mean refusing to use them, but only refusing to assume their prior knowability and stability; and Butler's 1999 introduction to *Gender Trouble* goes so far as to stage an autobiographical, politically engaged "I" (going to meetings, "sitting on Rehoboth Beach," etc.), even while noting its "difficulty" (xvi–xxvi). "Despite the dislocation of the subject that the text performs," Butler writes in the late 1990s, "there is a person here" (xvi).

13. For more on fluidity as queer theory's characteristic trope (especially in Butler), see Brad Epps, who shares my concern that "what goes with this flow is gender, race, age, class" (413) and, more generally, words, things, and bodies. Epps also argues that, despite its emphasis on fluidity, queer theory has its own rigidities (414).

14. Alongside Butler, it is relevant here to mention Diana Fuss's influential book, *Essentially Speaking* (1989). The express design of this work is to question the essentialism/constructionism binary; Fuss demonstrates that each of these categories contains elements of the other and argues that neither is inherently conservative or radical. This entails a defense of "essentialisms" as actually variable and not necessarily reactionary. But it also entails a stronger and more memorable case for the complementary proposition that most constructionisms, and notably feminist ones, simply relocate "essence" in the social. What sticks about this book is the sense that avowedly antiessentialist feminisms inevitably contain a residue of essentialist thinking. And since essentialism remains heavily stigmatized, despite Fuss's efforts to the contrary, one effect of her argument is to move the widest possible range of feminist thinking over into a discredited category. Once this occurs, the long-fetishized feminist distinction between the biological and social becomes moot, enabling even feminisms on the far constructionist end of the spectrum to be tainted with biologism.

15. See also Julie Thompson's *Mommy Queerest: Contemporary Rhetorics of Lesbian Maternal Identity* (2002), which explores and debunks the mainstream view that "lesbian motherhood" is a contradiction in terms. As a corrective, Thompson agrees with me in stressing the need for notions of legitimate motherhood beyond the strictly biological, and for "a cultural space that allows mothers to engage in non-procreative erotic practices" (119). Our purviews are different, however. Thompson's topic is negative portrayals of lesbian motherhood within the press, the courts, and even the academy. But queer theory as a distinct oppositional discourse (with its claiming of a "queerness" *opposed* to standing notions of the "lesbian") does not figure in her discussion.

16. For another critical response to "The Future is Kid Stuff," see John Brenkman's "Queer Post-Politics." Leaving aside Brenkman's disagreement with Edelman about whether the political can be a site of social transformation as well as reproduction, I note that Brenkman understands Edelman's notion of queerness in relation to "gay male promiscuity" (179) and to "the bars and the baths" (180). Although Edelman insists, in response, that "queerness" in his essay is a trope—not a person, place, or practice—Brenkman's ready assumption that this category is tied to queer masculinity would seem to support my reading.

17. Edelman's wonderful analysis of George Bush's throwing up on the Japanese prime minister also turns on the word "pregnant," which he argues arose in this context to sanitize the scene of Bush with his face in another man's lap (*Homographesis* 138–47). Once again, I am wholly persuaded by this reading but still feel that, within Edelman's own discourse, the continual citing of *pregnancy* as shorthand for spiritualized, sentimentalized heterosexuality effectively locates the antithesis of queerness within the female body.

18. This might seem to contradict the Lacanian axiom, which Edelman would presumably accept, about the maleness of the symbolic order. But I think it's possible to recognize phallogocentrism at one level and still, at a deeply ingrained psychological level, to represent and resent the tyranny of conventionality as "feminine." In fact, the latter structure of feeling may be crucial in helping dissimulate and perpetuate the former. The coexistence of these two seemingly contradictory viewpoints can be seen in most of my "cool men," who typically share a "feminist" if not Lacanian awareness of male domination, even as they direct their oppositional anger toward a feminized object.

19. Of course the other thing that gets left out is *queer kids*. In this sense, the strategy of "Kid Stuff" differs sharply from that of Sedgwick's essays in *Tendencies*, which do not reject the trope of the child but choose instead to redeploy it in various ways: to explore "sissiness" in Willa Cather's "Paul's Case" (167–72), to advocate for effeminate boys (154–64), and to protest the high rates of HIV transmission and suicide among queer teens (1–2).

20. Edelman's point is to recognize and resist the homophobia produced by the racial logic of castration: if black men are seen as castrated and so feminized, then antiracism naturally takes the form of asserting black male "virility"

through zealous heterosexuality. Nevertheless, while challenging some aspects of this logic, Edelman still seems to credit the idea that racism's most egregious effect has been the disabling of black manhood, citing Ishmael Reed and others to this effect (*Homographesis* 53). This view recalls the infamous 1965 "Moynihan Report," which derived black social ills from mother-headed households, and resonates as well with various Afrocentric discourses, from 1970s nationalism to 1990s Million Man-ism (recall my previous chapter). It is a view that has drawn fire from many feminists for the extent to which it disregards, when it does not blame, the sufferings and strengths of black women.

21. As Sedgwick so concisely puts it, "*There has been no important and sustained Western discourse in which women's anal eroticism means.* Means anything" (*Tendencies* 204). Edelman cites this essay for its observation that the expression "a piece of ass" references female genitalia (Fuss, *Inside/Out*, 116). His argument is that, for men, anality suggests vaginality, conjuring up a dangerous likeness to the mother (106). Unlike Sedgwick, however, he takes for granted that the ass in question is male, whereas she pauses to regret that this phrase by no means "pretends to name or describe (never *mind*, value) the anus as a site of *women's* active desire" (205). As I say, for me the Wolf Man text is a (missed) opportunity precisely to describe and value the anus as a site of active female desire.

While Sedgwick laments the devalued female anus in "A Poem," in "Is the Rectum Straight?" she complains about Kaja Silverman's assertion that the mother is indispensable to the primal scene. Here Sedgwick echoes Edelman in regarding the mother only as a normativizing figure within a homoerotic fantasy (though at least she sees the father in similar terms) (*Tendencies* 97–98).

For another reading of the Wolf Man case history, see Leo Bersani, who resists the emphasis in Freud on the son's repression, for fear of castration, of his desire for the father. Like Edelman, Bersani would recover the male homoeroticism hinted at but suppressed by Freud's account: the son's pleasure (rather than terror) in imagined penetration by the father (*Homos* 109); the Wolf Man's "dream" as a fantasy of gentle and generous erotic exchange between men (112). Note that in this version too, however, the mother is quickly dispensed with. Indeed, Bersani doesn't even bother to decipher and transpose her anality, much less dwell on the rest of her; rather, the son's immediate and complete displacement of her as his father's lover is taken for granted.

22. On Bersani's gender politics, see the prologue to *Homos* (1995), in which he admits and defends (from feminist complaints) the extent to which his work specifically concerns "gay men's love of the cock" (8). At the same time, he continues, if this particular "we" arises from his own white male perspective, the book also employs other, more inclusive "we's"—for example, the one "alluding to both gay men and lesbians as targets of homophobic aggression" (9). But it is just this shifting, having-it-both-ways use of "we" that troubles me, since it so closely resembles conventional sexist usage: it is a tentatively universal "we" that, when it comes to actual instances, quickly emerges as masculine. Thus in

the prologue itself, Bersani moves continually between seemingly general references to "gays," "sexuality," or "homosexuality" and, as specific examples of these categories, "a boy" (2), "a gay man," or "gay men" (6). I do, however, as I have already suggested, share much of Bersani's skepticism regarding queer refusals of gay identities (4–7). I think he is right that "The discrediting of a specific gay identity . . . has had the curious but predictable result of eliminating the indispensable grounds for resistance to, precisely, hegemonic regimes of the normal. . . . [These regimes] don't need to be natural in order to rule; to demystify them doesn't render them inoperative" (4).

23. For an example of Edelman's solidarity with feminism, see especially "Redeeming the Phallus" (*Homographesis* 24–41), where Edelman breaks down the retrograde sex/gender politics driving Frank Lentricchia's attack (in his notorious Wallace Stevens essay) on both feminism and gay liberation.

24. Thanks to one of the anonymous readers for Columbia University Press, who stressed Halberstam's *difference* (as a woman writing on women) from the figures preceding her. Heather Love has also helped me to appreciate the major ethnographic contribution of Halberstam's work and made many other valuable suggestions concerning this chapter. Jonathan Flatley's wise and rigorous criticism has likewise been indispensable to my thinking about queer theory and feminism.

25. Elsewhere in *Female Masculinity* Halberstam observes that "today's [male] rebel is tomorrow's investment banker" (5), but she doesn't see the young rebel himself as conventionally masculine in his disparagement of the feminine. Moreover, when she turns from the boy rebel to the rebel tomboy, her emphasis is on gender defiance *tout court* (5–9).

26. In contrast to my earlier critique of Butler, here I am the one advocating a deconstructive view over against Halberstam's frequent reliance on rather essentialist notions of gender, even within a project framed in broadly poststructuralist terms. In one sense, I appreciate the fact that Halberstam is willing to compromise this framing by arguing, in effect, for a queer identity politics. Like me, she describes herself as "trying to get away from the tendency within queer popular culture and some queer writing to privilege gender fluidity," and she argues instead that sexual and gender identities, while not fixed, are in fact "remarkably rigid" (147). I admire her frankly political goal of validating women with identities like her own, women whose gender ambiguity is frequently a source of shame (xi). I would, however, distinguish between the theoretical implications of my willingness to essentialize women in order to promote their devalued rights and culture, and Halberstam's willingness to essentialize "masculinity" (if not men) for the sake of an inferiorized subset of the masculine. Within a culture that esteems femininity and masculinity in such grossly asymmetrical ways, the first strategy challenges this asymmetry while the second, however well-intentioned, ultimately reinforces it.

27. I see additional signs of this exclusivity in the "male" bonding and rivalry casually referenced in Halberstam's book and explicitly defended in her essay "Between Butches" (1998). This essay sets out to value butch bonding and mentoring with-

out "reproducing the fateful triangle of heterosexual male bonding that Sedgwick has described" (57). Halberstam realizes her project may be "unpopular" (58) and seeks to reassure Biddy Martin that focusing on butch homosociality doesn't necessarily mean ignoring femmes. I have already made clear, however, that I share Martin's concerns on this point: I am arguing that butch bonding in Halberstam does indeed reproduce not only the fateful subordination of the feminine but also the fetishizing of male competition. As she observes in chapter 5 of *Female Masculinity*, "the border wars between transgender butches and FTMs presume that masculinity is a limited resource" (144), and her book offers many less self-conscious examples of butches vying to be the most masculine. These include the final discussion of boxing, a perfect trope for the premise that masculinity is a coveted prize won through successful battle with other "males." Masculinity as scarce resource is also illustrated by a scene Halberstam describes from the movie *Aliens*: a male soldier aggressively asks a butch who is working out if she's ever been mistaken for a man, to which she replies, "No, have you?" (181) Halberstam suggests that the "tough comeback," given "mid-pull-up," "nicely denaturalizes gender" (181). In spite of the butch's denial, however (no, she hasn't been mistaken for a man), the humor and pleasure of this moment are clearly produced by masculine one-upmanship. By debunking the soldier's manhood, the butch implicitly gains hers. In this sense, the joke does not denaturalize gender so much as illustrate two of its basic premises: one, you get masculinity by having more than the next guy; two, not being manly (i.e., being womanly) is the ultimate humiliation.

28.   For more along these lines, turn again to "Between Butches," where Halberstam dismisses "grumblings that we have now heard too much about butches and not enough about femmes." As in *Female Masculinity*, her claim here is that "not only have we *not* heard enough about butches, but that we know barely enough about female masculinity to locate its specific relationship to lesbianism" (58). A more recent essay suggests, however, a new and welcome willingness to look at femininity, at least among men. In "The Good, the Bad, and the Ugly: Men, Women, and Masculinity" (2002), Halberstam hopes that attention to female masculinity will "force us to look anew upon male femininities and interrogate the new politics of manliness that has swept through gay male communities in the last decade" (345).

29.   In another version of the opposition between "boring mothers" and "sexy men," Halberstam demonizes lesbian feminist forbearers of the 1970s and 1980s in precisely the terms that so anger Faderman and others—as tending, she says, "to cede raw sexuality to men, equate femininity with intimacy rather than sexuality" (135). Recalling Andrew Ross, Halberstam assumes that a feminist desire for sexual reciprocity takes the "rawness" out of sex, that butch-femme roles are self-evidently sexier than "sameness." As I have said in reference to Ross, this kind of blanket critique not only simplifies feminist views of sexuality but also relies on a sexual essentialism of its own.

30.   Halberstam's point in her chapter on stone butchness is to recuperate an identity pathologized even by queer discourses and to see it, instead, as a viable, functional sexuality, legible as a type of female masculinity. My difference is less with her

view of this sexuality than with her reading of *Stone Butch Blues*. For while Halberstam describes stoneness as both "problematic" and "powerful" for Feinberg's narrator, her concern, as I say, is to stress the latter. I agree that Jess is a "powerful" rather than simply dysfunctional figure, but I want to locate her charisma not in her stoneness but in her combination of hard and soft, "masculine" and "feminine," butch and maternal. Halberstam specifically refutes an opinion expressed by Butler—that the butch who "provides" sexually may also, in sacrificing her own pleasure, fall into "the most ancient trap of feminine self-abnegation" (Butler, "Imitation," 25; Halberstam 127). I follow Butler in wishing to bring out the "feminine" aspects of Jess's butchness, but I see these less as a "trap" than as an attractive addition to her "masculinity." For an essay interested, as I am, in valuing butch feelings, see Ann Cvetkovich's "Untouchability and Vulnerability: Stone Butchness as Emotional Style" (1998), which describes butch reticence not as the absence of emotion but rather as a particular emotional style.

31. Joan Nestle's collection, *The Persistent Desire: A Femme-Butch Reader* (1992), is full of femme testimonials both to femme strength and to the appealing vulnerability as well as power of butches. See, for example, Melinda Goodman's poem in which "butches are vulnerable/It's the femmes that are fierce/ . . . Butches are the sweet ones" (235); or the poem by Lee Lynch asking (like Butler), "Who is more womanly/than the stone butch?/who knows better/how to deny her own/feelings" (405). Finally, for my purposes here, see especially Sima Rabinowitz's femme disidentification with her butch's longing to bear and mother a child: "Your butch wants to have a baby. You don't know what she must be feeling, because you have never imagined a baby in your belly. . . . But she has. For as long as she can remember, she says. . . . She wants to feel a baby growing in her womb. She wants to hold a baby to her breast. She wants to watch a baby learn to crawl, to walk, to run, to shoot hoops" (391).

32. In Jess's case, the preoedipal tie is not to her birth mother, who immediately shunned her, but to her Native American neighbors, "the Dineh women," who assisted at her birth and cherished her as a baby (13–15). See Kath Weston's *Families We Choose: Lesbians, Gays, Kinship* (1991) for more on structures of queer kinship that are nonbiological.

33. Jess has breast-reduction surgery as well as male hormone therapy and feels that she "comes home" to her masculinized body (224). In this sense, as Jay Prosser argues, her passing as a man is more than a "disguise" assumed by a woman/lesbian to escape harassment (Prosser 183). But Prosser goes on to suggest that Jess's story swerves away from a simply transsexual one, since Jess decides to stop taking hormones and ultimately claims the identity of a "transgendered woman" rather than that of a female-to-male transsexual (185–87). Prosser notes that "Jess has maintained to herself while passing as a man the stability of her identity *as a masculine woman*, that transgendered ambivalence" (185). My discussion too is concerned with bringing out the "maternal" identity that Jess retains, for herself and for Kim, who immediately recognizes her even as she passes for male.

WORKS CITED

Abraham, Julie. *Are Girls Necessary? Lesbian Writing and Modern Histories.* New York: Routledge, 1996.

———. "I Know What Boys Like: Tales from the Dyke Side." *Voice Literary Supplement* (June 1992):20–21.

Afzal-Khan, Fawzia. Untitled review of *Cultural Imperialism. World Literature Today* 68.1 (Winter 1994): 229–30.

Ahmad, Aijaz. *In Theory: Classes, Nations, Literatures.* London: Verso, 1992.

Ansell-Pearson, Keith, Benita Parry, and Judith Squires, eds. *Cultural Readings of Imperialism: Edward Said and the Gravity of History.* New York: St. Martin's, 1997.

Aptheker, Bettina, ed. *Lynching and Rape: An Exchange of Views.* Occasional Paper No. 25. San Jose, CA: American Institute for Marxist Studies, 1977.

Austen, Jane. *Mansfield Park.* London: Penguin, 1966.

———. *Persuasion.* Harmondsworth: Penguin, 1966.

———. *Northanger Abbey.* Harmondsworth: Penguin, 1972.

Awkward, Michael. "A Black Man's Place(s) in Black Feminist Criticism." In *Representing Black Men*, ed. Marcellus Blount and George P. Cunningham. New York: Routledge, 1996, 3–26.

Baughman, Cynthia, and Richard Moran. "'A Moment of Clarity': Retrieval, Redemption, Resurrection, and Narrative Time in *Pulp Fiction.*" *Creative Screenwriting* 1.4 (1994): 108–18.

Baumgardner, Jennifer and Amy Richards. *Manifesta: Young Women, Feminism, and the Future.* New York: Farrar, Straus & Giroux, 2000.

Bersani, Leo. *Homos.* Cambridge: Harvard University Press, 1995.

————. "Is the Rectum a Grave?" In *AIDS: Cultural Analysis, Cultural Activism*, ed. Douglas Crimp. Cambridge: MIT Press, 1988, 197–222.

Blair, Sara. "*Pulp Fiction*: Any Good?" Unpublished paper, 1995.

Boone, Joseph A. "Vacation Cruises; or The Homoerotics of Orientalism." *PMLA* 110.1 (Jan. 1995): 89–107.

Bové, Paul A., ed. *Edward Said and the Work of the Critic: Speaking Truth to Power*. Durham: Duke University Press, 2000.

Brenkman, John. "Queer Post-Politics: On Edelman's 'The Future is Kid Stuff.'" *Narrative* 10.2 (May 2002): 174–80.

Brown, Susan, Theresa Collier, and Prayon Meade. Interview Series with Charlayne Hunter-Gault. *MacNeil/Lehrer Newshour*. PBS. WNET, New York, 2 Oct. 1990; 16 Jan. 1991; 11 Feb. 1991; 15 May 1991.

Brownmiller, Susan. *Against Our Will: Men, Women and Rape*. Middlesex: Penguin, 1976.

Buhle, Mari Jo. *Women and American Socialism, 1870–1920*. Urbana: University of Illinois Press, 1981.

Butler, Judith. *Bodies That Matter: On the Discursive Limits of "Sex."* New York: Routledge, 1993, 57–91.

————. "Contingent Foundations." In *Feminists Theorize the Political*, ed. Judith Butler and Joan W. Scott. New York: Routledge, 1992, 3–21.

————. *Gender Trouble: Feminism and the Subversion of Identity*. 1990; reprint, New York: Routledge, 1999.

————. "Imitation and Gender Insubordination." In *Inside/Out: Lesbian Theories, Gay Theories*, ed. Diana Fuss. New York: Routledge, 1991, 13–31.

Carby, Hazel V. *Race Men*. Cambridge: Harvard University Press, 1998.

————. *Reconstructing Womanhood: The Emergence of the Afro-American Woman Novelist*. New York: Oxford University Press, 1987.

————. "Telling Fruits from Roots." *Times Literary Supplement* 29 Dec. 1989:1446.

Case, Sue-Ellen. "Toward a Butch-Feminist Retro Future." In *Cross-Purposes: Lesbians, Feminists, and the Limits of Alliance*, ed. Dana Heller. Bloomington: Indiana University Press, 1997, 205–20.

Castle, Terry. *The Apparitional Lesbian: Female Homosexuality and Modern Culture*. New York: Columbia University Press, 1993.

Chapman, Rowena, and Jonathan Rutherford, eds. *Male Order: Unwrapping Masculinity*. London: Lawrence & Wishart, 1988.

Chodorow, Nancy. *The Reproduction of Mothering: Psychoanalysis and the Sociology of Gender*. Berkeley: University of California Press, 1978.

Clarke, John. "The Skinheads and the Magical Recovery of Community." In *Resistance Through Rituals: Youth Subcultures in Post-War Britain*, ed. Stuart Hall and Tony Jefferson. London: Hutchinson, 1975, 99–102.

Clarkson, Wensley. *Quentin Tarantino: Shooting from the Hip*. London: Piatkus, 1995.

Cleland, John. *Memoirs of a Woman of Pleasure*. Ed. Peter Sabor. New York: Oxford University Press, 1985.

Clover, Carol J. *Men, Women, and Chainsaws: Gender in the Modern Horror Film.* Princeton: Princeton University Press, 1992, 21–64.

Cohan, Steven. "Masquerading as the American Male in the Fifties: Picnic, William Holden and the Spectacle of Masculinity in Hollywood Film." In *Male Trouble,* ed. Constance Penley and Sharon Willis. Minneapolis: University of Minnesota Press, 1993, 202–33.

Crafts, Hannah. *The Bondswoman's Narrative.* Ed. Henry Louis Gates Jr. New York: Warner, 2002.

Crenshaw, Kimberle. "Beyond Racism and Misogyny: Black Feminism and 2 Live Crew." *Boston Review* 16 (Dec. 1991).

Cvetkovich, Ann. "Untouchability and Vulnerability: Stone Butchness as Emotional Style." In *Butch/Femme: Inside Lesbian Gender,* ed. Sally R. Munt. London: Cassell, 1998, 159–69.

Daly, Mary. *Gyn/Ecology: The Metaethics of Radical Feminism.* Boston: Beacon, 1978.

Dargis, Manohla. "Quentin Tarantino on *Pulp Fiction.*" *Sight and Sound* (Nov. 1994):16–19.

Davis, Angela Y. "Rape, Racism, and the Myth of the Black Rapist." In *Women, Race and Class.* New York: Random House, 1983, 172–201.

Decker, Jeffrey Louis. "The State of Rap: Time and Place in Hip Hop Nationalism." In *Microphone Fiends: Youth Music and Youth Culture,* ed. Andrew Ross and Tricia Rose. New York: Routledge, 1994, 99–121.

Deemer, Charles. "The Screenplays of Quentin Tarantino." *Creative Screenwriting* 1.4 (1994): 59–83.

de Lauretis, Teresa. "Fem/Les Scramble." In *Cross-Purposes: Lesbians, Feminists, and the Limits of Alliance,* ed. Dana Heller. Bloomington: Indiana University Press, 1997, 42–48.

———. *The Practice of Love: Lesbian Sexuality and Perverse Desire.* Bloomington: Indiana University Press, 1994.

———. "Queer Theory: Lesbian and Gay Sexualities, an Introduction." *differences* 3.2 (1991): iii–xviii.

De Palma, Brian, dir. *Casualties of War.* Columbia, 1989.

Dever, Carolyn. "Obstructive Behavior: Dykes in the Mainstream of Feminist Theory." In *Cross-Purposes: Lesbians, Feminists, and the Limits of Alliance,* ed. Dana Heller. Bloomington: Indiana University Press, 1997, 19–41.

Didion, Joan. "New York: Sentimental Journeys." *The New York Review of Books* 17 Jan. 1991:45–56.

Dittmar, Linda and Gene Michaud, ed. *From Hanoi to Hollywood: The Vietnam War in American Film.* New Brunswick: Rutgers University Press, 1990.

Doan, Laura, ed. *The Lesbian Postmodern.* New York: Columbia University Press, 1994.

Doane, Mary Ann. *The Desire to Desire: The Woman's Film of the 1940s.* Bloomington: Indiana University Press, 1987.

duCille, Ann. "The Occult of True Black Womanhood." *Signs* 19.3 (Spring 1994): 591–629.

———. "'Who Reads Here?': Back Talking with Houston Baker." *Novel* (Fall 1992):97–105.

Duggan, Lisa. "Making It Perfectly Queer." In *Sex Wars: Sexual Dissent and Political Culture*, ed. Lisa Duggan and Nan D. Hunter. New York: Routledge, 1995, 155–72.

Duggan, Lisa and Kathleen McHugh. "A Fem(me)inist Manifesto." *Women and Performance* 8.16 (1996): 150–60.

The Economist (unsigned, untitled review of *Culture and Imperialism*) 27 Feb. 1993:95.

Echols, Alice. *Daring to Be Bad: Radical Feminism in America 1967–1975.* Minneapolis: University of Minnesota Press, 1989.

———. *Shaky Ground: The '60s and Its Aftershocks.* New York: Columbia University Press, 2002.

Edelman, Lee. "The Future is Kid Stuff: Queer Theory, Disidentification, and the Death Drive." *Narrative* 6.1 (Jan. 1998): 18–30.

———. *Homographesis: Essays in Gay Literary and Cultural Theory.* New York: Routledge, 1994.

———. "Post-Partum: Response to Brenkman." *Narrative* 10.2 (May 2002): 181–85.

———. "Seeing Things: Representation, the Scene of Surveillance, and the Spectacle of Gay Male Sex." In *Inside/Out: Lesbian Theories, Gay Theories*, ed. Diana Fuss. New York: Routledge, 1991, 93–116.

Ehrenreich, Barbara. *The Hearts of Men: American Dreams and the Flight from Commitment.* Garden City, NY: Anchor, 1983.

Enloe, Cynthia. *Bananas, Beaches and Bases: Making Feminist Sense of International Politics.* Berkeley: University of California Press, 1990.

Epps, Brad. "The Fetish of Fluidity." In *Homosexuality and Psychoanalysis*, ed. Tim Dean and Christopher Lane. Chicago: University of Chicago Press, 2001, 412–31.

Estrich, Susan. *Real Rape.* Cambridge: Harvard University Press, 1987.

Faderman, Lillian. Afterword. In *Cross-Purposes: Lesbians, Feminists, and the Limits of Alliance*, ed. Dana Heller. Bloomington: Indiana University Press, 1997, 221–29.

———. *Odd Girls and Twilight Lovers: A History of Lesbian Life in Twentieth-Century America.* New York: Columbia University Press, 1991.

Faue, Elizabeth. *Community of Suffering and Struggle: Women, Men, and the Labor Movement in Minneapolis, 1915–1945.* Chapel Hill: University of North Carolina Press, 1991.

Favor, J. Martin. *Authentic Blackness: The Folk in the New Negro Renaissance.* Durham: Duke University Press, 1999.

Feinberg, Leslie. *Stone Butch Blues.* New York: Firebrand, 1993.

Felski, Rita. "Images of the Intellectual: From Philosophy to Cultural Studies." In *Doing Time: Feminist Theory and Postmodern Culture.* New York: New York University Press, 2000, 154–74.

Fennessey, Scott. "Conjunctions of Geography and Society in Austen's *Mansfield Park.*" Unpublished paper, 1994.

Ferguson, Moira. *Colonialism and Gender Relations from Mary Wollstonecraft to Jamaica Kincaid.* New York: Columbia University Press, 1993.

Fiedler, Leslie. *What Was Literature? Class Culture and Mass Society.* New York: Simon & Schuster, 1982.

Foner, Philip S., ed. *Frederick Douglass on Women's Rights.* Westport, CT: Greenwood Press, 1976.

Foucault, Michel. *History of Sexuality: Volume I.* Trans. Robert Hurley. New York: Vintage, 1980.

Fraiman, Susan. "Catharine MacKinnon and the Feminist Porn Debates." *American Quarterly* 47.4 (1995): 743–49.

Frank, Thomas. *The Conquest of Cool: Business Culture, Counterculture, and the Rise of Hip Consumerism.* Chicago: University of Chicago Press, 1997.

Freud, Sigmund. *Beyond the Pleasure Principle.* Ed. James Strachey. New York: Norton, 1961.

Fuller, Graham. "Quentin Tarantino: Answers First, Questions Later." In Reservoir Dogs *and* True Romance. New York: Grove, 1994, ix–xviii.

Fuss, Diana. *Essentially Speaking: Feminism, Nature and Difference.* New York: Routledge, 1989.

Garber, Linda. *Identity Poetics: Race, Class and the Lesbian-Feminist Roots of Queer Theory.* New York: Columbia University Press, 2001.

Gates, Henry Louis, Jr. "Affirmative Reaction: A Conversation with Cornel West on Talent, Tradition, and the Crisis of the Black Male." *Transition* 5.4 (Winter 1995): 173–86.

———. *Colored People: A Memoir.* New York: Vintage, 1995.

———. "Delusions of Grandeur: Young Blacks Must Be Taught That Sports Are Not the Only Avenues of Opportunity." *Sports Illustrated* 75.8 (Oct. 1994).

———. *Figures in Black: Words, Signs, and the "Racial" Self.* New York: Oxford University Press, 1987.

———. Introduction to *Black Male: Representations of Masculinity in Contemporary American Art,* ed. Thelma Golden. New York: Whitney Museum, 1994.

———. *Loose Canons: Notes on the Culture Wars.* New York: Oxford University Press, 1992.

———. *The Signifying Monkey: A Theory of African-American Literary Criticism.* New York: Oxford University Press, 1988.

———. *Thirteen Ways of Looking at a Black Man.* New York: Random House, 1997.

———. "'What's Love Got To Do with It?': Critical Theory, Integrity, and the Black Idiom." *New Literary History* 18.2 (Winter 1987): 345–62.

———. *Wonders of the African World.* New York: Knopf, 1999.

Gates, Henry Louis, Jr., ed. *Afro-American Women Writers.* Boston: G. K. Hall, 1998.

———. *Oxford-Schomburg Library of Nineteenth-Century Black Women Writers.* New York: Oxford University Press, 1991.

———. *Reading Black, Reading Feminist: A Critical Anthology.* New York: Penguin, 1990.

Gates, Henry Louis, Jr. and K. Anthony Appiah, eds. *Africana: The Encyclopedia of the African and African-American Experience.* New York: Basic, 1999.

Gates, Henry Louis, Jr. and Nellie McKay, eds. *Norton Anthology of African American Literature.* New York: Norton, 1996.

Gates, Henry Louis, Jr. and Cornel West. *The Future of the Race.* New York: Knopf, 1996.

Gilligan, Carol. *In a Different Voice: Psychological Theory and Women's Development.* Cambridge: Harvard University Press, 1982.

Gorra, Michael. "Who Paid the Bills at Mansfield Park?" *New York Times Book Review* 28 Feb. 1993:11.

Grossberg, Lawrence. *We Gotta Get Out of This Place: Popular Conservatism and Postmodern Culture.* New York: Routledge, 1992.

Gunning, Sandra. *Race, Rape, and Lynching: The Red Record of American Literature, 1890–1912.* New York: Oxford University Press, 1996.

Halberstam, Judith. "Between Butches." In *Butch/Femme: Inside Lesbian Gender,* ed. Sally R. Munt. London: Cassell, 1998, 57–65.

———. *Female Masculinity.* Durham: Duke University Press, 1998.

———. "The Good, the Bad, and the Ugly: Men, Women, and Masculinity." In *Masculinity Studies and Feminist Theory: New Directions,* ed. Judith Kegan Gardiner. New York: Columbia University Press, 2002.

Hall, Jacquelyn Dowd. "'The Mind that Burns in Each Body': Women, Rape, and Racial Violence." In *Powers of Desire: The Politics of Sexuality,* ed. Ann Snitow, Christine Stansell, and Sharon Thompson. New York: Monthly Review Press, 1983, 328–49.

———. *The Revolt Against Chivalry: Jessie Daniel Ames and the Women's Campaign Against Lynching.* New York: Columbia University Press, 1979.

Hall, Stuart, et al., eds. *Culture, Media, Language.* London: Hutchinson, 1980.

Harper, Phillip Brian. *Are We Not Men? Masculine Anxiety and the Problem of African-American Identity.* New York: Oxford University Press, 1996.

Hartman, Saidiya V. *Scenes of Subjection: Terror, Slavery, and Self-Making in Nineteenth-Century America.* New York: Oxford University Press, 1997.

Hartmann, Heidi. "The Unhappy Marriage of Marxism and Feminism: Towards a More Progressive Union." In *Women and Revolution,* ed. Lydia Sargent. Boston: South End Press, 1981, 1–33.

Hebdige, Dick. "The Meaning of Mod." In *Resistance Through Rituals: Youth Subcultures in Post-War Britain,* ed. Stuart Hall and Tony Jefferson. London: Hutchinson, 1975, 87–96.

Heller, Dana, ed. *Cross-Purposes: Lesbians, Feminists, and the Limits of Alliance.* Bloomington: Indiana University Press, 1997.

Hennessy, Rosemary. "Queer Theory, Left Politics." In *Marxism Beyond Marxism,* ed. Saree Makdisi, Cesare Casarino, and Rebecca E. Karl. New York: Routledge, 1996, 214–42.

Henry, Annette. "Stuart Hall, Cultural Studies: Theory Letting You Off the Hook?" In *Feminist Engagements: Reading, Resisting, and Revisioning Male Theorists in Education and Cultural Studies,* ed. Kathleen Weiler. New York: Routledge, 2001, 165–82.

Hernton, Calvin. *The Sexual Mountain and Black Women Writers.* New York: Anchor, 1987.

Hilferty, Robert. "Reservoir Dogs." *Cineaste* 19.4 (1992): 79–81.

Holcombe, Lee. *Wives and Property: Reform of Married Women's Property Law in Nineteenth-Century England.* Toronto: University of Toronto Press, 1983.

hooks, bell. *Black Looks: Race and Representation.* Boston: South End Press, 1992.

———. "Cool Tool." *Artforum* (March 1995): 63–66, 108.

Hopkins, Robert. "General Tilney and Affairs of State: The Political Gothic of *Northanger Abbey.*" *Philological Quarterly* 57.2 (Spring 1978): 213–24.

Howe, Irving. "History and Literature." *Dissent* (Fall 1993):557–59.

Hunter-Gault, Charlayne. *In My Place.* New York: Farrar, Straus & Giroux, 1992.

Huyssen, Andreas. "Mass Culture as Woman: Modernism's Other." In *Studies in Entertainment: Critical Approaches to Mass Culture,* ed. Tania Modleski. Bloomington: Indiana University Press, 1986, 188–207.

Indiana, Gary. "Geek Chic." *Artforum* (March 1995):63–66, 104, 108.

Irigarary, Luce. "Commodities Among Themselves." In *This Sex Which is Not One,* trans. Catherine Porter. Ithaca: Cornell University Press, 1985, 192–97.

Jardine, Alice. "Men in Feminism: Odor di Uomo or Compagnons de Route?" In *Men in Feminism,* ed. Alice Jardine and Paul Smith. New York: Methuen, 1987, 54–61.

Jefferson, Tony. "Cultural Responses of the Teds: The Defense of Space and Status." In *Resistance Through Rituals: Youth Subcultures in Post-War Britain,* ed. Stuart Hall and Tony Jefferson. London: Hutchinson, 1975, 81–86.

Jeffords, Susan. "Protection Racket." *The Women's Review of Books* July 1991:10.

———. *The Remasculinization of America: Gender and the Vietnam War.* Bloomington: Indiana University Press, 1989.

Jeffreys, Sheila. "The Queer Disappearance of Lesbians: Sexuality in the Academy." *Women's Studies International Forum* 17.5 (1994): 459–72.

Johnson, Claudia L. *Jane Austen: Women, Politics, and the Novel.* Chicago: University of Chicago Press, 1988.

Johnston, Claire. "Women's Cinema as Counter-Cinema." In *Notes on Women's Cinema,* ed. Claire Johnston. *Screen* Pamphlet. London: SEFT, 1973, 24–31.

Joyce, Joyce A. "The Black Canon: Reconstructing Black American Literary Criticism." *New Literary History* 18.2 (Winter 1987): 335–44.

———. "'Who the Cap Fit': Unconsciousness and Unconscionableness in the Criticism of Houston A. Baker, Jr., and Henry Louis Gates, Jr." *New Literary History* 18.2 (Winter 1987): 371–84.

Kipnis, Laura. *Bound and Gagged: Pornography and the Politics of Fantasy in America.* New York: Grove, 1996.

Kirkham, Margaret. *Jane Austen, Feminism, and Fiction.* Sussex: Harvester Press, 1983.

Koenig, Rhoda. Untitled review of *Culture and Imperialism. New York* 1 March 1993:119–20.

Lang, Daniel. *Casualties of War.* New York: McGraw-Hill, 1969.

Leavis, Q. D. "A Critical Theory of Jane Austen's Writings." *Scrutiny* 10 (1942): 61–75.

Lee, Spike, dir. *Do the Right Thing*. Universal, 1989.

———. *School Daze*. Columbia, 1988.

Lee, Spike. "Final Cut." With Henry Louis Gates Jr. *Transition* 52 (1991): 176–204.

Leonard, John. "Novel Colonies." *The Nation* 22 March 1993:383–90.

Lévi-Strauss, Claude. *The Elementary Structures of Kinship*. Boston: Beacon Press, 1969.

Lewis, Lisa A. *Gender Politics and MTV: Voicing the Difference*. Philadelphia: Temple University Press, 1990.

Lichtenstein, Nelson. *State of the Union: A Century of American Labor*. Princeton: Princeton University Press, 2002.

Lipsitz, George. "We Know What Time It Is: Race, Class and Youth Culture in the Nineties." In *Microphone Fiends: Youth Music and Youth Culture*, ed. Andrew Ross and Tricia Rose. New York: Routledge, 1994, 17–28.

Lott, Eric. *Love and Theft: Blackface Minstrelsy and the American Working Class*. New York: Oxford University Press, 1993.

———. "White Like Me: Racial Cross-Dressing and the Construction of American Whiteness." In *Cultures of United States Imperialism*, ed. Amy Kaplan and Donald Pease. Durham: Duke University Press, 1993, 474–95.

Lowe, Lisa. *Critical Terrains: French and British Orientalisms*. Ithaca: Cornell University Press, 1991.

Lubiano, Wahneema. "But Compared to What?: Reading Realism, Representation, and Essentialism in *School Daze*, *Do the Right Thing*, and the Spike Lee Discourse." In *Representing Black Men*, ed. Marcellus Blount and George P. Cunningham. New York: Routledge, 1996.

MacAdams, Lewis. *Birth of the Cool: Beat, Bebop, and the American Avant-Garde*. New York: Free Press, 2001.

MacKinnon, Catharine A. *Only Words*. Cambridge: Harvard University Press, 1993.

Majors, Richard and Janet Mancini Billson. *Cool Pose: The Dilemmas of Black Manhood in America*. New York: MacMillan, 1991.

Mao, Douglas. "*Pulp Fiction*: The Anxiety of Evacuation." Unpublished paper, 1995.

Martin, Biddy. *Femininity Played Straight: The Significance of Being Lesbian*. New York: Routledge, 1996.

Mayne, Judith. "Walking the *Tightrope* of Feminism and Male Desire." In *Men in Feminism*, ed. Alice Jardine and Paul Smith. New York: Methuen, 1987, 62–70.

McClintock, Anne. *Imperial Leather: Race, Gender, and Sexuality in the Colonial Contest*. New York: Routledge, 1995.

———. "Sex Workers and Sex Work: Introduction." *Social Text* 37 (Winter 1993): 1–10.

McClintock, Anne, Aaimir Mufti, and Ella Shohat, eds. *Dangerous Liaisons: Gender, Nation, and Postcolonial Perspectives*. Minneapolis: University of Minnesota Press, 1997.

McDowell, Deborah E. *"The Changing Same": Black Women's Literature, Criticism, and Theory*. Bloomington: Indiana University Press, 1995.

————. "In the First Place: Making Frederick Douglass and the Afro-American Narrative Tradition." In *Critical Essays on Frederick Douglass*, ed. William L. Andrews. Boston: G. K. Hall, 1991, 192–214.

McRobbie, Angela. *Feminism and Youth Culture: From "Jackie" to "Just Seventeen."* London: MacMillan, 1991.

————. "Shut Up and Dance: Youth Culture and Changing Modes of Femininity." *Cultural Studies* 7.3 (October 1993): 406–26.

McRobbie, Angela and Jenny Garber. "Girls and Subcultures: An Exploration." In *Resistance Through Rituals: Youth Subcultures in Post-War Britain*, ed. Stuart Hall and Tony Jefferson. London: Hutchinson, 1975, 209–22.

Mercer, Kobena. *Welcome to the Jungle: New Positions in Black Cultural Studies*. New York: Routledge, 1994, 189–219.

Meyer, Susan L. *Imperialism at Home*. Ithaca: Cornell University Press, 1996.

Miller, D. A. "Anal *Rope*." In *Inside/Out: Lesbian Theories, Gay Theories*, ed. Diana Fuss. New York: Routledge, 1991, 119–41.

————. *The Novel and the Police*. Berkeley: University of California Press, 1988.

Mitchell, W. T. J. "In the Wilderness." *London Review of Books* 8 April 1993:11–12.

Modleski, Tania. *Feminism Without Women: Culture and Criticism in a "Postfeminist" Age*. New York: Routledge, 1991.

————. *Loving with a Vengeance: Mass-Produced Fantasies for Women*. 1982. New York: Methuen, 1984.

————. *Old Wives' Tales and Other Women's Stories*. New York: New York University Press, 1998.

————. *The Women Who Knew Too Much: Hitchcock and Feminist Theory*. New York: Routledge, 1988.

Moraga, Cherrié. *Waiting in the Wings: Portrait of a Queer Motherhood*. Ithaca: Firebrand, 1997.

Moraga, Cherrié and Gloria Anzaldúa, eds. *This Bridge Called My Back: Writings by Radical Women of Color*. 1981; reprint, New York: Kitchen Table, 1983.

Morris, Meaghan. "Things to Do with Shopping Centres." In *Grafts: Feminist Cultural Criticism*, ed. Susan Sheridan. London: Verso, 1988, 193–225.

Mulvey, Laura. *Visual and Other Pleasures*. Bloomington: Indiana University Press, 1989.

Munt, Sally R., ed. *Butch/Femme: Inside Lesbian Gender*. London: Cassell, 1998.

Neale, Steve. "Masculinity as Spectacle: Reflections on Men and Mainstream Cinema." *Screen* 24.6 (1983): 2–16.

Nelson, Cary. "Men, Feminism: The Materiality of Discourse." In *Men in Feminism*, ed. Alice Jardine and Paul Smith. New York: Methuen, 1987, 153–72.

Nestle, Joan. *The Persistent Desire: A Femme-Butch Reader*. Boston: Alyson, 1992.

O'Dair, Sharon. "Academostars are the Symptom; What's the Disease?" *The Minnesota Review* 52–4 (Fall 2001): 159–74.

Painter, Nell. Review of Gates and West, *The Future of the Race*. *The Nation* 262.18 (May 1996): 38.

Payne, Charles. *I've Got the Light of Freedom: The Organizing Tradition and the Mississippi Freedom Struggle.* Berkeley: University of California Press, 1995.

Pellegrini, Ann. "Star Gazing." *The Minnesota Review* 52–4 (Fall 2001): 209–14.

Pierson, Ruth Roach and Nupur Chaudhuri, eds. *Nation, Empire, Colony: Historicizing Gender and Race.* Bloomington: Indiana University Press, 1998.

Perera, Suvendrini. *Reaches of Empire: The English Novel from Edgeworth to Dickens.* New York: Columbia University Press, 1991.

Pollitt, Katha. "Are Women Morally Superior to Men?" *The Nation* 28 Dec. 1992:799–807.

Pountain, David and David Robins. *Cool Rules: Anatomy of an Attitude.* London: Reaktion, 2000.

Prosser, Jay. *Second Skins: The Body Narratives of Transsexuality.* New York: Columbia University Press, 1998.

Radway, Janice A. *Reading the Romance: Women, Patriarchy, and Popular Literature.* Chapel Hill: University of North Carolina Press, 1984.

Rich, Adrienne. "Compulsory Heterosexuality and Lesbian Existence." In *Blood, Bread, and Poetry: Selected Prose 1979–1985.* New York: Norton, 1986, 23–75.

Robbins, Bruce. "Celeb-Reliance: Intellectuals, Celebrity, and Upward Mobility." *Postmodern Culture* 9.2 (1999): <muse.jhu.edu/journals/postmodern_culture>

Roiphe, Katie. *The Morning After: Sex, Fear, and Feminism on Campus.* Boston: Little, Brown, 1993.

Roof, Judith. *A Lure of Knowledge: Lesbian Sexuality and Theory.* New York: Columbia University Press, 1991.

Rose, Tricia. *Black Noise: Rap Music and Black Culture in Contemporary America.* Hanover, NH: Wesleyan University Press, 1994.

Rosen, Ruth. "Women's Liberation." In *Encyclopedia of the American Left,* ed. Mary Jo Buhle, Paul Buhle, and Dan Georgakas. 2nd ed. New York: Oxford University Press, 1998, 882–89.

Ross, Andrew. "Back on the Box: Weather Report on the Rap Channel." *Artforum* (May 1995):17, 112.

———. "Ballots, Bullets, or Batmen: Can Cultural Studies Do the Right Thing?" *Screen* 31.1 (1990): 26–44.

———. *The Celebration Chronicles: Life, Liberty, and the Pursuit of Property Value in Disney's New Town.* New York: Ballantine, 1999.

———. *The Chicago Gangster Theory of Life: Nature's Debt to Society.* London: Verso, 1994.

———. "Cowboys, Cadillacs, and Cosmonauts: Families, Film Genres, and Technocultures." In *Engendering Men: The Question of Male Feminist Criticism,* ed. Joseph A. Boone and Michael Cadden. New York: Routledge, 1990, 87–101.

———. "Demonstrating Sexual Difference." In *Men in Feminism,* ed. Alice Jardine and Paul Smith. New York: Methuen, 1987, 47–53.

———. "Dress to Oppress: Weather Report on the Return of the Sweatshop." *Artforum* (March 1996):18, 119.

———. "The Everyday Life of Lou Andreas-Salomé: Making Video History." In *Feminism and Psychoanalysis*, ed. Richard Feldstein and Judith Roof. Ithaca: Cornell University Press, 1989, 142–63.

———. *The Failure of Modernism: Symptoms of American Poetry*. New York: Columbia University Press, 1986.

———. "The Gangsta and the Diva: Poverty Meets Performance." *The Nation* 22/29 August 1994:191–94.

———. Introduction to *Microphone Fiends: Youth Music and Youth Culture*, ed. Andrew Ross and Tricia Rose. New York: Routledge, 1994, 1–13.

———. "Introduction." *Social Text* 46/47 ("Science Wars" Issue, ed. Andrew Ross) 14.1 and 14.2 (Spring/Summer 1996): 1–13.

———. "No Question of Silence." In *Men in Feminism*, ed. Alice Jardine and Paul Smith. New York: Methuen, 1987, 85–92.

———. *No Respect: Intellectuals and Popular Culture*. New York: Routledge, 1989.

———. *No Sweat*. Ed. Andrew Ross. London: Verso, 1997.

———. *Real Love: In Pursuit of Cultural Justice*. New York: New York University Press, 1998.

———. "The Right Buff." *Artforum* (November 1995):27–28.

———. *Strange Weather: Culture, Science, and Technology in the Age of Limits*. London: Verso, 1991.

———. "This Bridge Called My Pussy." In *Madonnarama: Essays on Sex and Popular Culture*, ed. Lisa Frank and Paul Smith. Pittsburgh: Cleis Press, 1993, 47–64.

———. "Undisciplined: An Interview with Andrew Ross." With Jeffrey Williams and Mike Hill. *Minnesota Review* 45/46 (1996): 77–94.

———. "Weather Report: The World Cup." *Artforum* (September 1994):14–15.

Ross, Marlon B. "Race, Rape, Castration: Feminist Theories of Sexual Violence and Masculine Strategies of Black Protest." In *Masculinity Studies and Feminist Theory: New Directions*, ed. Judith Kegan Gardiner. New York: Columbia, 2002, 290–343.

Rottnek, Matthew, ed. *Sissies and Tomboys: Gender Nonconformity and Homosexual Childhood*. New York: New York University Press, 1999.

Rubin, Gayle. "The Traffic in Women: Notes on the 'Political Economy' of Sex." In *Toward an Anthropology of Women*, ed. Rayna R. Reiter. New York: Monthly Review Press, 1975, 157–210.

Rutherford, Jonathan. "Who's That Man." In *Male Order: Unwrapping Masculinity*, ed. Rowena Chapman and Jonathan Rutherford. London: Lawrence & Wishart, 1988, 21–67.

Said, Edward W. *Covering Islam: How the Media and the Experts Determine How We See the Rest of the World*. New York: Pantheon, 1981.

———. *Culture and Imperialism*. New York: Knopf, 1993.

———. *Out of Place: A Memoir*. New York: Vintage, 1999.

Sánchez-Eppler, Karen. *Touching Liberty: Abolition, Feminism, and the Politics of the Body*. Berkeley: University of California Press, 1993.

Sedgwick, Eve Kosofsky. *Between Men: English Literature and Male Homosocial Desire.* New York: Columbia University Press, 1985.

————. *Epistemology of the Closet.* Berkeley: University of California Press, 1990.

————. *Tendencies.* Durham: Duke University Press, 1993.

————. "Jane Austen and the Masturbating Girl." *Critical Inquiry* 17 (Summer 1991): 818–37.

Segal, Lynne, and Mary McIntosh. *Sex Exposed.* New Brunswick: Rutgers University Press, 1992.

Shumway, David R. "The Star System in Literary Studies." *The Minnesota Review* 52–4 (Fall 2001): 175–84.

Silverstein, Olga and Beth Rashbaum. *The Courage to Raise Good Men.* New York: Penguin, 1994.

Silverthorne, Jeanne. "Recidivist Dames." *Artforum* (March 1995):63–66, 108, 110.

Smith, Valerie. "Gender and Afro-Americanist Literary Theory and Criticism." In *Speaking of Gender.* New York: Routledge, 1989, 56–70.

————. "Split Affinities: The Case of the Interracial Rape." In *Conflicts in Feminism,* ed. Marianne Hirsch and Evelyn Fox-Keller. New York: Routledge, 1990, 271–87.

Spillers, Hortense J. "Mama's Baby, Papa's Maybe: An American Grammar Book." *Diacritics* 17.2 (Summer 1987): 65–81.

Spivak, Gayatri Chakravorty. *In Other Worlds: Essays in Cultural Politics.* New York: Routledge, 1987.

————. *The Post-Colonial Critic: Interviews, Strategies, Dialogues.* Ed. Sarah Harasym. New York: Routledge, 1990.

Spurgin, Tim. "The *Times Magazine* and Academic Megastars." *The Minnesota Review* 52–4 (Fall 2001): 225–37.

Stansell, Christine. *American Moderns: Bohemian New York and the Creation of a New Century.* New York: Henry Holt, 2000.

Staves, Susan. *Married Women's Separate Property in England, 1660–1833.* Cambridge: Harvard University Press, 1990.

Stearns, Peter N. *American Cool: Constructing a Twentieth-Century Emotional Style.* New York: New York University Press, 1994.

Suleri, Sara. *The Rhetoric of English India.* Chicago: University of Chicago Press, 1992.

————. "The Secret Sharers: Edward Said's Imperial Margins." *Voice Literary Supplement* 8 June 1993:31.

Swindells, Julia, and Lisa Jardine. *What's Left? Women in Culture and the Labour Movement.* London: Routledge, 1990.

Tanner, Tony. Introduction to *Mansfield Park,* by Jane Austen. London: Penguin, 1966.

Tarantino, Quentin. *Pulp Fiction.* New York: Hyperion, 1994.

————. *Reservoir Dogs and True Romance.* New York: Grove, 1994.

Tate, Claudia. *Domestic Allegories of Political Desire: The Black Heroine's Text at the Turn of the Century.* New York: Oxford University Press, 1992.

Terry, Don. "A Week of Rapes: The Jogger and 28 Not in the News." *The New York Times* 29 May 1989:25.

Thompson, Julie M. *Mommy Queerest: Contemporary Rhetorics of Lesbian Maternal Identity.* Amherst: University of Massachusetts Press, 2002.

Tyler, Carole-Anne. "Boys Will Be Girls: The Politics of Gay Drag." In *Inside/Out: Lesbian Theories, Gay Theories,* ed. Diana Fuss. New York: Routledge, 1991, 32–70.

Vermeule, Blakey. "Is There a Sedgwick School for Girls?" *Qui Parle* 5.1 (Fall/Winter 1991): 53–72.

Vogel, Lise. *Marxism and the Oppression of Women: Toward a Unitary Theory.* New Brunswick: Rutgers University Press, 1983.

Wald, Priscilla. *Constituting Americans: Cultural Anxiety and Narrative Form.* Durham: Duke University Press, 1995.

Wallace, Michele. *Black Macho and the Myth of the Superwoman.* 1979; reprint, London: Verso, 1990.

——. *Invisibility Blues: From Pop to Theory.* London: Verso, 1990.

Walters, Suzanne Danuta. "From Here to Queer: Radical Feminism, Postmodernism, and the Lesbian Menace (Or, Why Can't a Woman Be More Like a Fag?)" *Signs* 21.4 (1996): 830–69.

Weed, Elizabeth. "A Man's Place." In *Men in Feminism,* ed. Alice Jardine and Paul Smith. New York: Methuen, 1987, 71–77.

——. "The More Things Change." In *Feminism Meets Queer Theory,* ed. Elizabeth Weed and Naomi Schor. Bloomington: Indiana University Press, 1997, 266–91.

Weed, Elizabeth and Naomi Schor, eds. *Feminism Meets Queer Theory.* Bloomington: Indiana University Press, 1997.

Weigand, Kate. *Red Feminism: American Communism and the Making of Women's Liberation.* Baltimore: John Hopkins University Press, 2001.

Wells, Ida B. *Crusade for Justice: The Autobiography of Ida B. Wells.* Chicago: University of Chicago Press, 1970.

——. *On Lynchings: Southern Horrors; A Red Record; Mob Rule in New Orleans.* New York: Arno Press, 1969.

Weston, Kath. *Families We Choose: Lesbians, Gays, Kinship.* New York: Columbia University Press, 1991.

Wicke, Jennifer and Michael Sprinker. "Interview with Edward Said." In *Edward Said: A Critical Reader,* ed. Michael Sprinker. Cambridge: Harvard University Press, 1992, 221–64.

Wiegman, Robyn. *American Anatomies: Theorizing Race and Gender.* Durham: Duke University Press, 1995.

——. "Melville's Geography of Gender." *American Literary History* 1.4 (1989): 735–53.

Williams, Jeffrey J., ed. *The Minnesota Review* (special "Academostars" issue) 52–4 (Fall 2001).

——. "Name Recognition." *The Minnesota Review* 52–4 (Fall 2001): 185–208.

Williams, Linda. *Hard Core: Power, Pleasure, and the "Frenzy of the Visible."* Berkeley: University of California Press, 1989.

Williams, Patricia J. *The Alchemy of Race and Rights.* Cambridge: Harvard University Press, 1991.

Williams, Raymond. *The Country and the City.* New York: Oxford University Press, 1973.

Williamson, Judith. "Woman Is an Island: Femininity and Colonization." In *Studies in Entertainment: Critical Approaches to Mass Culture,* ed. Tania Modleski. Bloomington: Indiana University Press, 1986, 99–118.

Willis, Sharon. *High Contrast: Race and Gender in Contemporary Hollywood Film.* Durham: Duke University Press, 1997.

Willis, Susan. *A Primer for Daily Life.* New York: Routledge, 1991.

Wilson, Ann. "Cautious Optimism: The Alliance of Women's Studies and Cultural Studies." *University of Toronto Quarterly* 65.2 (1996): 366–75.

Wilson, Harriet. *Our Nig; or, Sketches from the Life of a Free Black.* Ed. Henry Louis Gates Jr. New York: Vintage, 1983.

The Wilson Quarterly (unsigned, untitled review of *Culture and Imperialism*) 18.2 (Spring 1993): 86–87.

Witt, Doris. *Black Hunger: Food and the Politics of U S. Identity.* New York: Oxford University Press, 1999.

Wittig, Monique. "The Straight Mind." *Feminist Issues* (Summer 1980):103–11.

Women's Studies Group (Centre for Contemporary Cultural Studies, University of Birmingham). *Women Take Issue: Aspects of Women's Subordination.* London: Hutchinson, 1978.

Wood, Michael. "Lost Paradises." *The New York Review of Books* 3 March 1994:44–47.

Wood, Robin. "Slick Shtick." *Artforum* (March 1995):63–66, 110.

Yeazell, Ruth Bernard. "The Boundaries of *Mansfield Park.*" *Representations* 7 (Summer 1984): 133–52.

Zimmerman, Bonnie. "'Confessions' of a Lesbian Feminist." In *Cross-Purposes: Lesbians, Feminists, and the Limits of Alliance,* ed. Dana Heller. Bloomington: Indiana University Press, 1997, 157–68.

INDEX